THE POLITICAL ECONOMY OF
— WORKPLACE INJURY —
IN CANADA

LABOUR ACROSS BORDERS

Series Editors: **Ingo Schmidt and Jeff Taylor**

Labour studies once had a national and institutional focus
that rarely allowed for "border crossings" that linked labour
movements in different countries. A New Labour History
arose that challenged both the national and institutional
narratives, focusing instead on gender, occupational, racial,
and regional divisions among workers. *Labour Across
Borders* attempts to resurrect both social class analysis and
the perspective of labour as a potentially liberating social
force. The series features analyses that at once recognize
the divisions among workers that the New Labour History
examined and explore possibilities of overcoming them.

SERIES TITLES

The Political Economy of Workplace Injury in Canada
by Dr. Bob Barnetson

— LABOUR ACROSS BORDERS SERIES —

the POLITICAL
ECONOMY of
WORKPLACE INJURY
IN CANADA

Dr. Bob Barnetson

© 2010 Bob Barnetson

Published by AU Press, Athabasca University
1200, 10011 – 109 Street
Edmonton, AB T5J 3S8

Library and Archives Canada Cataloguing in Publication

Barnetson, Bob, 1970 –
The political economy of workplace injury in Canada / Bob Barnetson.

(Labour across borders series, ISSN 1922-3552)
Includes bibliographical references and index.
Also issued in electronic format (978-1-926836-01-0).
ISBN 978-1-926836-00-3

1. Industrial safety – Economic aspects – Canada.
2. Industrial hygiene – Economic aspects – Canada.
3. Industrial accidents – Canada – Costs.
4. Occupational diseases – Canada – Costs.
5. Workers' compensation – Canada.
I. Title.
II. Series: Labour across borders series

HD7658.B37 2010   363.110971   C2010-903243-8

Cover and book design by Natalie Olsen, kisscutdesign.com.
Printed and bound in Canada by Marquis Book Printing.

A volume in the Labour across borders series:
ISSN 1922-3522 (Print)
ISSN 1922-3560 (Online)

LET ME REMIND YOU WHAT FASCISM IS. IT NEED NOT WEAR A BROWN SHIRT OR A GREEN SHIRT—IT MAY EVEN WEAR A DRESS SHIRT. FASCISM BEGINS THE MOMENT A RULING CLASS, FEARING THE PEOPLE MAY USE THEIR POLITICAL DEMOCRACY TO GAIN ECONOMIC DEMOCRACY, BEGINS TO DESTROY POLITICAL DEMOCRACY IN ORDER TO RETAIN ITS POWER OF EXPLOITATION AND SPECIAL PRIVILEGE.

— **TOMMY** *Douglas*

THREE
Critique of OHS in Canada [47]

FOUR
Political Economy of Preventing Workplace Injury ⌈ **89** ⌉

FIVE
Compensation of Workplace Injury ⌈ *105* ⌉

EIGHT
Conclusion ⌈ *173* ⌉

Acknowledgements

While accepting that this book (and its errors) reflect my own particular views about the prevention and compensation of workplace injury and, more broadly, the employment relationship, I would be remiss in not acknowledging the assistance I received in completing this manuscript.

The idea for this book started when I was writing Athabasca University courses on workers' compensation and industrial relations. Winston Gereluk provided useful guidance in both processes, including extensive research support for the compensation course. He, along with Bruce Spencer, Ingo Schmidt, and Jeff Taylor in the Centre for Work and Community Studies, provided useful commentary on particular aspects of my argument and sheltered me from some of the administrative work while I completed research and writing.

The staff at the Alberta Labour Library and at the Athabasca University Library provided much appreciated help in tracking down required materials and volunteering some rather obscure "stuff we just had in the back." Thanks are also due to Athabasca University's Research Incentive Grant program, which funded the acquisition of a small library.

Jason Foster, formerly of the Alberta Federation of Labour, provided useful commentary on some of the arguments and the issue of compensating occupational cancer. Also deserving credit (although perhaps not wanting it) are the staff at the Alberta Workers' Compensation Board and the Department of Employment, Immigration and Industry whom, during my brief stays there, provided a useful introduction to the practicalities and politics of workers' compensation and occupational health and safety.

I cannot adequately thank the two anonymous reviewers of an early version of this manuscript. Their comments were exceptionally insightful and broadened my perspective significantly. Similar assistance was patiently provided by the editorial board and staff of the AU Press. Thanks in particular to Alvin Finkel and Jay Smith for providing helpful guidance to a first-time author.

Finally, thanks are due to my wife, who never once rolled her eyes (that I saw...) when I hijacked the dinner conversation to work out some argument or other about workplace injury.

Introduction

On 21 October, 2009, Patrick Clayton, an injured carpenter, entered the Alberta Workers' Compensation Board in Edmonton with a rifle. To some, Clayton is an object of scorn — a violent man who held nine people hostage. To others, Clayton — an injured worker jerked around for years by an uncaring bureaucracy — is symptomatic of how injury prevention and compensation efforts in Canadian workplaces do little to protect or aid workers. This book examines prevention and compensation to see whether sceptics have reason to be concerned.

Consider the number of workers injured each year. In 2003, six hundred and thirty thousand Canadian adults were injured on the job severely enough to limit their activity. Approximately 300,000 of these injured workers required time off to recover.[1] Disturbingly, this is an underestimate of the actual number of work-related injuries. It ignores injuries that did not limit activity — such as minor cuts, burns, bruises, and strains. It also excludes injuries to minors, repetitive strain injuries, workers injured multiple times, and unreported injuries.

It is hard to grasp the magnitude of this number. Instead, consider the case of Philippa Thomas.[2] In January 2006, she cut her thumb working at a horse stable. The cut became infected and Thomas now has a rare nerve disease. Her right hand often swells to twice its normal size. She experiences pain that seven surgeries (including a spinal cord implant) and drugs cannot dull. She cannot work and rarely leaves her home.

In some ways, Thomas' story is unique. Yet it is also similar to the stories of the 630,000 workers who are significantly injured every year. Thomas went to work and was injured doing her job. She now has to bear the physical, emotional, and financial costs of that injury. Some workers have it better—they eventually make a full recovery or get workers' compensation. And some workers have it worse. More than 1000 Canadian workers die every year.

PERSPECTIVES ON WORKPLACE INJURY

How you react to the vast number of workers injured and killed each year reflects your values and beliefs. Are these injures inevitable? Are they just the cost of doing business? One way to look at workplace injuries is from an economic perspective. This view sees the risk of injury as minimal, unavoidable and, ultimately, acceptable. Is it the price we (or at least workers) must pay for a "healthy" economy? If we are going to lower the risk of injury, we need to ensure the cost is less than the benefit we'll receive. And the people best positioned to decide that are employers.

This economic perspective dominates the debate about workplace health and safety. It is the *lingua franca* of employers, bureaucrats, politicians, and most academics. There are, of course, alternative perspectives. An alternative advanced by workers views workplace injuries as the result of choices employers make in order to maximize profitability. Contrary to the slogan "safety pays," it is usually cheaper for employers to organize work unsafely. This is especially true if employers can (with the tacit consent of government) pass along the cost of occupational injuries and disease to workers.

This political economy approach to workplace injury focuses attention on the ways groups with a common economic interest — such as employers — advance their interests by political means. This perspective reflects a (and my) Marxist view of social, political, and economic relationships. In this tradition, capitalist states are subject to antagonisms between capital and labour. These can be seen in the workplace in terms of contests over wages and control of work.

These antagonisms operate more broadly in society as a tension between the imperatives of production and social re-production. Production is the process by which we make stuff (including profit). Social reproduction is the process by which the social arrangements necessary for production are perpet-uated. This includes ensuring there are workers and consumers. It also means ensuring workers accept being subordinate to employers in the production process.

Employers' desire for maximum profitability often conflicts with the need to perpetuate a compliant workforce. It is certainly possible to arrange things such that workers earn starvation wages or die on the job in droves. But such an arrangement comes with two risks: there will be no more workers, and workers may revolt and take what they believe is rightfully theirs. Some political economists believe that the state was developed, in part, to manage the tensions that emerge around production and social reproduction.

In this view, one of the roles of government is to ensure the accumulation of capital through production continues with minimal impediment.[3] Governments cannot afford policies that deter private investment. At the same time, the state needs to maintain political legitimacy among its citizens. Governments must get re-elected and workers must accept their place within the system. The state, then, must also address specific conflicts (e.g., over workplace injury) within these constraints.[4] The state's need for legitimacy precludes the routine use of coercion, (although the threat is always there). Instead, the state has created policies and programs that assist with social reproduction.[5]

PURPOSE OF THIS BOOK

This book is aimed at students and practitioners seeking to understand the political and economic aspects of workplace injury—aspects of injury often ignored in other texts. For this reason, this book focuses on how Canadian governments try to prevent and compensate workplace injury, who benefits from this approach, and how they benefit. It starts from the premise that injury prevention and compensation occurs within a larger political and economic context. This context puts pressure on governments to address workplace injury and shapes how governments do so.

This analytical approach to workplace injury shows (among other things) that government strategies for preventing injuries don't do a very good job of it. It also reveals how ineffective regulation can benefit governments and employers, and how the state has contained the ability of workers to resist this agenda, by shaping the discourse around injury and the operation of these systems. Analysis of injury compensation highlights how seemingly neutral aspects of claims adjudication and management advantage employers and limit the ability of workers to resist unsafe work. This approach to workplace injury is important because it reveals that the prevention and compensation of workplace injuries are not solely technical or legal undertakings, but intensely political ones that entail serious consequences — most often for workers.

Examining workplace injury through the lens of political economy is relatively uncommon in Canada. The majority of books, conferences, and courses focus on technical issues (e.g., hazard identification and mitigation, accident investigation, hazardous material handling, managing returns to work) or the workings of institutions, formal rules, and the legal relationships between players. That approach has value. It does a good job of describing what we do to prevent and compensate injuries. It also explains how the system works, and indeed how it can be worked to one's advantage. But it fails to explain why things work as they do or examine how certain arrangements differentially benefit workers and employers. These are among the objectives of this book.

PREVENTING WORKPLACE INJURY

Canadian governments have enacted programs to both prevent and compensate workplace injuries. Occupational health and safety (OHS) laws seek to prevent workplace injuries, in part by raising the cost to employers of organizing work in a dangerous manner. These laws are enforced by the state — sometimes by inspectors who are part of government and sometimes through workers' compensation boards (WCBs). The effectiveness of this system is the topic of much debate. Can a system where more than half a million workers are seriously injured each year be described as effective?

We examine government injury-prevention efforts in the first four chapters. Chapter 1 sets out the political and economic dynamics of employment. These dynamics help explain why and how governments seek to prevent and compensate work-related injuries. This discussion casts employment as a relationship of power, wherein employers use their labour market and legal power to maximize the profit they can extract from workers' efforts. One outcome of this arrangement has been the (sometimes-intentional) injury or death of workers. Chapter 1 also considers the "logic" and some of the history of transferring production costs to workers via workplace injury.

Not surprisingly, workers don't like being injured and killed at work. At various times and in different ways, Canadians have pressured governments to reduce the incidence of workplace injury. Chapter 2 looks at how Canadian governments have sought to prevent workplace injuries over time. Various approaches to injury prevention — leaving it to the market, state regulation, and partial self-regulation — are examined and evaluated. Among the constants is the reluctance of governments to interfere significantly with employers' rights to decide what is produced when, where, and how. It is these decisions that determine which and when workplace injuries occur.

In Chapter 3, we examine contemporary injury prevention efforts. We begin by discussing the absence of good data on the number of injuries and how injury recognition is an intensely political process. We then consider the effectiveness of present-day internal and external responsibility systems. Finally, we look at state-employer partnerships and the notion that "safety pays." This includes exploring how governments create the appearance that workplaces are safer than they really are.

Chapter 4 provides some preliminary discussions about the political economy of regulating workplace injuries. Among the conclusions drawn are that employers remain able to transfer production costs to workers through injury, despite state efforts to limit this behaviour. The use of ineffective regulatory strategies contributes to this failure. Finally, we see that governments legitimize prioritizing profitability over safety by blaming workers for injuries, arguing intervention is not economically feasible, and by creating the appearance that workplaces are safer than they are.

COMPENSATING WORKPLACE INJURY

As part of their response to workplace injuries, governments have developed systems to compensate injured workers. Workers receive more immediate, predictable, and stable compensation for injuries via workers' compensation than they did when they had to sue their employer. But it is also important to consider the benefits workers' compensation provides to employers. Collective liability protection makes injury costs predictable and insulates individual employers from the full cost of injuries in the workplace. And the state benefits because an important source of social instability—financial ruin following an injury —is largely eliminated.

Chapter 5 considers the historical development of workers' compensation in Canada, including the way injuries are determined to be compensable or not. While seemingly neutral, adjudication is a political process wherein the interests of employers and workers conflict. This conflict is particularly evident in decisions around occupational diseases and psychological injuries. These injuries are often adjudicated in ways that limited employer liability. This is particularly the case for injuries that emerge over or after a long period of time, do not demonstrate a clear pathology, tap into an existing social prejudice, and/or entail significant costs for employers.

Limiting employer costs recurs as a theme in Chapter 6. Workers' compensation boards seek to minimize employer compensation costs by limiting benefit entitlements. Deeming of wages and the use of early-return-to-work programs are two ways to limit employer costs. These behaviours are justified by reference to the widely accepted view that workers will malinger, that being off work because one is sick is somehow unhealthy, and that work is indeed rehabilitative. A similar analysis is applied to experience-rating schemes for employer premiums. These systems appear to encourage employers to manage claims aggressively, more so than reduce injuries. One outcome is a transfer of the costs of work-related injuries onto workers, their families, and government-funded medical and social assistance programs.

Chapter 7 examines how workers' compensation is used to manage workers. While decision-making and appeal processes offer workers a way to address incorrect decisions about individual claims, at the same time they appear to reduce workers' collective ability to resist workplace injury. Claims adjudication and management isolate workers from one another, thereby reducing the potential for worker resistance. And the appeals process allies employers and WCBs against workers. Worker groups seeking change to compensation must consider that change could also bring the privatization or abolition of workers' compensation. This pressures workers to limit their demands for reforms. At the same time, employers are altering employment relationships as a way of evading workers' compensation obligations to their workers for coverage.

MAJOR CONCLUSIONS

The last chapter of the book considers some important themes that emerge from this analysis of workplace injury. Regarding the prevention of workplace injuries, three conclusions can be drawn:

1. Injuries occur in high numbers despite prevention efforts. This is explained partially by the state's use of demonstrably ineffective prevention strategies.

2. Injury prevention schemes channel worker energy and workplace conflict into mechanisms that manage and diffuse such conflict. This reduces the threat posed by workplace injuries to the capital accumulation and social reproduction processes. It also allows unsafe working conditions to persist.

3. Governments legitimize prioritizing profitability over safety in three ways: they blame workers for injuries; they make cost-benefit arguments, which implicitly adopt an economic perspective on workplace injury; and they create the appearance that workplaces are safer than they are.

Similarly, it is possible to draw three conclusions regarding the compensation of workplace injuries:

4. Workers' compensation provides most workers with predictable, stable, and immediate compensation. This

reduces the threat that the financial and social consequences of workplace injury historically posed to the legitimacy of a capitalist social formation. It also limits the effect of workplace injury on the production process. In this way, workers' compensation is a substitute for injury prevention.

5. Where workers' compensation results in conflict, worker energy is directed into mechanisms that manage and diffuse the conflict. This further reduces the threat posed by workplace injury to the production process.

6. Governments legitimize limiting compensation in two ways. They rely upon a biomedical conception of injury. And they focus on the belief in moral hazard to legitimize limiting compensation. Where this is ineffective, the state may rely upon the implicit threat of reducing or eliminating compensation as a way of containing workers demands.

These conclusions do not (necessarily) suggest that governments are conspiring with employers to imperil workers' health and safety. Rather, the existing system is one solution to conflict over workplace injury that threatens the existing economic and social arrangement. Historical contingencies have influenced the options available to governments as they tried to maintain both production and social reproduction. It may be that some degree of injury is unavoidable. And perhaps compensation systems are never going to compensate all injuries perfectly. Yet these possibilities ought not to blind us to the pattern that emerges from our analysis. Occupational health and safety laws don't make workplaces safe. And workers' compensation does not fully compensate workers for their injuries.

— ONE —

EMPLOYMENT RELATIONSHIPS IN CANADA

Having a job usually means being in an employment relationship. These relationships entail both conflicting interests and unequal power. This dynamic influences who is injured and how they are injured. It also affects whether and how an injured worker will be compensated. As you read this discussion, keep in mind the case of 17-year-old Yvon Poulin.

In January 2004, Poulin was killed after he fell headfirst into a bailer while working near Peace River, Alberta.[1] During his three months on the job, Poulin complained about a lack of training. He was also looking for less dangerous work elsewhere. After his death, inspectors found Poulin's employer had failed to ensure an alarm system was installed to warn workers when the machine was in operation. Poulin's employer used a legal loophole to have charges under the *Occupational Health and Safety Act* dismissed.

This situation raises some compelling questions. Why would Poulin continue working at a dangerous job? Why would Poulin's employer not provide a safe workplace? What does the ability of Poulin's employer to evade liability say about why and how we regulate and compensate workplace injuries? The context in which work occurs helps us answer these questions.

EMPLOYMENT IN A CAPITALIST ECONOMY

Employment is normally discussed as an economic relationship. Workers trade their time and skills to their employer in exchange for wages. In Canada, this exchange occurs in the context of a capitalist economy. A capitalist economy is characterized by the private ownership of capital. Resources are allocated through market mechanisms. And the profit motive guides employer decision-making.[2]

For workers, this means three things. First, the employer is risking capital by operating a business. To protect this investment, the employer has been given the right to organize and direct work. Consequently, the employer issues orders and workers obey them. As we'll see below, the employer's right to manage is codified in the common law. This gives employers significant power in the workplace.

Second, employers must profit or fail. Unprofitable companies go out of business. Less profitable companies cannot attract investors. The profit imperative pressures employers to minimize costs. Labour is expensive and has unique properties. This makes employers want to cheapen and intensify labour. Third, maximizing profitability can run contrary to workers' interests. Workers typically want to maximize their wages and control how and how hard they work — the opposite of what most employers want.

This description suggests employment is not only an economic relationship, but is also a social one. By accepting employment, workers accept the employer's authority. That is to say, workers agree to do as they are told, even when this runs contrary to their own interests.[3] The importance of managerial authority is a recurring issue in workplace injury.

THE LABOUR MARKET AND THE WAGE-RATE BARGAIN

Employment begins in a labour market. In a labour market, employers buy and workers sell the workers' capacity to work.[4]

Historically, labour markets were physical places. For example, in nineteenth-century England, agricultural labour was bought and sold at hiring fairs:

> Just fancy the spectacle of a large concourse of people, of varying ages and both sexes, standing, under every variety of weather, in a public market place, and, like so many cattle, or so much common merchandise, open to the inspection, and too frequently, rude handling, of persons in want of them — the great desiderata being straightness of limb, breadth of shoulder, development of muscle...[5]

Buyers and sellers negotiated wages based upon what they knew or could find out about one another. Wages were determined by the supply of and demand for workers. That is to say, there was a generally agreed to wage rate for different types of work. But the wage rate could go up if there was a shortage of labourers, such as during harvest or war, or after a plague or famine. Similarly, the wage rate could go down if there was a surplus of labour.

Today, the labour market is more of a concept than a real place. And modern workers are often screened based upon their education, experience, and the results of standardized tests rather than through poking and prodding. Yet the modern and historical labour markets are not that different. Employers and workers try to strike the best bargain possible. What is sold is the employees' capacity to work. And the price of work — called the wage-rate — is greatly influenced by supply and demand.

THE LABOUR PROCESS AND THE WAGE-EFFORT BARGAIN

When a worker accepts a job, the employer has rented the worker's time and skills. The employer must then utilize the worker's capacity to work. But labour has unique properties. It is not concrete and interchangeable like other inputs, such as oil or grain. Rather, workers are highly variable in the skills, knowledge, and attitudes they bring to the job. And the characteristics of workers may not be apparent when they are hired. Further, ownership of workers does not pass from the seller to the buyer (anymore). All that an employer has purchased is the worker's ability to work during the time the worker attends the workplace.[6] Whether the worker actually produces anything and whether the worker produces what the employer wants are uncertain.

Converting the capacity of work into actual work is known as the labour process. Employers do this by defining the nature of the job, matching workers to the job, and regulating workers' performance and behaviour. As we saw above, the interests of employers and workers may differ when it comes to just how hard and in what ways a worker will work. In this way, the wage-rate bargain is supplemented by a wage-effort bargain. An understanding emerges about how hard and productively a worker is going to work. The wage-effort bargain is a far more intangible and problematic bargain than agreeing on a wage-rate.

POWER AND RULES IN EMPLOYMENT

One has power when one possesses or exercises influence or authority. For example, if an employer gets a worker to complete a distasteful task at work, the employer has likely exercised some form of power. Perhaps the employer bribed or threatened the worker. Both workers and employers possess power. They differ, though, in the source and strength of their power, the perceived legitimacy of their power, and how they exercise that power.

The labour-market power of workers and employers shapes the wage-rate bargain. When there are more workers than jobs (the usual situation), employers gain power. They can be fussy about whom to hire. They can drive down wages by pitting prospective workers against one another. Employers can threaten to replace workers who resist their demands while on the job.

Workers, of course, can refuse to work if they believe the employer is being unfair. This source of worker power is mitigated, however, by workers' need for wages to buy food, shelter, and clothing. In this way, employers' labour-market power can be used to affect the wage-effort bargain. In the short-term, the supply of and demand for workers is usually beyond the control of employers. But employer power has roots in both the labour market and the law.

THE COMMON LAW

When an employer and a worker strike a wage-rate bargain, the employer and worker have entered into a contract. A contract is a legally enforceable set of promises. Employment contracts are known as common law contracts of employment.[7] When there is a dispute about what precisely has been agreed to between an employer and a worker, the courts turn first to the written employment contract. When there is a written contract (and there often isn't), the contract usually contains only the barest information. When the terms of an employment contract are silent or ambiguous, the courts use certain common law rights and obligations to interpret the contract. An employer's common law obligations include the duty to provide:

> **Work and remuneration:** An employer is required to provide a worker with the wages (often called *consideration*) the two parties negotiated. Indeed, there can be no contract of employment without consideration. An employer is also required to provide the worker with an opportunity to work as per their agreement.

> **Notice of termination:** Employment relationships are normally considered to be for an indefinite period of time

unless otherwise specified. Assuming the employment is indefinite, an employer wishing to terminate the contract must normally give the employee reasonable notice of termination (or pay in lieu of the notice). Employers who find they have just cause for terminating the worker (e.g., they catch the worker stealing from them) do not have to provide reasonable notice.

A safe worksite: Employers are required to provide a reasonably safe system of work.

Employers are also vicariously liable for their workers' actions. That means that the employer is responsible for negligent acts or omissions of workers when workers are carrying out job-related duties.

By contrast, a worker's common law obligations include:

Obligations of good faith and fidelity: A worker must act in a manner that is consistent with advancing the employer's business interests. For example, a worker cannot normally operate a business on the side that competes with the worker's employer. Nor can a worker act in a way that undermines the fundamental trust relationship that exists by, for example, stealing from the employer.

The duty to obey: Once employed, the worker is the employer's to command. While there are limits on what an employer can demand of a worker, generally speaking, the worker must obey lawful commands of the employer.

The obligation to perform work competently: A worker must competently perform the duties assigned by the employer.

Requirement to provide resignation notice: Workers are required to provide the employer with notice of their intent to terminate the employment contract.[8]

A contract is (notionally) a voluntary agreement between two free and equal parties. Yet the common law rights and obligations attached to employment suggest otherwise. Workers must advance their employer's interests, even when the employer is not paying them. And workers reap no benefit from their work other than their wage. By contrast, the key enforceable obligation of employers is simply to pay for work done.

Further, workers' rights only exist if the employer recognizes them or the worker is prepared to enforce those rights in court. Suing one's employer is expensive, slow, and often career limiting. This fundamental asymmetry in common-law obligations "is only explicable on the basis that courts do not see the contract of employment as one of cooperation or mutuality, but rather as one between a superior and an inferior or, if you will, a master and a servant." [9]

The legal rights and obligations associated with employment also suggest that the law is not neutral. Instead, it enhances the labour market power of employers. Not only do workers need a job to feed themselves, but also the law requires them to do as they are told by their employer, on pain of immediate termination. By contrast, if contested, worker rights can only be asserted through costly litigation. In this way, employment is a relationship of power, wherein power is distributed asymmetrically.

Questioning the impartiality of the law can seem heretical, especially if you believe the law is created and administered by a neutral state in the public interest. Nevertheless, procedural impartiality (e.g., due process in the judicial system) does not require the substantive content of the laws be balanced or fair. The marked power imbalance between those who own and control the means of production (capitalists) and those who do not (labour) is clearly reinforced in the law of employment. Employers decide when, where, and how to produce something. Workers just do as they are told.

CHANGING DEFINITIONS OF WORK

Whatever your thoughts about the fairness of employment, it is difficult to image a world without it. Our job is how we pay our bills. Many of us also identify with our occupation — we're welders, daycare workers, salespeople. But we are also all simply workers. That is to say, we trade our time, effort, and skill to someone else for money. Those who do the work, however, have not always been "workers."

Prior to 1850, most Canadian "jobs" were in agriculture, fishing, and fur trading. Families completed much of this "work," often on a subsistence basis. What manufacturing existed occurred in small workshops. Waged work certainly did exist — in canal construction, logging, shipbuilding, and domestic service — but it was not the norm and might be seasonal. After 1850, farm debt, investment in manufacturing, and increasing costs associated with self-employment began to create both a pool of unskilled workers and waged employment opportunities for them. In this way, waged work increased and, in doing so, created demand for products (and the infrastructure to meet these demands). This led, in turn, to more waged work.[10]

Over time, employers have used their power to implement many of the defining features of the modern employment experience. For example, manufacturing and other forms of work were often concentrated in factories. This allowed employers to better control workers.[11] From this change comes our experience of work as normally done away from home and under the direct supervision of our employer. Similarly, the introduction of scientific management saw employers (instead of workers) determine how production occurs.[12] This pattern continues in modern systems of job design and performance evaluation. The introduction of the assembly line further increased the employer's control over how and how fast work was done. Workers were rooted to the spot and their work paced by the speed of the line. These changes all seek to, in part, cheapen and intensify labour — goals consistent with the profit motive of capitalism.

WORKPLACE SAFETY AND THE PROFIT MOTIVE

Most people recognize that one outcome of work is the injury of workers. Fewer people accept the notion that employers intentionally harm workers to make a buck, in part because this assertion appears to paint (inaccurately) all employers as amoral, malevolent, and greedy. Yet, before dismissing the notion that employers may knowingly injury workers because it is distasteful, let's take a moment to consider the incentive and opportunity employers have to transfer costs to workers, their families, and communities via injury.

Capitalism pressures employers to maximize their profitability. Profitability is an important criterion when employers decide what sort of work to do or which inputs or processes to use. One way to increase profitability is to externalize costs. For example, if a company can pass on the cost of pollution to the environment or the state, rather than building it into the cost of the product, the company can gain a competitive advantage. They can price their goods lower and thus be more profitable. There is significant evidence that corporations seek to minimize regulation and liability for the health effects of their products and production processes.[13] And, if a company's competitors can also externalize costs in this way, the pressure on every company to do so will be almost overwhelming.

Injuring or killing a worker is one way of externalizing cost. For example, increasing the pace of production may increase profitability. Workers can be made to work faster. Or, production processes can be re-organized to minimize the distance materials are moved. Or volatile chemicals can be used to speed up processes or cut supply costs. These decisions may increase the chance and/or severity of a work-related injury. Working faster can cause or exacerbate repetitive strain injuries (RSIs) or result in worker error. Using cranes to move materials over or through workspaces can increase the risk of a worker being struck by an object. Chemicals can leak, off-gas, or explode, causing burns or occupational diseases.

In theory, injuring or killing workers should entail an offsetting cost for employers. Injured workers might sue the employer. The workplace might be shutdown to remove a body, repair damaged equipment, or investigate an accident. Other workers might demand higher wages, become de-motivated, or quit. Workplace injury, however, does not occur in a perfect world. Temporarily halting production and the psychological effects of injuries on workers do seem to have a negative effect on profitability.[14] But the continued occurrence of such events suggests the costs of such injuries are lower than the benefits employers reap. Otherwise, employers would take steps to reduce the number of accidents further. Costs of prevention may exceed the benefits of prevention, which may reflect that, in part, the ability of workers to refuse work (which might get them fired) or quit is limited by their need to earn a wage. In this way, workers must trade their need for wages against their desire for health.[15] And workers' ability to gain compensation for their injuries has been limited.

COMPENSATION THROUGH THE COURTS

Prior to the development of industrial capitalism, families bore and mitigated the effects of work-related injuries — most of which occurred in the course of operating a family workshop or farm. The shift to industrial capitalism resulted in more injuries occurring in more clearly delineated employment relationships.[16] Setting aside the unique properties of labour, within a capitalist framework, labour is simply a commodity that is exchanged through contract. So how does one handle a workplace injury or fatality in such a framework?

The employers' obligation to provide a safe workplace has been firmly rooted in English common law for many years. The 1837 appeal case of *Priestley v Fowler* was heard by the English Court of the Exchequer. The court determined that only where an employer was negligent could an injured worker recover damages.[17] This decision adopted the view that workers consent to employment-related risks, other than those caused by negligence. Canadian judges were bound by the constitution, habit, and convenience to follow this lead.[18]

Consequently, injured workers seeking compensation in the courts had to demonstrate that an employer had failed to exercise due care — the standard of care that would be exercised by a reasonable person.[19] Even when employers were found guilty of failing to exercise due care, they could still put forward three arguments, or "common law defences," to escape liability:

Contributory negligence: If it could be shown that the injured worker failed to exercise reasonable care, and thereby contributed to the accident, the worker would assume full liability for the injury, and no compensation in the form of damages would be awarded.

Fellow-worker doctrine: Under this doctrine, employers could not be held liable for accidents caused by co-workers; the focus of any action for damages would therefore have to shift to that worker.

Assumption of risk: This doctrine assumes that workers are compensated for accidents via a wage rate. That is to say, high-risk occupations are better paid and, in accepting this, workers knowingly and voluntarily assumed the greater risk.[20]

There are problems with the "unholy trinity" of defences. For example, it is unclear how workers can know the risks of a job before accepting it or whether they can reasonably be expected to act without error. A lack of knowledge about risk and the need to earn a wage suggests workers' ability to negotiate a risk premium or seek other work may be largely notional. And the ability of injured workers' to recover damages from fellow workers or the employer is limited by the cost and time involved in an unpredictable civil action.[21]

Even a successful suit might not result in compensation as an employer might simply go bankrupt.[22] It is not possible to determine the success rate of cases brought under the tort system. Morley Gunderson and Douglas Hyatt suggest that between 15 percent and 30 percent of suits were successful, but do not substantiate this claim.[23] For the most part, the cost of legal counsel, the time involved, and the slim prospects of success meant that injured workers either did not bother or were unable to pursue claims. Consequently, employers were able to transfer production costs onto injured workers, their families, charities, and in rare cases, government.

ALTERNATIVES TO LITIGATION

When discussing the legalities of workplace injuries, it is easy to lose sight of the fact that society and workers grappled with workplace injuries in a variety of ways. Often it fell to families to pay for medical treatment and burial expenses. Families might also be forced to support injured workers and their families until and unless a worker recovered. In the United States, co-operative insurance schemes were a popular option at the turn of the twentieth century.[24]

Workers also developed mutual aid societies (often under the auspices of trade unions) to pay for medical care, wage loss, and burial costs.[25] One of the more elaborate efforts was by coal miners in the Pacific Northwest, who set up their own hospital in the late nineteenth century.[26] Some employers took to providing medical care and injury compensation to workers. This strategy was more common among large employers, such as railroads.[27] Such benefit schemes — often funded by deductions from worker salaries — also increased employer power over workers.[28] In Canada, most of these strategies were superseded by state-run workers' compensation and medical systems.

DO EMPLOYERS INTENTIONALLY TRANSFER COSTS?

So far, we've seen employers can transfer costs to workers. But do they? The short answer is yes, at least sometimes. For example, employers have hidden the health effects of hazardous substances resulting in asbestos-, uranium- and silica-related diseases in the mining industry. Similar behaviours can be seen in the chemical industry. Employers have also sought to resist regulation designed to protect worker health. This behaviour is canvassed in Chapter 2.

Most times, though, things are not so clear-cut. Workers may, for example, be struck by lightning or injured when a component fails. Are these freak and unavoidable accidents? Perhaps. Yet the injury occurred only because the worker was doing work. And the employer — who controlled what was produced, when, where, and how — could have stopped work when the thunderheads built up. Or could have inspected the machine more frequently.

Such suggestions are often dismissed as not being cost effective. This may be true. But, in making the argument that it is more cost effective to work unsafely, employers are admitting two things. First, it is possible to work more safely. And, second, employers choose to transfer risk to workers because it is cheaper to do so than remove the source of the risk. This cost-benefit analysis reflects an economic perspective on the risk of injury — something we'll also discuss at length in Chapter 2.

Risks are also sometimes discussed as being unavoidable. But almost every workplace risk could be avoided by organizing work differently or simply not engaging in risky work. The decision about what to produce and how to do it is one taken by employers, with an eye to making a profit. Passing off responsibility for the resulting injuries by saying risk is "just the nature of the job" simply deflects responsibility away from the employer. Again, we see the economic perspective on risk lurking in the background: risk of injury is minimal, unavoidable, and acceptable.

Employers may legitimately not know about certain workplace risks. This can be a particular issue with hazardous substances. The effects of the workplace exposure may not be immediately apparent. Or there may appear to be multiple causes (some not work-related) of an illness. Yet, governments choose to allow employers to introduce substances without any testing of their hazards (thereby making workers guinea pigs), a political decision that prioritizes employer profitability over worker health. And that employers do so is a choice to pursue profit at the expense of workers.

CONCLUSION

So let's go back to the case of Yvon Poulin. Why did he work at a dangerous job? Like most of us, he had a job so that he could feed, clothe, and house himself. In return for wages, he agreed that his employer could tell him what to do and how to do it. In this, we see that employment is a relationship of power. Employers' power has both legal and practical limits — workers pushed too hard resist in a variety of ways. Yet, when the whip of hunger is combined with the legal right to manage, workers mostly fall into line.

Why did his employer not provide a safe workplace? Likely, his employer used power to respond to the profit imperative. Labour is a significant cost that employers have sought to cheapen over time. Organizing work in a dangerous manner usually increases profitability by externalizing costs to workers, their families, and society. Not installing a warning device or providing adequate training saved the employer money and facilitated faster work, by allowing workers to work while the machine was in operation.

What does the ability of Poulin's employer to evade liability say about why and how we regulate and compensate workplace injuries? In theory, the savings employers realize by injuring or killing workers are offset by the cost of those injuries. But the common law has historically allowed employers to transfer costs to workers, their families, and communities. In this case, Poulin's employer sought exemption from prosecution on the grounds that, as an agricultural operation, it was outside the ambit of occupational health and safety laws. This cost transfer is a source of significant social instability because injury and death reveal so clearly where the interests of workers and employer conflict.

The state has sought to prevent open conflict over workplace injury in two main ways. First, it began regulating working conditions in the late nineteenth century, with an eye to remedying the worst excesses of employers. When that proved ineffective, it created a workers' compensation system in the early twentieth century to limit the financial effects of injury. Further regulation efforts followed in the late twentieth century. In these ways, the state has attempted to address (or at least paper over) the political problems created by workplace injury. In Chapter 2, we'll examine how the state tries to prevent workplace injuries.

—TWO—

PREVENTING
WORKPLACE INJURY

Each province and territory tries to prevent workplace injuries. But these efforts aren't very successful. Every year, hundreds of thousands of workers are injured. To understand why prevention efforts don't work, we need to look at how governments approach the problem. This chapter begins by examining how employers and workers view risk in the workplace. Do they view the risk of injury as inevitable, minimal, and acceptable? Or is risk as something imposed upon workers by employers? The perspective adopted affects subsequent approaches to prevention.

The economic perspective that risk is minimal, unavoidable, and acceptable dominates prevention efforts. As a result, state intervention in the operation of workplaces has been limited, creating the perception of safety more so than the reality of it. Employers are obligated to address hazards, but face little incentive or pressure to do so. When this hasn't silenced worker demands, the state has tried to buy off workers with injury compensation. It has also made workers partially responsible for workplace health and safety — all the while limiting workers' ability to protect themselves.

This pattern is rarely acknowledged. To do so would be to

admit awkward truths about the exploitative nature of employment and the role the state plays in maintaining this arrangement. Instead, safety is discussed as socially desirable and even profitable. Yet, in this chapter and the one that follows, we'll see that workers continue to be injured in droves and safety is only taken seriously when workplace injuries imperil production and social reproduction.

DEVELOPMENT OF OCCUPATIONAL HEALTH AND SAFETY IN CANADA

Perspectives on risk

Employers and workers view the risk of workplace injury differently. This isn't surprising. Workers shoulder most of the consequences of injury while employers and their investors reap most of the rewards. For employers, risk is mostly an economic issue.[1] And the risk of workplace injury is cast as minimal, unavoidable, and acceptable. This economic perspective dominates popular discussion and public policy.[2]

One implication of this economic approach is that, since perfect safety is unattainable, safety initiatives should be assessed on a cost-benefit basis.[3] Put bluntly, safety should only be improved when it costs less to prevent the injury than the injury itself costs.[4] Employers assert that they ought to make these decisions. Government regulation is said to cause rising prices, job losses, and a declining standard of living. On the surface, this economic perspective appears quite sensible. Every activity does entail some risk. And risk reduction can be very expensive.

Nevertheless, workers — those most often injured and killed — tend to see things differently. Workers note that workplace injury is not a natural phenomenon that no one can control. Rather, the risks workers face reflect decisions employers make: decisions about what, when, where, and how goods and services are produced. As we saw in Chapter 1, employers make these decisions with the goal of maximizing profitability. In this way, injury is a cost imposed on workers by employers. And allowing employers to do this is a political choice by the state.

Workers also know that the most important consequence of health and safety risks is not economic, it is the injury and death of workers. Reducing injury, disease, and death — not maximizing cost-effectiveness — is the pre-eminent goal of occupational health and safety activities. That is not to say that workplace injuries don't have economic consequences. Clearly they do. Injured workers cannot earn a living and thus lose their houses. Society must pay for medical treatment. Employers profit from dangerous work. But these economic outcomes are secondary effects — by-products of workers being exposed to the risk of injury and death by their employers.

The political perspective and the economic perspective on risk start with contradictory views about the nature of risk in the workplace. Employers see risk as natural; workers see it as imposed. Consequently, their prescriptions for reducing risk differ. How governments choose to regulate workplace injury reflects the respective abilities of workers and employers to influence public policy.

Market model of occupational health and safety

Provincial governments began regulating Canadian workplaces in the late nineteenth century. This intervention reflected growing concern about the effects of industrialization on workers and society — including the effects of workplace injuries. Before governments began regulating employment, workplace injury was the purview of the courts and the subject of the common law of negligence.[5] Under this market model of safety, employers had to provide a safe workplace. Workers (theoretically) received higher wages for hazardous work. They could also sue their employers for workplace injuries. This created an incentive — albeit a weak one — for employers to operate safety.

Whether workers could actually get hazard pay is unclear. To demand hazard pay, workers need to know job risks before being hired. To compel hazard pay, workers need a means to survive unemployment for a period of time — perhaps a long time, in a loose labour market. Once hired, workers who found their jobs too hazardous faced significant costs if they changed employers. There was also no guarantee that any other job entailed less risk than their current one.[6] For their part, employers may have preferred to pay higher wages if the cost was less than the cost of operating safely. This all suggests that getting hazard pay was unlikely.

Workers also had a hard time gaining compensation for injuries via the courts. The requirement to demonstrate employer negligence combined with the assumption of risk, contributory negligence, and fellow-worker doctrines meant few lawsuits were successful.[7] Yet despite these barriers, workers still sought redress primarily by suing. Relying on the (unreliable) courts is hard to understand. This behaviour may reflect that a civil suit was one of the few socially legitimate ways injured workers could seek redress.[8] The important point is that legal hurdles and the difficulty workers had in getting hazard pay created little incentive for employers to make workplaces safe.

Inevitability and the careless worker

Two inter-related narratives bolstered the market model: the careless worker and the inevitability of injuries. The notion of worker carelessness underlies the belief that some workers or groups of workers (often discussed in terms of ethnicity) are accident prone, careless, or even reckless.[9] This idea remains important. For example, a 2005 study found that 76 percent of Canadian employers believed that most accidents and injuries are the result of worker carelessness or lack of attention.[10] Similarly, the majority of Canadians broadly accept the idea that workplace injuries are inevitable and acceptable.[11]

The careless worker narrative has a long pedigree. American companies used it in the 1920s to counter opposition to the introduction of leaded gasoline. Lead poisoning among workers making the tetraethyl lead additive made people leery of using leaded gasoline. General Motors, DuPont, and Standard Oil responded to critics, in part, by blaming injuries on workers not following safety precautions.[12] In this case, carelessness was not the root cause of worker injuries and death—exposing workers to a toxin at work was. Indeed, analysis of injury causation suggests that unsafe conditions, not carelessness, is the cause of most accidents.[13]

DuPont, Standard Oil, and General Motors combined the careless worker narrative with the assertion that innovation and economic progress demand risk. In effect, workplace injuries are inevitable and necessary. This argument radically (and bizarrely) reframes the debate about the cost of workplace injury. Workplace injury is not about the cost of injuries to workers. Instead, it is about the cost to society of not injuring workers! This neatly sidesteps the awkward fact that employers (and their investors) reap the economic benefits of these injuries while workers bear the costs.

Suggesting injuries are inevitable also deflects attention from the fact that workplace injuries are not random events that defy prediction. And they are not unpreventable. Patterns of injury are clearly discernable. In agriculture, for example, the most common injuries requiring hospitalization include fractures of the limbs, spine, and trunk, and open wounds on upper limbs. The most common injury mechanisms include animals, becoming entangled in a machine, falling from a height, being pinned or struck by a machine or another object, and falling from a machine.[14] Anyone who has worked on a farm could tell you about these patterns.

Injury mechanisms are well known to employers, as are many ways to prevent injuries. The problem is that eliminating or containing hazards is expensive. It is cheaper and much easier to blame the victim.[15] Focusing attention on the victim protects cherished beliefs or powerful actors. We do this all the time. Victims of sexual assault were (and are) often blamed for their injury. Blaming rape victims is easier than grappling with seemingly intractable issues such as the objectification and victimization of women by social and legal forces. Similarly, it is easier to blame workers than grapple with the idea that injuries are the by-product of employer decisions.

The social construction of accidents

Worker carelessness and injury inevitability are a recurring refrain in popular debate. They also make an important contribution to the social construction of a workplace accident. A social construction is an understanding about something that emerges over time based on the behaviour of various actors. In this case, it defines what an "accident" means and what response is appropriate. Such understandings become embedded in the institutional fabric of society. The resulting social reality makes it hard even to think seriously about alternatives.

The idea of a social construction is a bit hard to grasp, so consider how we measure time. There are 60 seconds in a minute, 60 minutes in an hour and 24 hours in a day. Extrapolating, we get 365 days in a year, unless the year is divisible by four, and then we have a leap year with one extra day. Mind you, if that leap year number is divisible by one hundred, then we don't add the extra day. Unless the year is divisible by four hundred and then we do.

The point is that how we measure time is arbitrary (not to mention confusing). It is a social construction that reflects the historical evolution of time keeping. There is no real reason that we have a base-60 system for measuring time. A system based on tens would much simpler. But no one seriously considers a base-10 system because the base-60 system is embedded in the institutional fabric of society. We all have a base-60 watch, computers run on base-60 time, and so on.[16] This same dynamic operates in how we socially construct workplace injuries. The idea that injuries are caused by "accidents" is embedded in the institutional fabric of society and makes it hard even to think seriously about alternatives.

Saying a workplace injury is the result of an "accident" implies a lack of intentionality. This terminology implicitly absolves employers of responsibility for an injury because they did not explicitly set out to injure a worker. This is not, however, the full picture. While the exact moment individual injuries occur can be difficult to predict, the circumstances in which injuries occur and mechanisms of injury are typically well known. In deciding how work is designed and performed, employers place workers in circumstances that routinely give rise to the injury in the pursuit of profit. Using the term "accident" obscures, and indeed legitimizes, this behaviour. Accidents happen, after all. Now get back to work.

Bizarrely, the concept of an "accident" is also used to support to the idea that employers should be able to manage safety. Employers know the most about work processes. And they appear to bear the financial costs of accidents.[17] Thus, so the argument goes, employers are best positioned to prevent accidents. This line of thinking sidesteps two important points. First, injuries are by-products of employer decision-making: that is to say, employers already have the power to prevent injuries, but they don't. And, second, the fact that employers don't prevent injuries reflects the reality that the interests of workers (safety) and employers (profit) conflict. Not surprisingly, leaving safety to employers doesn't usually work out very well for workers — they keep having these "accidents." This was as evident in the late nineteenth century as it is today. And thus the state began experiencing and responding to pressure from workers to regulate the workplace directly.

Pressure for state regulation

Government regulation of employment is closely tied to the emergence of employment relations typical of a modern industrial society.[18] The rapid industrialization of Europe and North America in the nineteenth and early twentieth centuries led to an increasing number of work-related accidents.[19] For example, in 1925, the Workers' Health Bureau noted that the introduction of spray painting meant that 18 workers could now spray-paint 1200 car chassis per day. Formerly, 20 workers could only hand paint 275 chassis. This increased efficiency came at a cost, though: every spray-painting worker was poisoned within a year of starting.[20]

Industrialization also led to the emergence of an organized, self-conscious, and politically potent working class.[21] It was also a time when there was growing interest in socialism as an alternative to capitalism.[22] As a result, there was growing pressure for government to respond to the needs of injured workers and address the deteriorating credibility of capitalism and capitalists.[23] Subsequently, various forms of regulation were introduced that (partially) limited the employer's right to manage as it saw fit.

Among these regulations were standards governing such matters as hours of work, wages, and child labour. Union membership and collective bargaining were also legalized.[24] Workers were not the only group demanding regulation of factories. Middle-class reformers sought state regulation as a way to maintain the sexual segregation and child educational goals they desired.[25]

The Factory Acts

Ontario began regulating working conditions in 1874 and passed *The Ontario Factories Act* in 1884.[26] Upon coming into force in 1886, this Act regulated working conditions for women and children. It prohibited unsafe factories or factories where persons were likely to be permanently injured (although temporarily injuring workers was apparently okay). Three inspectors were hired to enforce the Act.[27] Enforcement was, however, limited. Inspectors did little to affect the employer's right to manage.[28] Other jurisdictions followed suit.[29]

It is unclear why inspectors chose persuasion over prosecution. One explanation is that persuasion was the most efficient use of limited resources — limited resources being a political choice by the state. Persuasion was also consistent with the notions of inevitability and worker carelessness.[30] Workers were given no role in occupational health and safety, reflecting their subordinate role in employment relationships.[31]

There is no evidence that early state regulation appreciably reduced workplace injury. While obviously a concern to workers, high rates of workplace injury may also have given employers pause for thought. The horrific nature of workplace injury and the injustice of its (lack of) compensation may cause workers to reflect on whether their interests are really the same as their employers' interests.[32] Workers might well conclude that their health and safety is being systematically sacrificed to maximize the profitability of employers. Such a conclusion is a powerful critique of the capitalist system, posing a significant threat to social stability.

Injury compensation

In the late nineteenth century, Western governments began altering how injuries were compensated. Among the first changes was Great Britain's *Employer's Liability Act* (1880) — an act that limited the use of the three common law defences regularly used by employers to avoid liability.[33] Britain enacted additional legislation in 1887, which made individual employers liable for accidents but did not require any system of insurance.[34] Between 1884 and 1886, the Bismarck government of Germany created the first system of compulsory, no-fault workers' compensation insurance with liability borne collectively by employers.[35] Laws were also enacted in the United States[36] and New Zealand.[37]

In Canada, workers' concerns became more politically important during the early years of the twentieth century. Between 1900 and 1914, Canada saw rapid growth and a drift toward highly concentrated forms of corporate production.[38] This economic change, and the addition of over 2.2 million immigrants between 1903 and 1912, transformed the nature and position of class forces in Canadian society. It resulted in unprecedented confrontation on the shop floor and in the streets. Workers also found legislative voice with the election of labour candidates to seats in all levels of government.

Between 1902 and 1911, seven Canadian provinces instituted injury compensation reforms, although only Quebec implemented a collective liability model.[39] These changes began ameliorating one objectionable consequence of workplace injury: poverty caused by a legal system that was stacked against injured workers and their families. The widespread adoption of no-fault workers' compensation is typically identified as beginning with Ontario's 1914 legislation. While fully explained in Chapter 5, in brief, workers' compensation developed to provide for lost earnings as well as medical and rehabilitative benefits to workers whose injuries arose out of and occurred in the course of employment. Who was at fault for the accident was deemed irrelevant. All employers paid premiums to cover the costs and workers gave up the right to separately sue their employer.

Why workers' compensation?

While growing worker pressure was an important factor in the emergence of workers' compensation, it was not the sole reason for this change.[40] It is important to be cognizant of the advantages workers' compensation offered to employers, including liability protection and increased predictability in compensation costs. Further, there were societal shifts afoot. For example, studies demonstrating that structural factors, rather than specific acts of the worker or employer, were a significant cause of accidents.[41] This undermined the perception that the law of negligence was an appropriate way to compensate injury.[42]

Employer support may have made workers' compensation attractive to governments seeking to ameliorate worker grievances.[43] William Meredith's report that led to Ontario's workers' compensation legislation suggests this idea.[44] Meredith also used moral and political rationales that spoke to the stabilizing effect of no-fault workers' compensation:

> In these days of social and industrial unrest it is, in my judgment, of the gravest importance to the community that every proved injustice to any section or class resulting from bad or unfair laws should be promptly removed by the enactment of remedial legislation and I do not doubt that the country whose Legislature is quick to discern and prompt to remove injustice will enjoy, and that deservedly, the blessing of industrial peace and freedom from social unrest.[45]

He further commented on the potential of workers' compensation to mitigate worker demands and power in a speech to the Ontario Section of the Canadian Bar Association:

> The Legislature should be careful to put upon the statute books a fair law, not to be influenced by the pressure of a strong body which wields a powerful influence to temporize with the matter, to give only half justice. There are some who think that the manufacturers of this country are pretty well taken care of, and it seems to me it is bad policy on the part of the manufacturers to antagonize the workmen at a

time like this. There are sounds in the air of an attack upon their privileges, and I could not imagine a stronger weapon with which to attack than to say, "You protect the manufacturers but you will not protect the working man."[46]

Workers' compensation ameliorated a significant source of social instability by providing stable, predictable, and immediate compensation. In doing so, workers' compensation allowed governments to diffuse pressure for more aggressive regulation of occupational health and safety. In this way, workers' compensation can be viewed as a substitute for injury prevention.

Partial self-regulation

Subsequent to the introduction of factory acts, many jurisdictions enacted specific legislation to address safety in shops, construction, and mines.[47] Responsibility for enforcement was normally assigned to the government department most closely associated with the area of commerce being regulated. Until the Second World War, worker demands for further changes in the workplace were limited by conflict between craft and industrial unions, state and employer repression, and the Great Depression.

During the Second World War, workers forced a significant accommodation from the state. PC 1003 required employers to recognize and bargain in good faith with trade unions.[48] The resulting framework of labour relations reinforced the rights of employers to manage. Consequently, worker demands focused on wages, benefits, and union security. Combined with a recession in the 1950s, this dynamic meant that workers did not make health and safety a bargaining priority.[49] Fewer than half of the provinces had an occupational health and safety program in place before 1970.[50]

Beginning in the 1960s, workers across North America began agitating for better health and safety laws. Socially, there was increasing skepticism about the benevolence of employers and the state. In the workplace, occupational diseases took on new importance.[51] And employers' reluctance to share information about diseases or recognize them as work-related highlighted how the interest of employers and workers diverged and conflicted.[52] The introduction of Medicare in 1968 also focused state attention on the cost of workplace injuries and illness.[53]

Hoggs Hollow and Elliot Lake

Events at Hoggs Hollow and Elliot Lake, Ontario, catalyzed the Canadian occupational health and safety (OHS) movement during the 1960s and '70s. At Hoggs Hollow (now part of Toronto), five workers were killed constructing water mains in the soft soil beneath the Don River. The tunnel was 35 feet underground and 6 feet in diameter with a 36-inch water main running through it. To pass by one another, one worker was forced to curl into a ball beneath the pipe to make room. To keep the water and silt from entering, the employer pressurized the tunnels. On 18 March 1960, sparks from a blowtorch ignited a fire in the oxygen-rich environment.

> In the mass confusion and panic that ensued, rescue workers shut down the compressors that forced air into the tunnel, causing much of the tunnel to cave in, and leaving the men to suffer the tortures of the bends as nitrogen bubbles expanded within their blood. To make matters worse, the floor of the tunnel was not properly sealed with cement, so that when water was finally poured into the tunnel to quell the fire, behind the water came a torrential flood of quicksand and muck.

> For these five men, the dream of a better life died in a cramped, slimy tunnel beneath the Don River. The official cause of death was ruled acute poisoning by

carbon monoxide and suffocation due to the inhalation of smoke, sand, and water. It took three days of digging to free the bodies of these men from the tunnel as they were completely buried in silt and trapped under the 36-inch water main that lined the tunnel. The bodies of the Mantella brothers were found kneeling beside each other in the posture of prayer.[54]

The resulting coroner's inquest and a strike by Italian construction workers sparked changes that contributed to new occupational health and safety laws in Ontario.

Hoggs Hollow was followed by events at Elliot Lake, Ontario, in 1974. Alarmed by the high incidence of lung cancer and silicosis, uranium miners struck over health and safety conditions. Worker health concerns dated back to 1958, when the union began pressuring the federal and provincial government to reduce worker exposure to silica dust and radiation. A 1973 study of the workforce found that 3.6 percent of workers had silicosis and 5.6 percent had a pre-silicotic condition.[55] An 18-day wildcat strike and questioning in the Ontario legislature from provincial New Democrats eventually led to the formation of Ontario's Ham Commission, which recommended changes in health and safety laws.

The external responsibility system

As a result of political pressure, Canadian governments re-evaluated their approach to occupational health and safety during the 1970s.[56] Among the main changes were the establishment of single regulatory agencies, new legislation,[57] and increased worker involvement.[58] The external responsibility system created under this legislation explicitly adopted the economic perspective on risk commonly advocated by employers by limiting the obligations of employers to protect workers.

Saskatchewan, for example, requires employers to "ensure, insofar as is reasonably practicable, the health, safety and welfare at work of all of the employer's workers."[59] Similar language can be found in other legislation.[60] The legislation does not require employers to protect workers from every hazard or risk. Rather, employers must do everything that is "reasonably practicable" to protect workers. While this is an improvement, it also suggests that legislators continue to view the risk of workplace injury as unavoidable and acceptable. The relatively low fines historically assessed against violators supports this assertion. If injury were viewed as unacceptable, legislators would have enacted much higher fines and directed more frequent prosecution on the principle (embedded in all of the acts) that increasing the cost of injury increases employer motivation to reduce injury.[61]

By the 1990s, the effect of the neo-liberal prescription on government policies was being seen in OHS.[62] External regulation was de-emphasized, with fewer or lower quality inspections being conducted. Prosecutions also dropped off. Governments also began "partnerships" with industries, whereby employers could earn incentives (often rebates on workers' compensation premiums) based on their accident records.[63] These new partnerships move workers and unions to the periphery of occupational health and safety regulation.[64]

The internal responsibility system
New legislation in the 1970s also created three new worker health and safety rights. These included the right to know about workplace hazards, the right to participate in discussions about workplace health and safety, and the right to refuse unsafe work. These rights represented significant gains for workers. Among the reasons for emphasizing internal (i.e., firm-based) responsibility for health and safety is the state's purported inability to regulate the large number of workplaces.[65] It is, however, more accurate to say that governments were not prepared to undertake such intensive regulatory work. This unwillingness reflects a reluctance to expend resources and interfere

with employer management of the workplace—a long-standing feature in OHS. In this way, the economic perspective on risk underlies the internal responsibility system (IRS).

That said, the internal approach is also informed by a sense that workers have an important stake in occupational health and safety. Workers are made responsible for policing employer compliance with OHS standards. This is particularly important, as the number of workplace inspections has declined in many jurisdictions.[66] Joint health and safety committees (JHSCs) are designed to improve communication about health and safety within firms. Yet employers continue to control what, when, where, and how goods and services are produced — a power fettered only by a duty to consult with workers over safety matters. The conflicting nature of worker and employer interests is only partially recognized in IRSs.[67] In this way, state regulation has given way to partial self-regulation. This approach also pushed occupational health and safety issues out of the public spotlight by making them local workplace matters.

CANADA'S OHS SYSTEM TODAY
The history of injury prevention in Canada presented above clearly shows that the state and employers view the risk of workplace injury as inevitable, minimal, and acceptable. Governments have sought to limit the employer's right to manage as little as possible. This section briefly outlines how governments presently regulate workplace injuries. This includes providing a clearer picture of the internal and external responsibility systems and how they interact. In Chapter 3, we'll evaluate the effectiveness of this system in depth.

Duties and obligations
Each province and territory, as well as the federal government, has enacted laws addressing occupational health and safety. The

precise form of the law (e.g., act, regulation, guideline, code) varies. That said, every jurisdiction sets out employer duties and responsibilities, powers of enforcement, gives workers the right to refuse unsafe work, and protects workers from reprisal for doing so.[68]

Employers are made responsible for taking every reasonable precaution to ensure the safety of workers. This includes complying with statutory standards (e.g., providing fall protection), providing workers with adequate supervision, education, and training, ensuring equipment is properly maintained, and informing workers of potential hazards. Supervisors must ensure workers comply with legislative requirements, alert workers to hazards, and use safety equipment and devices. Workers, in turn, comply with the law, use safety equipment and devices, report hazards to their employer and report contraventions of the law to the government.

Health and safety standards

In addition to the basic rights and duties set out in legislation, governments establish standards addressing occupational hazards. These may address physical hazards. For example, Section 139 of Alberta's *Occupational Health and Safety Code* normally requires employers to use a fall protection system if a worker may fall more than 3 metres or if there is an unusual possibility of injury if a worker falls less than 3 metres. Specific standards for working over water and the type of equipment are specified.

Other standards address chemical and biological agents. Exposure to these agents causes the majority of occupational diseases and many workplace injuries. These standards usually include exposure limits. Exposure limits are frequently set in terms of an exposure (e.g., 50 parts per million) over a period of time (e.g., two hours, eight hours, a lifetime).[69] These exposure limits are the level of exposure at which it is believed that nearly all workers may be exposed without adverse effect.

Hazardous materials also come with manufacturer-provided Material Safety Data Sheet (MSDS). The federal Workplace Hazardous Materials Information System (WHMIS) implemented in 1988 required standardized labelling and MSDSs.[70] The availability of MSDSs for over 400,000 products increases the ability of workers to know what they are handling. Worker training programs on handling hazardous materials supplement this information.

External responsibility system

All provinces and territories employ inspectors to visit worksites, investigate workplace injuries, and enforce OHS standards. Responsibility for enforcement may rest within government or be delegated to an agency, such as a workers' compensation board (WCB). Canadian inspectors continue to focus on persuasion, rather than coercion. Inspectors may direct employers to remedy health and safety hazards via the issuance of an order. Inspectors may also recommend charges be laid against employers.[71]

In 2004, the federal *Criminal Code* was amended to allow prosecutors to bring charges against organizations and senior managers when there has been a serious breach of workplace safety standards. The first conviction occurred in March 2008 and imposed a penalty of $110,000 upon a Quebec company. To date, there has been no case law specifying the level of negligence required under the statute. Such charges can be laid in parallel with prosecutions under occupational health and safety legislation.

Some jurisdictions (e.g., Manitoba, British Columbia) have also experimented with allowing inspectors to issue tickets with fines attached to them. In Ontario, both employers and workers can be the subject of such tickets. Significant controversy attends this system, which appears to focus attention on the actions of individual workers and supervisors (indeed making them mostly responsible for workplace safety), rather than the decisions made by employers.[72]

Internal system and the three rights

In the 1970s, the introduction of the IRSs devolved much responsibility for regulating compliance with OHS standards to workers. Workers have three rights under the IRS: the right to know about health and safety hazards in the workplace, the right to participate (typically by selecting representatives to a joint health and safety committee), and the right to refuse unsafe work.

The most significant of these rights is the right to refuse unsafe work. The right to refuse runs contrary to workers' common law obligation to obey and the collective bargaining principle of "work now, grieve later." This exception reflects the immediacy and potential harm that health and safety hazards represent to workers.[73]

Official work refusals are relatively uncommon.[74] More typically, workers will quietly alter their work to avoid a hazard.[75] Issues may also be raised in joint health and safety committees. These committees may be required by legislation or collective agreements. They typically comprise an equal number of worker and employer representatives and are charged with examining health and safety issues and recommending remedies.

Partnership model and incentives

During the late 1980s, the idea of state–employer partnerships as a way to improve safety gained currency. This idea is similar to the notion of underlying IRSs: employers and workers are in the best position to know and remediate workplace risks. Where state–employer partnerships differ from IRS is that workers are largely excluded from these partnerships — except as the target of educational campaigns.

For example, faced with rising compensation costs, the

Government of Alberta issued a challenge to employers in 2002 to reduce workplace injuries by 40 percent within two years. Various government initiatives followed, including a system of incentives.[76] As part of the post-2002 injury reduction campaign, a Certificate of Recognition was linked to a 5 percent reduction in an employer's WCB industry rate through the Partnership in Injury Reduction (PIR) program on top of the WCB's own experience-rating system.[77]

CONCLUSION

Over time, governments have addressed injury prevention in various ways. In seeking to reduce the incidence of workplace injuries, governments have avoided significantly curtailing the rights of employers to manage. But there have been significant gains for workers. There are rules around working conditions. Employers are obligated to identify and remediate hazards. Workers have the right to know, participate, and refuse. And injured workers can gain more predictable, stable, and immediate compensation.

Yet, despite these efforts, hundreds of thousands of Canadians continue to be injured each year. In Chapter 3, we will examine this apparent inconsistency in some depth. Among the issues we'll consider is the degree to which conflict between maintaining production and social reproduction retards effective injury prevention. Also of interest is the degree to which regulation affects an employer's ability to decide what is produced when, where, and how. The importance of the economic perspective on risk will also be highlighted. Of particular interest is how this perspective is used to justify prioritizing profitability over safety.

— THREE —

CRITIQUE OF
OHS IN CANADA

On 27 July 2009, 37-year-old Darryl Binder died at Athabasca University after falling five meters and being impaled by rebar. Binder was a construction foreman at Athabasca's new research building and left behind five children.[1] Alberta's occupational health and safety (OHS) regulations require workers to use fall protection if they could fall more than three meters or face an increased risk of injury because of the surface onto which they could fall. Despite this requirement, Binder was not adequately protected and he died.

Binder's death is, unfortunately, not unusual. Despite OHS laws, over half a million Canadians are significantly injured at work each year. And more than 1000 workers — likely many more — die as a result of work-related injury and disease. These very crude indicators are a good place to start examining the reality of occupational health and safety in Canada. These numbers (and their deficiencies) reveal interesting things about what workplace injuries and hazards are recognized in Canada.

From this discussion, we turn our attention to specific injury prevention activities. This includes examining the effectiveness of internal and external safety systems. Of particular concern is the degree to which workers can and do exercise their rights under health and safety legislation. We will also examine the degree to which government standards and external enforcement work. Finally, we look at the effectiveness of state–employer partnership programs and the perception that they create regarding workplace safety.

RECOGNIZING INJURY AND HAZARDS

How many injuries?

To determine whether OHS efforts are effective, it is useful to consider the rate and severity of injuries and fatalities. We might then look at changes over time. Or we might compare industries in different provinces or other countries.[2] Such comparisons can be tricky — it is difficult to know whether any two things are comparable, no matter how similar they appear on the surface. Yet even crude indicators of injury and death are a useful place to start.

Unfortunately, we simply don't know how many workers are injured and killed each year. In the Introduction, we saw that 630,000 Canadian adults reported being injured on the job in 2003 severely enough to limit their activity. This number is a significant underestimate of workplace injuries. It ignores injuries that did not limit activity, such as minor cuts, burns, bruises, and strains. It also ignores injuries to minors, repetitive strain injuries, multiple injuries, and unreported injuries.[3] Despite these problems, 630,000 injuries is likely closer to the truth than almost any other number available.

This difficulty exists because most "injury statistics" are actually the number of compensation claims accepted by workers' compensation boards (WCBs).[4] Injuries not reported to or rejected by a WCB are not counted. Frequently, injuries that did not cause time off work are also excluded. Injuries to the 10 to 20 percent of workers not enrolled in workers' compensation are also missing. On top of this, there appears to be significant under-reporting of potentially compensable workplace injuries.[5] Consequently, the injury numbers commonly used are low. For example, in 2003, the Association of Workers' Compensation Boards of Canada (AWCBC) reported 348,715 accepted time-loss injury/disease claims. That same year, the AWCBC reported 963 work-related fatalities.[6]

This suggests three things. First, injury statistics commonly do not report the true level of workplace injury and death. Second, this under-reporting distorts our perception about the frequency of injury: there are many more injuries than we "see." Third, injury rates are a social construction. That is to say, how we define injury affects the level of injury we see. WCB claims data is the easiest way to "see" injuries. But, in accepting these statistics, we accept the definitions and biases built into them.

Who gets hurt affects injury recognition

A workplace injury is damage a worker sustains at work. Many injuries are easy to see, such as cuts, bruises, broken bones, and burns. Depending on how a worker gets hurt, the relationship between work and the injury may also be obvious. In these cases — such as that of Darryl Binder — it is easy to agree there is an injury and that it was caused by work. But this is not always so. Consider injuries caused by repetitive motions.

Repetitive strain injuries (RSIs) became an important public policy issue in the 1980s. But they began appearing in factory and office workers during the early nineteenth century. Often referred to as writers' cramp or telegraphists' cramp, these RSIs received uneven treatment over time — often depending on who was experiencing them. For example, research by Dr. George Phalen contributed to chronic hand disorders not being recognized as work-related for nearly 40 years. His assertion was that many women experienced these disorders but, since women did no "manual" work, such injuries could not be work-related.[7]

The Phalen example illustrates that who gets injured plays an important role in the recognition of hazards and injuries.[8] The physical demands of women's work in the home and on the job are often downplayed. And much of the "science" of workplace health and safety is based upon studies of healthy men. Exposure limits to chemical and biological agents have historically been set with little consideration that there may be meaningful physiological differences between men and women, as well as between healthy and unhealthy individuals.

The type of injury and its cost also affect recognition
We limit workers' exposure to chemical and biological agents because these agents cause occupational diseases, as well as injuries (such as burns). But recognition of the exposure–disease relationships has not come easily or quickly. Occupational diseases typically have long latency periods that make it difficult to see the relationships between work and the injury. The presence of other potential causes or contributory factors can make it even harder to determine definitively that work contributed to the disease in other than a minimal way.[9] While governments and employers often cite the complex causation of such diseases as a reason for delay or refusals, there is evidence that concerns about financial liability drive these decisions.

Fluorspar miners in St. Lawrence, Newfoundland, for example, struggled for 30 years to gain adequate health and safety protections, as well as compensation for work-related silicosis and lung cancer. Government concern about the economic impact of accepting such diseases played a part in delaying and limiting compensation. Only mounting public pressure and workplace disruption triggered change.[10] Uranium miners at Elliott Lake, Ontario, faced similar barriers to gaining recognition of the link between their work and silicosis and cancer and used similar tactics to gain redress.[11]

Employers may impede injury recognition

Employers withholding information about an occupational hazard also contributes to delays in recognizing such hazards. The danger of asbestos exposure was well known in the industry[12] but Bendix Automotive, for example, withheld this information from brake plant workers in Windsor, Ontario. When political pressure finally resulted in both health and safety enforcement and compensation claims, Bendix closed its plant in 1980.[13]

Bendix is not an isolated case of an employer withholding information and then abandoning its workers. In the United States, the Johns-Manville Company engaged in a decades-long pattern of denying asbestos was a hazard and repressing information about its effects in order to maximize its profitability.[14] During this time, hundreds of its workers fell ill and died from asbestos-related diseases. The 1980 shutdown of the Johns-Manville plant in Scarborough, Ontario, allowed the employer to externalize the costs of compensating asbestos-related injuries by removing itself from the workers' compensation rate-group to which those injuries would be charged.[15]

The social construction of injury and hazards

These examples indicate that injuries, like accidents, are a social construction. That is to say, factors other than "science" contribute to what we consider legitimate work-related injuries. Workers, employers, and governments have much at stake when defining an injury. They are also differently able to cause or impede the recognition of workplace injuries.

Eric Tucker notes that constructing what is considered "normal" in the workplace is a fundamentally political act, because the expectations that are generated arise out of divergent and competing interests.[16] Thus, the recognition of and response to injuries depends on positions taken by the state and other players, such as corporations and trade unions. Naturally, those who are more powerful are better situated to have their versions of reality become the dominant ones. And in our society, capital is very much more powerful and better organized than workers are.

Health and safety hazards are also social constructions. They grow (in part) out of what we consider legitimate injuries. Over time, substances and activities that we once did not consider hazardous have been redefined. Asbestos, coal dust, and silica all come to mind. More recently, we've come to see activities such as sitting in one position for hours or making repetitive motions as hazardous. And new hazardous substances, such as photocopier and printer toner, have been identified.

Employer tactics in contesting injury recognition

As with injuries, employers, workers, and the state often contest what work and substances are considered hazardous. Angela Nugent traces the plight of young women who died from radium poisoning after painting luminescent paint on watch faces. These workers experienced severe anemia, lesions of the gums, and necrosis of the jaw before dying.[17] The United States Radium Corporation responded by engaging researchers to determine if radium was indeed the cause of these deaths. This research indicated that it was.

The employer's response exemplifies how employers can evade responsibility for such injuries. The employer requested additional research, criticized the methods, prohibited publication of the research, misrepresented the findings to government, hired a more compliant researcher to create evidence that there was no risk, blamed the workers for their exposure, and then argued that the deaths of the young women was an acceptable price to pay for glow-in-the-dark watch faces.[18] Eventually the employer was forced to address these hazardous conditions. It chose to alter how watches were made to provide more protection to workers, rather than eliminate the hazard from the workplace.

Radium poisoning demonstrates that some hazards are easier to find agreement about than others are. An unguarded saw blade poses an obvious hazard. The way a subcontracting system pressures workers to work unsafely is more difficult to see. For example, the effect of the subcontracting system used in Australia's long-haul trucking system on workplace safety has been largely ignored because of the dispersed and incremental nature of fatalities — fatalities were not viewed through the lens of work.[19] This subcontracting system exacerbated normal demands on drivers, compelling them to work excessive hours, speed, and use drug stimulants.

Ignoring the context in which the accidents occurred meant the hazard was constructed as driver error. Regulation then became focused on drivers and not on the system of work. This construction benefited employers because it ignored how employers caused accidents through the organization of work. It also benefitted the state by obscuring the role played by government deregulation of the trucking industry.

Perpetuating the careless worker myth

Focusing attention on worker behaviour is a recurring issue in the prevention of workplace injuries. As we saw in Chapter 2, the careless worker narrative has been a powerful tool for employers over time. Despite being largely discredited, it continued to inform state efforts to prevent workplace injuries. For example, Alberta ran an OHS awareness campaign in 2005 that showed workers engaging in or the consequences of unsafe work practices.[20] The common visual component of the campaign was the word "stupid." Its location in each poster (e.g., on a crate being moved unsafely, on a wall from which an unsecured ladder had fallen) was designed to focus attention on the contribution of worker behaviour to workplace accidents. In this way, the campaign implicitly blamed workers for their injuries.

Alberta launched a similar campaign in 2008, with graphic videos showing how workers' behaviour causes accidents.[21] In one vignette, a worker in high heels is injured when she falls from a ladder while trying to reach unstable stock on a high shelf. The video ignores the role of the employer in creating jobs that require workers to engage in risky behaviour to complete routine tasks. The employer required the worker to wear high heels to look fashionable. The employer gave the worker a rickety ladder. The employer placed stock high up and stacked it unsafely. That the worker was injured was entirely predictable and preventable—by the employer. The safety tips provided for *workers* at the end of this particular video all suggest alterations to how the job is designed—things entirely out of the control of workers. Missing is any indication that employees have a statutory right (and obligation) to refuse such obviously unsafe work.

Identifying occupational cancer
Occupational cancer provides an interesting example of how injuries and hazards are socially constructed in ways that endanger workers. Occupational cancer is important because of the long-term growth in the proportion of work-related fatalities attributed to occupational diseases.[22] Discussion and research about occupational cancer typically focuses more on treatment than prevention.[23] When preventing occupational cancer is discussed, it typically focuses on determining "safe" levels and types of exposure to carcinogens, rather than discussing whether exposure ought to occur at all. These discussions also tend to emphasize the importance of lifestyle factors (e.g., diet, exercise) in preventing cancer—in doing so, making workers' implicitly responsible for cancer prevention.[24] Framing the discussion this way ignores that involuntary and even unknowing exposure to carcinogens (for which, incidentally, there are no definitively safe levels of exposure) frequently occurs as a result of job-design decisions made by employers.

There is significant debate over the percentage of cancers that are occupationally linked. Although estimates range from 4 percent to 40 percent, and obviously vary by type of cancer and country, there is widespread acceptance of numbers between 8 percent and 10 percent.[25] Occupationally linked cancers are not evenly distributed through the workforce, more commonly affecting blue-collar workers and having gendered elements.[26] Yet these numbers are not reflected in government statistics, which are derived from worker's compensation claims.

For example, in 2005, approximately 13,100 Albertans were diagnosed with cancer and 5,500 Albertans died from cancer.[27] The Alberta Cancer Board estimates that 8 percent of all cancers are occupationally caused.[28] This suggests just over 1,000 of Alberta's 2005 cancers were occupational cancers and about 440 deaths were occupationally related. Yet, in 2005, the WCB accepted only 29 claims for cancer and reported just 38 cancer-related fatalities. This example is consistent with the pattern over the previous 10 years.[29] The vast majority of cancer cases accepted by the WCB are lung cancer (mesothelioma) with benefits going mostly to firefighters, coal miners, and workers exposed to asbestos. In this way, the prevalence of occupational cancer is hidden.

Preventing occupational cancer

Not surprisingly, discussion of occupational cancer has been largely absent from Alberta's occupational health and safety system, which — like workers' compensation — is designed to address more traditional accidents and injuries. The word carcinogen appears only three times in the 539-page *Occupational Health and Safety Code*. One mention requires the labelling of asbestos storage units. The other two instances require documentation of workplace and non-workplace exposures to asbestos, silica, or coal dust during a health assessment of such a worker.

While it may seem facile to criticize legislation based on the (dis)appearance of a single word, this forms part of a broader pattern of ignoring cancer in the workplace. The *Occupational Health and Safety Code* does require employers to keep exposures to chemicals, biological hazards, and harmful substances (many of which are carcinogens) as low as reasonably practicable and below certain threshold levels.[30] Yet, relying on such exposure thresholds for carcinogens simply sets an "acceptable" level of occupational cancer, rather than preventing it.

When workers get cancer from legal and/or illegal workplace exposures to carcinogens, the state then frames these (as at least partially) the consequence of worker behaviour. *Cancer in the Workplace*, a 2005 publication by the Alberta Cancer Foundation and Work Safe Alberta, notes how lifestyle and genetic factors are influential factors in the development of cancer.[31] The document acknowledges that job design is a pivotal factor in exposing workers to carcinogens, but then fails to follow that logic through in its recommendations.

Instead, workers are provided with tips, some of which are useful in limiting occupational exposures (e.g., wear personal protective devices, wash your hands) and some of which are not (e.g., eat lots of vegetables, get some exercise). While workers are encouraged to limit their exposure to hazardous substances, this is indeed something over which they have little control or even knowledge about. Employers, who do have control and knowledge, are recommended to "ensure that the products being used in the workplace are the least hazardous possible for the intended use" and that engineering controls and other equipment can be used to reduce exposures.[32]

Constructing cancer as a non-issue

In this example, we see occupational cancer and carcinogens being (de)constructed as a low-priority issue. The medical community pays little attention to the occupational origins of cancer.

When causation is discussed, the multi-factorial nature of cancer is (legitimately) raised as a barrier to identifying causes, which then seems to preclude effective prevention. This assertion is vexing in several ways. First, unequivocal evidence regarding causation in individual cases is likely impossible to find. Yet, this does not preclude taking action to eliminate exposure to known carcinogens immediately. Second, many non-occupational exposures to carcinogens that confound causation are the result of workers using or ingesting the products produced by employers, such as cigarettes, alcohol, pesticides, and herbicides on food, and fumes and other residue from industrial plants or manufactured products.

When an occupational link becomes established in the public's mind, compensation is provided.[33] Yet, overall, there is little regulation of carcinogens and the method of regulation legitimizes questionable levels of exposure. The state prefers advising workers to wear protective gear and eat well to requiring the redesign of work processes. In these ways, Alberta has constructed a (non)response to occupational cancer. This approach is common and advances the economic interests of employers. Many carcinogens are fundamental to industrial processes and eliminating them entails significant additional costs (resulting in higher prices and/or reduced profitability) and significant liability. Acknowledging that corporations knowingly expose workers to carcinogens and that the government allows this to continue is also a significant threat to both social stability and the legitimacy of the state. Thus, this topic receives little attention.

Conceptual models of injury

Embedded in legislation, policy, and practice are beliefs about the cause and nature of injuries. Three basic assumptions about work-related injuries underlie efforts to prevent and compensate workplace injuries:

· The mechanism of injury will be discernable, or at least mostly distinguishable from other events or disease processes,

· The injury will manifest itself at the time of or reasonably soon after the injury occurs, such that the injury can be causally related to a work-place event, and

· The course and treatment of the injury will be broadly similar from one person to the next.

This biomedical model asserts that illness has a biological source (or pathology). Further, the degree of illness is proportional to the degree of biological malfunction. Objective medical knowledge (e.g., test results, observations, functional evaluations) is more valued than patient self-reports.[34] This model plays a significant and useful role in both occupational health and safety and workers' compensation.

Limits to the biomedical model

Yet, this model also has some serious drawbacks. Determining whether a worker concern can be medically substantiated takes time and money. Employer resistance can impede such a determination. Until a determination is made, workers continue to be exposed to the hazard. Further, worker-identified injuries or illnesses that cannot be validated by such tests are not given much credence, and thus prevention and compensation may be denied. This, however, does not eliminate any hazard that exists or injury that occurs — it simply transfers these costs to workers.

This model also runs afoul of recent research that suggests (1) injuries are often multi-factorial, and (2) work exerts significant effects on health and a broad range of diseases have work-related components.[35] Attempting to classify injuries as work-related and non-work-related (thereby ignoring the interactive effect between occupational and broader environmental factors) is likely an impossible task.[36] Yet this biomedical approach remains commonplace.[37] Consequently, instead of triggering a broader effort to reduce unsafe work practices and the use of toxic substances in society, discussions define these hazards out of existence — uncertainty is used to preclude action.

Workers may take a different approach to constructing illness and injury. Many rely upon their own observations of how the workplace affects them and their co-workers to draw conclusions about health and safety.[38] The reliance of workers on this form of knowledge may have implications for the regulation of occupational health and safety.[39] Where injuriousness is contested, medical knowledge is typically given precedence over worker knowledge. Knowing this, workers may not engage in OHS systems knowing that they will fail, or they may engage it in a way they believe they can succeed at, even if the outcome is less than optimal.[40]

REGULATING WORKPLACE HAZARDS

Approaches to regulation

Chapter 2 suggested that the state has intervened in injury prevention because workplace injuries threaten production and social reproduction. Governments can intervene in the operation of society in several ways. It is useful to think about these policy instruments as falling into four different categories of increasing invasiveness.[41] States can use *hortatory instruments* to signal priorities and propel actions by appealing to values via symbols. Campaigns like "Bring 'em back alive" attempt to convince motorists to drive safely in order to protect their children.[42]

States can also use *capacity-building instruments*, such as investing in intellectual, material, or human resources to enable activity. For example, governments can offer educational campaigns, such as Alberta's online ergonomic training programs, to improve the knowledge of workers and managers.[43]

Alternately, the state could provide training materials, safety equipment, or trainers to build the capacity of workers and managers to act safety.

Incentive-based instruments use inducements, sanctions, charges, or force to encourage action. This could include financial incentives to employers for reducing workplace injuries, such as Alberta's Partners in Injury Reduction program (discussed below) or ticketing workers and employers for unsafe acts or circumstances, such as Ontario's 2005 initiative.[44] Prosecutions under health and safety legislation as well as the 2004 amendment to the federal Criminal Code are other examples.

Finally, states can use *authority-based policy instruments* that grant permission, or prohibit or require action. They can also change the distribution of authority of power within a system. So a state could sanction the creation of a no-fault system of injury compensation that displaces tort law. It could also compel employers to participate in that system. It could impose duties upon employers that are greater than their common law duties. It could set standards regarding chemical exposures.

Limits on regulation

Governments often use several policy instruments to achieve a goal, such as making workplaces safer. The exact choice of instrument(s) can be constrained by political pressure, such as employers wanting to minimize regulation. The state may also be limited by popular conceptions about the appropriate role of the state and the effectiveness of particular forms of regulation. Constraints are often categorized as political and practical. This division is false and obscures how "practical" constraints reflect earlier political decisions.

For example, many people believe that the state must rely upon employers and workers to make workplaces safe because there aren't enough inspectors. In this way, the internal responsibility system is cast as a reaction to a practical problem:

inspectors can't be everywhere. Is that really true? The number of inspectors that the state chooses to hire is a political decision. This decision reflects how many inspections the government believes is desirable. More broadly, it also reflects the degree of state interference in the operation of workplaces that the government thinks is required (or is politically palatable). Viewed this way, the seeming practical problem of not enough inspectors is actually a political decision.

It is also useful to be mindful that the ability of the state to regulate is compromised by the multiple goals that regulatory agencies must often pursue. In addition to adjudicating disputes and enforcing compliance, OHS agencies may undertake research, provide policy advice, distribute funding or compensation, or collect premiums. Such agencies may need to trade off how and how aggressively they enforce rules in order to achieve other organizational objectives.[45]

The internal responsibility system

Beginning in the 1970s, Canadian governments began emphasizing the internal responsibility system (IRS), with workers having the right to know, participate, and refuse. The IRS was adopted when the influence of labour was near its peak and the standard employment relationship was widespread.[46] In practice, those workers most able to benefit from the IRS have been unionized workers and non-unionized workers in workplaces where employers are prepared to cooperate.[47] With Canadian unionization rates hovering at around 30 percent, the IRS clearly does not equally benefit all workers.

In order to participate in decision-making about safety and exercise the right to refuse, workers need to be aware of the hazards they are facing. It is unclear whether workers are aware of hazards and whether the hazards workers identify are accepted as such. Workers may also be reluctant to ask for information. For example, only one in five Ontario workers with a health and safety concern asked for information about it — with the majority of workers asking their supervisors.[48]

Workers may also not know their rights. For example, a 1988 Ontario study found that 44 percent of workers knew nothing about their rights.[49] Workers who did know about their rights were those already most advantaged in the workforce: highly educated and/or unionized men.[50] More recently, a 2007 study found that only 21 percent of new Canadian workers received health and safety training in their first year with a new employer.[51] This suggests that most employers do not take safety issues seriously enough to train workers.

Knowledge is power?

A popular refrain among health and safety activists during the 1970s was "Knowledge is not power. Power is power."[52] While this slogan is incisive, there is good reason to believe that knowledge is power — for employers. Specifically, when there is a large difference in what workers and employers know about health and safety, the rights to know and participate may actually increase employer power in the workplace.[53]

This seemingly counterintuitive outcome occurs in two ways. First, employers can influence which hazards workers pay attention to by what knowledge they choose to share. Employers may be more likely to acknowledge or provide information about hazards that are easy to address rather than hazards that require more involved remediation.

The ability of employers to influence what hazards are recognized is heightened by having a designated group that is "responsible" for workplace health and safety issues, such as a joint health and safety committee (JHSC). This arrangement channels health and safety concerns in a single venue that the employer can dominate. Having an official place to discuss health and safety also delegitimizes discussion that occurs elsewhere, such as in a union hall or on the shop floor.

Second, employers can influence how workers think about hazards by how the employer frames an issue or the solution. For example, workplace air quality may be an issue. An employer may frame this as a worker "concern," thereby subtly contesting whether there is indeed a hazard. The employer can then quite reasonably suggest evidence needs to be collected (or provided by the workers) to substantiate the "concern." This delays, and possibly derails, action. In the meantime, workers continue to be exposed to the hazard.

Should a hazard be identified, the employer can shape the solution(s) considered by using its managerial power. For example, it can require the use of personal protective equipment (PPE) such as respirators (or other low-cost solutions) in lieu of altering the production process to eliminate the hazard. Without some way for workers to compel a specific remedy (e.g., collective bargaining, direct action on the shop floor), workers must accept the employer's solution.

Joint health and safety committees

The JHSC is a central feature of the IRS. Committees typically comprise an equal number of employer and worker representatives. When consensus on health and safety issues can be found, the JHSC can make non-binding recommendations to the employer. Data from the UK, U.S., and Canada suggest that such committees are associated with a reduction in workplace injuries.[54] The effectiveness of the committees appears, however, mediated by union representation, involvement of workers, management attitudes, and the degree of external regulation.[55] The most frequent criticism of JHSCs is that they lack the authority to compel employers to act on safety issues.[56] In short, the potentially positive effects of JHSCs only occur if employers accept the work of the committees.[57]

This is not to say that workers are entirely helpless. Recent research at the University of Windsor found that how worker safety representatives behave has an important effect on what can be achieved. When worker representatives gather their own research on hazards, emphasize worker knowledge, and mobilize workers around safety issues, significant improvements in working conditions were more likely to occur.[58] Workers with a more politically active orientation tend to challenge the way employers shape and limit discussion, recognizing that remedy often required action beyond simply identifying concerns to the employer.[59]

By contrast, the Windsor study also suggests that workers with a technical-legal orientation typically focused their attention on basic housekeeping and maintenance issues — concerns that are neither disruptive nor costly to address.[60] This finding builds upon the observation by Vivienne Walters that worker representatives on JHSCs are often drawn into technical, collaborative discussions shaped by employer notions of what risks are reasonable, and what costs are affordable.[61]

This research suggests two things. On the one hand, employers can use JHSCs to limit the impact worker of participation rights by controlling information flow, shaping discussion about safety, and ignoring recommendations they do not agree with. On the other hand, workers prepared to engage in more overtly political action could use JHSCs as a platform from which to exert pressure on employers. In short, employers continue to enjoy a structural advantage. But the effectiveness of participation rights for workers is determined, in part, by how those rights are exercised.

Despite (or perhaps because of) these shortcomings, JHSCs remains an important part of most provincial OHS systems. This is not the case everywhere though. In Alberta, for example, statutory JHSCs are formed at the order of the Minister. There were about 321,000 significant occupational injuries in Alberta in 2007 — an average year.[62] Despite this, the Minister did not order any committees formed. In fact, there are no

Minister-ordered JHSCs in Alberta. Committees that operate do so where workers are unionized (about 20 percent of the workforce) and have bargained them into place or where the employer allows a committee to function. Voluntary committees are not, however, subject to the provision of Alberta's *Health and Safety Act*. Without specific collective-agreement language, employers set the rules for such committees.[63]

The right to refuse

The right to refuse unsafe work is the most powerful right workers have under the IRS. It is one of the few instances where workers can legally disobey their employer. A refusal can compel the employer to pay attention to safety concerns. Yet, despite staggering numbers of injuries and deaths each year, workers do not refuse unsafe work very often.[64] To understand why workers don't refuse requires us to consider the nature of this right in practice.

A refusal is a reactive right. It operates only after the employer has made many decisions about the organization of work — some of which have made the work unsafe. And scope of the right is simply to work or not. The right to refuse confers no ability on workers to influence what hazards exist in the workplace — only to absent themselves from those hazards they know about and believe unsafe. By contrast, the employer has significant latitude to (re)organize work in ways that make it minimally acceptable to — although perhaps not entirely safe for — the worker. In this way, employers have significantly more discretion and flexibility around work refusals than workers do.

Formal work refusals are not the only kind of work refusal. An Ontario study found that only 1 percent of workers exercised their legislative right to refuse unsafe work, although 40 percent informally refused.[65] An informal work refusal may be confrontational (i.e., a refusal without triggering the formal legislative process) or non-confrontational (e.g., altering the work process).[66] Such behaviour may pressure the employer to alter unsafe work. Or, if the employer ignores or is unaware of a worker's resistance, an informal refusal may result in somewhat less unsafe work.

Workers and employers may also differ in their sense of what is "safe" and "unsafe" in the workplace. The right to refuse may also be affected by broader dynamics of industrial relations. Employers, for example, may often raise the spectre that workers might use their statutory right to exert pressure on the employer during collective bargaining — although there is no evidence of this in Canada.[67]

Employer responses to refusals

One outcome of a refusal is that the employer may simply assign the task to another worker, perhaps without telling the second worker about the hazard that has been identified. This may trigger cynicism about the efficacy of the right to refuse, potentially reducing workers' willingness to exercise this right in the future. Employers may also haggle with workers — applying pressure such as "you're holding up the line" or "we have to make this deadline." Indeed, fellow workers may also apply such pressure.[68]

Pressuring workers is effective because refusing unsafe work entails significant risk for workers. Workers who refuse may be disciplined for insubordination. Knowing that they may face discipline for exercising their right, workers may be reluctant to do so.[69] When such discipline is appealed to an administrative tribunal or arbitrator, the burden of proving the work is unsafe — whatever the actual rules about the burden of proof are — may well fall to the worker. A worker with a good work record whose refusal is measured and appears reasonable tends to fare best when he or she appeals discipline.[70]

The specific rules around refusals may also affect the ability of workers to exercise their rights. If the law says the refusal

is only legitimate if the hazard is abnormal, employers do not have to remedy long-standing or industry-wide OHS concerns. If the law says danger must be imminent, workers must wait until matters escalate and the risk to their safety is grave.

Refusal as a weak right

The unwillingness of workers to refuse unsafe work highlights that employers need not exert their power to get their way. That is to say, the powerful rarely have to prove their strength — simply the expectation that employers may exercise their power may be sufficient to gain compliance.[71] Consequently, the right to refuse is paradoxical. On the one hand, it provides workers with a rare opportunity to override employers' common law right to manage. Yet, on the other hand, workers face disincentives and barriers to exercising this right. And even if they do exercise the right, employers do not necessarily have to remedy the problem. In this way, the right to refuse is a weak right.

Yet it is difficult to see this weakness on the surface. It is (superficially) true that "workers have the right to refuse unsafe work" in Canada. This creates the appearance workers can to protect themselves. This, in turn, undermines the political power workers can derive from legitimate concerns about being injured or killed on the job. This appearance also protects employers from state interference: workers can (allegedly) protect themselves. And this appearance protects the state from political backlash when workers are injured because it makes workers appear responsible for their own injuries and death — why didn't the workers just utilize their right to refuse?

Effectiveness of the internal system

The internal system creates weak rights for workers. While workers have more protection than they would otherwise, much of the protection is notional. To exercise these rights — to make them real and meaningful — workers must take a chance in defying their employer and face dismissal.[72] The workers best able to exercise these rights are workers who are already advantaged in the workplace: educated and/or unionized men. In this way, the internal system is consistent with many of the legislative compromises between the interests of labour and capital brokered by the state during the twentieth century. Women, the ill-educated, the non-unionized, and those who have precarious employment (see Chapter 4) receive less protection than educated and/or unionized men do.

To the degree that workers can exercise their rights — perhaps with the cooperation of a sympathetic employer — there are significant limits on these rights. Health and safety rights tend to focus on quantifiable and obvious hazards to health. There is little scope to address qualitative issues in the work environment that may affect health and safety, such as pace, repetitiveness, and deskilling.[73] Workers can suggest changes to such factors through JHSCs, but employers are under no obligation to consider them. In short, "management" decisions about when, where, and how to produce things — the decisions that create risks and hazards — are out of workers' reach under the internal system.[74] Further, some commentators suggest that workers are slowly being squeezed out of an active role in the IRS as the state and employers increasingly adopt partnership models.[75]

Exposure levels and threshold limit values

Internal systems operate in conjunction with the external responsibility system. Governments set standards and obligations, conduct inspections and investigations, and then enforce their laws via orders, fines, and prosecutions. Among the standards set by the state are exposure limits to some of the chemical and biological agents found in the workplace. Workers clearly benefit from knowing to which chemical and biological agents they are being exposed. The limits used, however, raise many concerns.

There are more than 70,000 chemical substances in use in North America. Another 800 substances are introduced each year. There is no toxicity data available for 80 percent of these substances.[76] And the federal Workplace Hazardous Materials Information System (WHMIS) places no obligation on manufacturers or employers to determine the hazardous properties of products before introducing them into the workplace. Consequently, workers are often the first humans to experience prolonged and significant exposure to these substances.

The results of using workers as guinea pigs can be disastrous. As we saw in Chapter 2, workers were the first to experience lead poisoning as a result of adding tetraethyl lead to gasoline. Employers and the government wilfully disregarded these warnings. As a result, not only were workers injured, but also a hazardous product became widely used. The United States now faces an estimated four to five million metric tons of lead dust (8.8 to 11 billion pounds) deposited in soil from car emissions. This constitutes a significant hazard to children playing outdoors.[77]

Are exposure levels safe?

Exposure limits are theoretically supposed to be the level of exposure at which it is believed that nearly all workers may be exposed without adverse effect. There is, however, no scientific basis for this claim.[78] These limits are also largely based on data derived from research on healthy men. Consequently, there is little consideration of the effects of age and gender.[79] Also excluded is the effect of being unhealthy and on exposures from outside the workplace.[80] In this way, exposure limits are likely to overestimate what is a safe exposure.

A concerning trend is that these "safe" levels of exposure go down over time, often dramatically. The exposure level for benzene, for example, dropped from 100 parts per million (ppm) to 10 ppm between 1945 and 1988 and exposure limits on vinyl chloride dropped from 500 ppm to 5 ppm.[81] This phenomenon is not just a part of the distant past. Alberta reduced its exposure levels of chrysotile asbestos from 2 fibres per cubic centimetre (f/cc) in 1982 to 0.5f/cc in 1988 to 0.1f/cc in 2004.[82] These changes reflect that, in 90 percent of cases where threshold limit values (TLVs) have been set, there is insufficient data on the long-term effects of exposure from either animal or human studies.[83]

Barry Castleman and Grace Ziem have also exposed the corporate influence on the setting of TLVs in the United States. Nearly one sixth of all TLVs have been set based on unpublished corporate data, which raises concerns about the reliability of the results. Further, the committees that set these standards have included significant numbers of industry representatives and consultants — many of whose relationships to industry were hidden. This raises significant concerns about conflict of interest. Finally, TLVs have only been set for about 700 chemical substances — a fraction of the over 70,000 substances found in modern workplaces.

Why do exposure levels always go down?

The trend towards lower TLVs seems to indicate the system "works": regulators revise TLVs in response to emerging scientific discoveries. This conclusion is incorrect and misleading. The constant downward trend actually demonstrates a systemic underestimation of risk to workers by regulators. It is true that additional research should alter what is considered a "safe" level of exposure. The law of probability suggests that initial exposure levels will sometimes be too high and sometimes too low.[84] Yet it is rare for TLVs to be set too low — they are almost universally set too high. Why is this?

To be fair, regulators operate in some degree of uncertainty due to a lack of credible research on the effects of chemical substances. This is particularly true when employers hide evidence that substances negatively affect workers, sometimes by producing studies of questionable validity.[85] There is also little research on the synergistic effects of chemicals where there is a multi-agent exposure. For example, the chance of developing lung cancer following asbestos exposure increases dramatically if the worker also smokes cigarettes. Yet, these factors alone cannot explain the consistent underestimation of the hazards posed chemicals.

Regulators also operate in a political environment, where workers, employers, and the state all seek to advance their interests. It follows that regulators setting standards must ask what actions will be politically palatable. In this way, setting exposure limits is not a scientific process, but rather a political one. Among the findings of researchers is that most exposure limits have been set at levels industries were already achieving.[86] That is to say, "safe" appears to be defined in practice as "convenient for employers" rather than "posing no hazard to workers." Incorporating such standards into government regulations results in the incorrect belief that such exposures are safe.

This discussion expands our understanding of how hazards are socially defined concepts. By labelling levels of exposure as "safe" (even when they aren't), the state is able to define hazards out of existence. This benefits employers because many of these substances are integral to industrial processes and/or are the least expensive substance available to do the job. The effect of such hazardous substances on workers is ignored. After all, how can a "safe" substance cause harm to a worker?

Inspections and inspectors

As we saw in Chapter 2, Canadian workplace inspectors have historically favoured achieving compliance by means of persuasion, rather than sanction. Inspections are the main way inspectors identify workplace hazards and pressure employers to remediate them. It is difficult to find data on the number of inspectors. What information can be found suggests that the ratio of inspectors to workers and employers is low. For example, in 1983/84, Ontario had 360 inspectors and 20 occupational hygienists and a workforce of three million.[87] In 2008, Alberta had 84 health and safety inspectors and 144,000 employers.[88]

Inspection data is also difficult to come by. In British Columbia, the number of inspections decreased by 40 percent between 1995 and 2005.[89] By contrast, the total number of field visits in Ontario increased from 59,345 in 1996/97 to 101,275 in 2007/08, with static or declining field visits from 1996 to 2004, followed by a near doubling thereafter.[90] Some commentators have suggested, however, that this increase in inspections masks a reduction in the quality of the inspections.[91] It is difficult to use this data to draw any conclusions. Nationally, information is fragmentary and conflicting. Quantitative measures also exclude important qualitative details, such as the depth and rigour of the inspection.

These weaknesses do not entirely preclude analysis, however. Consider the case of Alberta. In 2005, the Government of Alberta inspected 5,237 worksites. These inspections are part of the province's plan to ensure workplaces are fair, safe, and healthy.[92] While 5,237 inspections seem like a lot, there are more than 140,000 employers in Alberta (many with multiple worksites). Assuming no worksites received multiple visits, this data indicates less than one out of every 26 worksites received a visit. Or, put another way, it would take more than 26 years for every worksite to receive a single visit.

That same year, more than 33,305 Alberta workers were injured so badly that they could not report to work the next day and at least 143 died from work-related injuries and disease.[93] Even if inspections focused exclusively on worksites with demonstrably hazardous conditions, only around one-sixth of these worksites would have received an inspection. It is difficult to believe that this level of inspection can lead to fair, safe, and healthy workplaces.

Bias in inspections

Setting aside the level and quality of the inspection, there is also reason to believe that inspections target traditional industries and work patterns. A 2007 CBC investigation found that inspectors were up to 10 times as likely to visit a traditionally inspected workplace (e.g., construction, manufacturing, mining, and forestry) as one not subject to traditional inspections (e.g., education, health care, office environment).[94]

Nurses, for example, are nearly 20 times less likely to be subject to inspections than workers in forestry are. While nursing is not normally considered an "unsafe" occupation, in 2005, there were 73,000 nurse assaults in Canadian hospitals and care facilities, affecting approximately one-fifth of all nurses. While focusing on workplaces that are traditionally inspected might be explained in terms of the potential dangers in each sector, the number of workers' compensation claims from traditionally and non-traditionally inspected workplaces are approximately equal.[95]

This same investigation found that most government inspections occurred during normal working hours. In Ontario, BC, Newfoundland, Nova Scotia, and New Brunswick, less than 1 percent of inspections occurred on weekends.[96] This ignores the increasing number of workers who work on weekends and evenings. And evidence suggests that their likelihood of having an accident increases during those times.[97]

The effect of orders

When an inspector identifies a hazard, the most common consequence is that the inspector directs the employer to remedy it. The idea is that (assuming the employer complies) this addresses the situation and maintains a good working relationship between the inspector and the employer.[98] Such direction can be verbal or can take the form of a written order. There is no data available comparing the incidence or circumstances when verbal directions become orders.

This approach of trading forbearance for compliance gets mixed reviews. Some suggest that by overlooking minor violations, not enforcing regulations that have a poor cost-benefit ratio, and/or delaying enforcement in return for an employer's promise to comply or mostly comply, inspectors are acting in a reasonable manner.[99] This approach makes inspection work much more cordial. It also reflects that inspectors generally have not had the power to issue on-the-spot fines. It may also reflect the fact that bureaucrats face political pressure that limits their access to prosecution. In this way, cajoling employers may be a reasonable (to their minds) trade-off. It may also reflect their orientation to capitalist relations, which emphasize the rights of the employer to direct work.

Yet this approach has its downsides. For example, this reluctance to deviate from cajoling undermines the effectiveness of workers seeking to address hazards via the internal responsibility system.[100] It also reduces the cost of non-compliance for employers. Employers begin to expect one or more opportunities to remedy deficiencies. This can't help but reduce their attention to safety because there is, in effect, no real penalty for operating a hazardous workplace. In effect, persuasion sends the message that non-compliance is only a problem when it results in injuries. That is to say, the state is legitimizing unsafe work practices so long as nothing bad happens.

Prosecution and fines

When employers don't comply with orders or legislation, governments may pursue prosecution. Prosecution has been relatively uncommon in Canada. The time and effort involved are significant. It also requires governments to get past their general reluctance to recognize or label anything done in the course of business as criminal.[101] When prosecuted, employers may employ the due diligence defence.[102]

Again, we're faced with fragmentary evidence about the number of prosecutions and level of fines. In British Columbia, the real-dollar value of fines declined from $2.3 million in 1995 to $1.4 million in 2005.[103] Ontario provides a contrast with a doubling of prosecutions and fines between 2004/05 and 2007/08.[104] Fine levels and prosecutions are, however, crude measures. The likelihood of being prosecuted and the relative level of fines is a more nuanced indicator of the effectiveness of enforcement.

In 2008, Alberta reported 22 successful prosecutions under the *Occupational Health and Safety Code* for violations going as far back as 2004. During this time, Alberta recorded approximately 700 occupational fatalities.[105] The largest fine was $419,250 for a 2004 violation. That sounds impressive. When compared to the company's annual revenues of $47 million in 2007, such fine is akin a person with an annual income of $50,000 getting a $440 ticket — about same fine you'd get for doing 80 kilometres per hour in a construction zone. The upshot is that Alberta employers face little chance of prosecution and a relative small fine, even when they horribly injure or kill a worker.

In a comprehensive review of the international literature, Canadian researchers Emile Tompa, Scott Trevithick, and Chris McLeod found limited evidence that health and safety inspections resulted in fewer or less severe injuries.[106] There was also only mixed evidence that the prospect of being penalized for health and safety violations lead to fewer or less severe injuries. The researchers suggest several possible explanations, including the fact that the penalties may not be significant enough to motivate compliance. It may also be that organizations do not always act rationally.

This conclusion is hardly surprising for workers. Inspections and the potential penalties have been demonstrably ineffective for decades, as evidenced by the ongoing high level of injury and death in the workplace. More interesting is the researchers' finding of strong evidence that actually being penalized led to a reduction in injuries. This suggests that enforcement of regulations can positively affect workplace safety.[107] Calls for enforcement (versus simple cajoling) were made as far back at 1898[108] and continue into modern times.[109]

Partnerships and the mantra of "safety pays"

Recently, governments and workers' compensation boards have begun creating partnerships with employers to improve workplace safety and reduce injuries. These partnerships are meant to encourage employers to undertake activities that will reduce workplace injuries. This encouragement often comes in the form of a financial incentive, such as a workers' compensation premium rebate. The government and employers may also benefit from the appearance that they are trying to reduce the number of workplace injuries. The Government of Alberta uses WCB claims data to allocate rewards in its partnership program and, indeed, to measure the success of its entire occupational health and safety program.

These programs are based on (and reinforce) the widespread belief that "safety pays." [110] This mantra asserts that organizations can increase profitability by reducing workplace injuries.[111] The most cited evidence for this perspective is a 1993, five-workplace study carried out by the British Health and Safety Executive (HSE).[112] The apparent and hidden costs of injuries were found to be as high as 37 percent of a transportation firm's annual profits, 8.5 percent of a construction project's tender cost for a second firm, and 5 percent of operational costs for a hospital.[113] Among the conclusions of the study is that, for every dollar of insurable costs triggered by an accident, employers faced between $8 and $36 of uninsured costs. The study's conclusion is, therefore, that it pays to improve safety.

This study has been criticized for several reasons.[114] First, the incidents that were selected for analysis were those deemed "economic to prevent" by a joint employer-state panel.[115] That is to say, the study's conclusion is more accurately stated as, "It pays to prevent accidents that are economical to prevent." This sort of circular reasoning makes the HSE results largely meaningless. Second, the study does not look at why injuries are occurring. There is no assessment of whether the injuries were caused by organizations responding to financial incentives to organize work unsafely. This omission makes it impossible to tell if the costs of the injuries were greater than the costs saved by allowing hazardous conditions to persist. That is to say, even in the cases where the accident was deemed economical to prevent, we don't know if that is true or not!

Finally, the notion that safety pays obscures the real message of "safety pays": improve safety only if it pays. In short, the "safety pays" narrative is simply sloganeering that obscures employers' traditional cost-benefit approach to health and safety issue. As we know, historically, this leads to the injury or death of hundreds of thousands of workers. Further, by suggesting safety is profitable, the "safety pays" narrative downplays the need for state regulation. Why would the state check to see if employers had acted in what is (allegedly) the employers' own best interest?

Similar studies have been done in other countries. For example, total injury costs in Australia were estimated at $20 billion in 1995.[116] As Andrew Hopkins points out, eliminating injuries does not make Australia $20 billion better off, because injuries also create benefits such as treating these injuries, replacing damaged equipment, and hiring new workers to replace injured or killed ones.[117] Further, these benefits are not evenly distributed among all stakeholders — 70 percent of the benefits accrue to workers and the state. This creates very little incentive for employers to reduce injury costs — particularly since organizing work in an injurious manner may be ultimately the most profitable choice for employers. Hopkins goes on to note that employers may not be affected (and may even benefit) from large-scale accidents. The death of 3000 and the injury of 300,000 people following a 1984 gas leak in Bhopal, India, resulted in large short-term costs to Union Carbide, however, restructuring led to record earnings per share in 1988.[118] Similar trends can be seen in other organizations.[119]

Interestingly, the Health and Safety Executive has changed its tune about whether safety pays. A 2003 report suggests that there is conflict between safety and other management priorities. And that safety is actually traded off against other priorities.[120] Further, the study confirms that employers are motivated to achieve health and safety standards by regulatory requirements and that "government regulations are necessary in order to protect employees against excessive levels of workplace risk." [121]

Creating evidence of safe workplaces

A significant issue with the safety pays narrative is that it is not likely to result in fewer accidents or injuries. This may undermine the legitimacy of particular governments and, more broadly, the capitalist social formation. Fortunately (for governments), data derived from OHS and workers' compensation programs can provide "evidence" that things are safer. Unfortunately (for workers), the measures used, however, obscure the actual injury rate, and erroneously suggest that workplaces are increasingly safe.[122]

Between 2002 and 2008, Alberta used the lost-time claim (LTC) rate as its main indicator of the level of occupational health and safety (i.e., whether workplaces were "safe and healthy"). The LTC rate is the number of times (per 100 person-years worked) that a worker sustained a compensable, work-related injury that made the worker unable to work beyond the date of injury as reported to the Alberta WCB. This measure is normally expressed as a number of claims (e.g., 2.9 claims per 100 person-years worked) and the results are listed in Table 3.1.

Table 3.1 Lost-time claims per 100 person-years worked, 1991–2008.[123]

Year	Lost-time claims
1991	4.1
1992	3.7
1993	3.5
1994	3.5
1995	3.4
1996	3.4
1997	3.4
1998	3.26
1999	3.21
2000	3.43
2001	3.13
2002	2.93
2003	2.78
2004	2.54
2005	2.41
2006	2.35
2007	2.12
2008	1.88

Table 3.1 makes it look like injury rates are falling. But there are a number of deficiencies with this measure.[124] For example, workplace "injury" is limited to injuries registered with the WCB that cause the worker to be unable to work beyond the date the injury occurred. This excludes approximately 17 percent of the workforce (approximately 325,000 workers) not covered by workers' compensation and ignores both injuries not requiring time off from work beyond the date of injury and injuries serious enough that workers are subsequently unable to do their job, but to whom their employer provides modified work. It also excludes unreported injuries. Further, it excluded LTCs filed but rejected. This percentage has increased from 2.3 percent of time-loss claims in 1996 to 7.8 percent in 2008.[125] Controlling for rejection rates reduces the degree of the LTC reduction over time.

Although the LTC rate has declined over time, the number of actual LTC injuries has remained relatively stable with 37,500 injuries in 2003 and 38,500 injuries in 2007.[126] Alberta's growing pool of workers masks this stability because the lost-time claim rate (i.e., the percentage of workers who experience lost-time claim injuries) is reported as a ratio. That said, stabilizing the number of LTCs during a period of workforce expansion might be a significant achievement. But some additional consideration is necessary.

Employers can reduce the number of LTCs by reducing the rate at which injuries occur or the severity of the injuries. Employers can also simply increase the rate at which they provide modified work, thereby causing the number or rate of lost-time claims to decrease.[127] This, in turn, can yield reductions in an employer's WCB premiums under both the Partnership in Injury Reduction program and the WCB's experience-rating system. It also creates the appearance an employer is "accident free," which can be an important perception to create when bidding on contracts (particularly in the construction industry) and attempting to hire workers. Since 2007, the government has attempted to discern whether employers are gaming the measure by also measuring the disabling injury rate.

Disabling injury rate and severity

A disabling injury "is a work-related injury serious enough to result in time lost from work beyond the day of injury, a modification of work duties, medical treatment beyond first aid, or an occupational disease." [128] In effect, this measure includes both lost-time injuries and instances where the employer provided modified work (and thereby avoided a lost-time claim). This measure does a better job of representing the actual rate of workplace injury, although it still excludes injuries that don't require time off beyond the first day, injuries that are not reported, and injuries to workers outside the ambit of the workers' compensation system.

The disabling injury rate is contrasted with the lost-time claim rate in Table 3.2. This table shows that, while the rate of lost-time claims has gone down over time, the overall rate of workplace injury (the disabling injury rate) has remained relatively stable.

Table 3.2 Disabling injury rate and lost-time claim, 1998–2008.[129]
Note: Rounding differences in data drawn from different publicly available sources results slight discrepancies in 2002–2004 disabling injury rates.

Year	Lost-time claims	Disabling injury rate
1998	3.26	unavailable
1999	3.21	unavailable
2000	3.43	unavailable
2001	3.13	unavailable
2002	2.93	3.8
2003	2.78	3.7
2004	2.54	3.9
2005	2.41	4.02
2006	2.35	4.14
2007	2.12	3.88
2008	1.88	3.50

Again, some additional consideration is warranted. While the disabling injury rate has remained stable, it may be that the seriousness of acute injuries has been reduced. This would explain why fewer workers are requiring time off from work. Further, declining severity might also be indicated by a decline in the duration of average lost-time claims, from 50.9 days in 2003 to 40 days in 2008.[130] But it may also be that employers are simply gaming their lost-time claims (i.e., offering employees modified work in lieu of time off) rather than actually reducing the incidence of serious injuries. The duration measure would also be affected by such gaming (motivated by the WCB's experience-rating mechanism, which is discussed in Chapter 6) thus does not, in itself, allow us to determine whether the seriousness of injuries has declined. Only a study of the seriousness of individual WCB claims would do so. Studies of seriousness almost all focus on lost-time claim rates, which do not control for the gaming behaviour of concern.

Another way to consider injury rates and severity is to examine work-related fatalities (the most serious kind of occupational injury). The number of workplace fatalities accepted by the WCB has increased over time, from 91 in 1996 to 165 in

2008.[131] That said, there is significant annual fluctuation in this number, in part due to its small size.[132] There has been consistent change in the type of fatality accepted over time, with the proportion of fatalities caused by motor vehicle accidents and workplace incidents declining and the proportion of fatalities caused by occupational disease has increased.[133]

Measures as conceptual technologies

Returning to the point made at the beginning of this chapter, a key weakness of accident statistics is that they are really workers' compensation claim statistics.[134] Injuries not reported to and accepted by a WCB are not counted. Even setting aside accidents where the employer is not enrolled in workers' compensation, there is still a significant potential for underreporting of potentially compensable workplace injuries.[135] Underreporting has the potential to significantly distort conclusions drawn from claims data about overall occupational health and safety.

In this case, the long-term care (LTC) and disability insurance (DI) rates used by Alberta may significantly underestimate accident rates and numbers. Further, when experience rating and other systems create incentives for employers to reduce the number and duration of claims through claims management, real accident rates and numbers will likely further diverge from those derived from compensation data.[136] In short, incentive programs designed to reduce injuries may in fact make injury data even less accurate over time.

In considering whether these measures are useful, it can be helpful to think of them as conceptual technologies. That is to say, the measures shape what issues we think about and how we think about those issues by embedding normative assumptions into the structure of the indicators.[137] For example, the act of measurement delineates what activity or outcome is valued and, by operationalizing it in measurable terms, shapes how that activity or outcome is conceptualized. In this case, measuring the LTC rate indicates that reducing lost-time claims (not necessarily reducing injuries) is the desire behaviour.

The recent development of the disabling injury rate partially addresses the issue of employers gaming the LTC rate by using modified work to avoid lost-time claims. But the disabling injury rate is not used to allocate incentives, either to employers in the Partnership in Injury Reduction (PIR) program or to bureaucrats through the government's accountability system. And, if it were, it still creates an incentive for employers to "hide" accidents, by failing to report them, by disputing claims, or by managing injuries such that they do not fall within the definition of a disabling injury. The potentially significant problem for both the LTC and DI rate of simple underreporting is not addressed at all.

By providing an easily communicated and apparently definitive measure of injury rates, the government creates the appearance that the number of injuries is decreasing. The actual number of time-loss injuries is surprisingly stable over time, but this is hidden because injuries are expressed as a rate.[138] Further, attention is focused on time-loss injuries. These injuries are important because of there are normally severe injuries, but these 34,000 timeline injuries in 2007 are also a minority of injuries. Alberta had approximately 321,000 injuries in 2007 — an overall injury rate 10 times what one "sees" when one looks at time-loss injuries. Creating a false impression of workplace safety raises difficult questions, such as why does the government not measure actual changes (ideally improvements) in workplace safety?

Why use inadequate measures?

It is unclear why the government continues to evaluate its programming and reward employers on the basis of a significantly deficient measure. Questions have been raised about the lost-time claim rate in particular so ignorance of the problem is not a particularly compelling explanation.[139] Examining how this measure (and the Partnerships in Injury Reduction program) advances the interests of some stakeholders and not others is insightful.

As noted in Chapter 2, the prevention and compensation of workplace injuries are issues that have galvanized workers to demand action. The resulting social programs (e.g., workers' compensation, occupational health and safety codes and bureaucracies, joint health and safety committees, criminal code amendments) have the potential to significantly impede the profitability of businesses. The state is thus placed in the awkward position of needing to take action on workplace safety to maintain its political legitimacy but not wanted to impede the capital accumulation process.

Measuring the LTC rate and the use of soft regulatory techniques (based on incentives) allows government to appear to be addressing the interests of workers (and perhaps even partially doing so) without requiring (costly) changes in employer operations. The LTC rate suggests that workplaces are getting safer, although the government has been careful never to quite make this assertion. Instead, the LTC rate is provided and individuals are left to infer what they will from it. Given that few Albertans have the knowledge or inclination necessary to analyze what this means, the impression conveyed is that workplaces are safer.

It is also important to be mindful that those who are regulated can sometimes capture regulators. Perhaps employers, in ways that are not readily apparent, are influencing government regulators. This is obviously not the "partnership" that the government wants to convey but there is historical precedent for industry calling the tune. For example, the introduction of fluorescent light bulbs by Sylvania in the 1940s resulted in a spate of workers dying from sarcoidosis, a disease now known to be caused by exposure to beryllium. Publicity about these deaths resulted in the United Electrical Workers Union requesting the government further investigate the hazards associated with making fluorescent bulbs. The government consulted with Sylvania's executives (who did not desire any further bad publicity about their product), who suggested Sylvania would not object to a statement by the government re-assuring workers that there was no undue risk to them. The government promptly complied.[140]

CONCLUSION

The discussion presented above raises serious questions about the degree to which current efforts to prevent workplace injuries are effective. While both the internal and external responsibility systems provide workers with better protections than those they would enjoy under common law, there are significant reasons to be concerned with their operation. Chapter 4 explores why the state would implement ineffective prevention methods. Before considering the explanation presented in Chapter 4, it is useful to consider how our answers to three questions affect the way we choose to frame workplace safety.

1. What hazards do we see in the workplace?

2. How and to what degree do we think these hazards should be addressed?

3. How much state oversight do we think is required to ensure standards are met?

Answering the first question is tricky. What hazards we see in the workplace depends upon how we construct concepts such as accidents, injuries, and hazards. There is broad agreement about many hazards that cause traditional injuries such as cuts, bruises, breaks, and burns — although this does not mean there is agreement about how and to what degree to address these hazards. There is less agreement about hazards that cause many occupational diseases and non-traditional injuries (e.g., RSIs, psychological injuries).

Our answer to the first question shapes how we answer the second. As we saw in Chapter 2, prevention efforts have focused more on hazards that cause traditional injuries. This emphasis reflects the interplay of worker and employer interests. Employers have, historically, sought to limit restrictions on their right to organize work as they see fit. It is more difficult to resist addressing hazards that cause traditional injuries than it is to resist hazards that cause occupational diseases and non-traditional injuries. This latter type of injury frequently entails a long latency period and murky causality that makes it easier to question whether the injury is real and whether it is work-related. Consequently, we focus much of our attention on obvious safety hazards. It easier to see, understand the implications of, gain agreement upon, and remedy the hazard posed by an unshored trench than it is to remedy the hazard posed by a chemical agent.

In determining how and to what degree hazards are remedied, employers retain significant discretion. Employers can approach hazard reduction in several ways. They can eliminate the hazard or, somewhat less effectively, implement engineering controls that contain the substance and thereby limit worker exposure (e.g., venting fumes before they reach workers).[141] Less effective still are human resource strategies (e.g., training and job rotation) and, finally, the use of personal protective equipment (PPE).[142] It is important to be mindful that the cost of each approach is typically related to its effectiveness: higher cost options result in better protection for workers. Employers can, of course, also do nothing and hope to transfer the costs of any resulting injuries to workers or to the state.

Our answer to the third question — determining the degree of state oversight required — is shaped by our sense of whether corporate behaviour ought to be regulated in the same way that we regulate the behaviour of individuals. The two extremes of this approach are embodied in the compliance and punishment schools. Compliance advocates view employers who injure workers as engaging in otherwise socially productive activities and as able to act responsibly. Consequently, persuasion and small fines are the most appropriate means of addressing "non-compliance" that results in injuries. By contrast, advocates of punishment suggest that aggressive policing and prosecution is required because, whatever socially productive activities are occurring, they do not warrant governments sanctioning the injury and death of workers via special treatment.[143]

Much of this debate turns on whether one believes that injuries are the result of amoral calculations designed to maximize profitability or are unintentional and unpredictable by-products of production. It is entirely possible for employers to make mistakes when determining how safe work is. And employers must often make production decisions in conditions of uncertainty. It is also possible for employers simply to act irrationally or without much thought to safety. Yet it is difficult to ignore the pressure on employers to organize production in the most profitable manner. And it is irresponsible to ignore the evidence that employers have responded to this pressure over and over by intentionally transferring productions costs to workers via injury and death.

Canadian governments clearly approach regulation from a compliance perspective. Education, persuasion, and the occasional prosecution are the primary methods by which the state ensures standards are met. By taking action only when workers are seriously injured or killed (and sometimes not even then), the state appears to be adopting the suggestion of compliance theorists that aggressive policing of minor infractions is counter-productive and not cost effective.

This ignores the fact that minor infractions can have significant consequences. A missing machine guard can result in amputation or death. A slippery floor can result in a bruise, concussion, or fracture. Minor infractions such as these are often hard to see. They can sometimes be identified by the occurrence of near misses. But a near miss is rarely reported and thus does not usually result in any change in the work process. This, in turn, creates a culture where safety is not particularly important. Workers learn about the hazards and try their best to avoid them. In doing so, responsibility for preventing accidents is shifted to workers. This, in turn, undermines the point of the occupational health and safety movement: hazards ought not to be a part of a workers' daily job and employers (and, failing that, the state) are responsible to ensure they are remedied.

— FOUR —

Political Economy of Preventing Workplace Injury

Canadian governments have assumed a central role in injury prevention. Unfortunately, their injury-prevention efforts are not very successful. As noted in Chapter 3, this lack of success often reflects inherent weaknesses in government strategies. To understand why governments adopt demonstrably ineffective approaches, it is necessary to consider the pressures, options and constraints governments must navigate when setting policy. That is the goal of this chapter.

The state, of course, is only one actor. The actions of employers and workers are also important. Employers have further intensified work during the past 30 years. They have also created increasingly precarious employment. The effects of increasing intensity and precariousness shed useful light on employer priorities in the modern workplace. This analysis allows us to draw some preliminary conclusions regarding injury prevention in Canada.

WHY REGULATE INEFFECTIVELY?
Context of state action
Canadian governments began directly intervening in the economy to prevent workplace injuries in the late nineteenth century.

To understand why and how the state chooses to intervene, we need to examine the contradictory demands governments face.[1] On the one hand, Canadian governments must facilitate the capital accumulation process. That is to say, they must act in ways that allow employers to produce goods and services in a profitable manner and thereby encourage private investment. Failing to do so may result in an economic downturn, for which the government may well be held responsible. This may have significant social consequences for society and electoral consequences for the government.

Typically, private investors want government regulation only to the degree that it facilitates the capital accumulation process. A legal system that enforces contracts is desirable because it facilitates investment and transactions.[2] On the other hand, regulation that limits managerial discretion in the workplace is undesirable for two reasons. First, funding regulation normally entails additional taxation, which may reduce profitability. Second, regulation impedes the ability of employers to — or at least increases the cost associated with — maximize their profitability through maximally efficient job design.

On the other hand, governments must maintain their own legitimacy with the electorate as well as the legitimacy of the capitalist social formation. The operation of capitalist systems often negatively affects workers, who comprise the majority of the electorate. We see this in the form of low pay, poor working conditions, and workplace injury and death. These effects can cause a loss of confidence in a particular government or in the capitalist social formation.

In order to gain re-election and perpetuate the capitalist social formation, the state has chosen to address these issues via employment laws and regulation. In doing so, government policy must navigate the contradictory demands of employers and workers. The importance of each demand is further shaped by the relative political power of the groups.

Regulation of workplace injury

It is tempting to begin talking about the political economy of injury prevention with what behaviour is regulated and how. It is more instructive, however, to begin with what isn't regulated. Most importantly, Canadian workers continue to have little or no control over what, when, where, or how goods and services are produced. These decisions are left largely to employers, although harmful decisions may provoke a response from workers. This policy choice means that employers determine what hazards exist in the workplace, who is exposed to them, and the nature of the exposure.

That governments don't challenge the notion of the employer's right to manage — despite employers' long record of managing in ways that harm their workers — is not a ground breaking observation. Yet, this basic fact is often lost in the rhetoric around the burdensome nature of government regulation. Further, this policy choice shows that employers have been able to shape in important ways how the state views workplace injury and responds to pressures for prevention.

The state has, of course, imposed some limits on employers' discretion. Governments have largely prohibited some activities, such as the employment of children.[3] They also set standards, give workers health and safety rights, and conduct workplace inspections. Despite this effort, hundreds of thousands of workers are injured on the job each year. The ineffectiveness of government injury-prevention efforts requires explanation.

Inadequate standards

One reason injury-prevention efforts are ineffective may be that regulations do not adequately address some hazards. Consider our discussion about exposure limits in Chapter 3. There is little data about and no exposure limits for 99 percent of chemical agents. Where there are limits, they are often set at levels easily achievable by employers but consistently too high to ensure worker safety. And there is no requirement for employers to ensure these substances are safe before exposing workers to them.

Clearly, governments are doing relatively little to regulate these hazards. It is unclear why states choose, through inaction, to prioritize profitability over safety, but several factors are likely at play. First, occupational diseases are difficult to "see" due to their long latency periods and murky causality. These characteristics have made it difficult for workers to gain recognition and compensation for their diseases. Similarly, many biological and chemical hazards are difficult for regulators detect. They require specific equipment and testing. And, when detected, such substances may exist at levels below (incorrectly) "acceptable" exposure levels. Further, the lack of agreement about what causes occupational diseases makes it easier to justify inaction than do traditional hazards, such as unguarded machinery.

Second, the effort workers must expend and the evidence they must gather to gain recognition for occupational diseases focuses debate at the level of individual diseases. In this way, effort and attention are channelled towards discussing specific diseases and exposures. Left largely unexamined is the widespread absence of information about the toxicity of substances and the lack of a requirement on employers to ensure substances are safe before introducing them to the workplace. Further, when pressure begins to mount, states have an alternative to strict regulation. By providing compensation, they can undermine the political potency of worker demands — the injury has, after all, already occurred.

This dynamic means the state can set exposure limits that pose little threat to the capital accumulation process without jeopardizing social reproduction. Of course, injuries and illnesses caused by biological and chemical agents are only one form of workplace injuries. It is also necessary to consider why regulation aimed at traditional workplace hazards doesn't work.

Regulation of hazards in the workplace

Occupational health and safety laws require employers to inform workers about workplace hazards and to prevent the injury of workers. Again, while it is tempting to focus on the specific requirements, it is more useful to begin by looking elsewhere. For example, why do legislators believe that employers must be compelled to tell workers about safety hazards? Similarly, why do legislators believe employers must be compelled to protect workers?

Our discussion in Chapters 2 and 3 sheds some light on these questions. Employers have a long track record of withholding information about hazards. In some cases, they have even withheld diagnoses of occupational diseases, thereby preventing workers from reducing their exposure or seeking treatment. Employers do this to limit corporate liability and facilitate continuing to expose workers to hazards that that they might not voluntarily accept.

In this behaviour, we see that slogans such as "workers are our most valuable resource" have an ironic truth to them. Employers do treat workers as resources and deploy them in the most beneficial manner to the employer. The impact of these decisions on workers' health and well-being are only considered if the cost of the decision to the employer exceeds the benefit. While clearly immoral, this behaviour is a rational response to the profit imperative under capitalism.

Ignorant and reckless?

This context is important because it places the commonplace belief that injuries are caused by worker ignorance or recklessness in a new light. Let's start with ignorance. Certainly, it is possible for workers not to know about a safety hazard or a regulation. But why did the employer not inform the worker about the hazard? Can we believe that the employer did not know? Perhaps. But the history of workplace injury suggests employers often do know about hazards and just don't say anything.

And what about the notion of worker carelessness? This narrative's recurring popularity has several explanations. It is premised on a negative view of workers — a view supported by (the few) instances where workers do seemingly stupid things. Of course, we don't generally look beneath the event to ask why the worker crawled under the conveyer belt without locking it out. Such explanations are slow to emerge, are tinged by concerns about liability, and are too complicated for a 15-second news clip. It is easier to blame the worker (who is likely dead).

The careless worker notion also places responsibility on individual workers for being safe. Blaming the victim allows us to avoid considering how injuries occur in the context of a relationship marked by significant differences in power and interests. This, in turn, allows us to avoid the uncomfortable fact that most of us are in this same position — our own ability to know about and resist workplace hazards is really quite limited. It also allows us to avoid uncomfortable questioning about the legitimacy of the capitalist social formation by deflecting attention away from the role that employers' largely unfettered right to manage plays in creating workplace hazards that injure and kill us.

Social sanction of workplace injury

There is significant evidence that government injury-prevention efforts fail because employers simply ignore them. Most forms of regulation are based, at least implicitly, on the premise that a penalty ought to reflect the seriousness of the behaviour being punished. This reflects notions of parity ("an eye for an eye"). It also rests on an expectation that individuals respond rationally to incentives and penalties. So, for example, if you want people to obey the speed limit in construction zones, increasing the penalty (e.g., higher fines, the threat of jail) is expected to increase compliance.

Health and safety penalties are rare. They are also overwhelming monetary in nature. The few prosecutions that occur rarely criminalize violators. The state may even allow the employer to donate the penalty to a charity or safety organization, instead of paying a fine as they would if they had broken any other law. This approach is rather surprising given that injuring and killing others outside of the workplace results in social disapprobation and a variety of criminal and civil sanctions.

It is unclear why employers are treated differently. Most probably, it is because worker injuries and deaths occur during economic activity that is considered (otherwise) socially useful. Further, employment appears to be a voluntary relationship between employers and workers, where each experiences some risk. Yet, as noted by Harry Glasbeek and Eric Tucker, the risks taken by employers and workers are very different: employers can, at worst, lose money; workers face the loss of their livelihood and/or life.[4] Further, employers are legally able to limit their liability by forming limited liability corporations.[5]

When the injury and death of workers is constructed as non-criminal behaviour, it follows that regulation need not be as intensive. This allows the state to implement injury-prevention regulations in ways that minimally impact the capital accumulation process. Limited regulation and monetary penalties then appear to be a proportional response to the issue.

Ineffective penalties

The monetary nature of the penalty also naturally results in employers considering the costs and benefits of compliance. Are the risk of being caught and the cost of the penalty worth whatever advantage noncompliance offers? For example, a company may save money by not buying safety equipment — betting they will never be inspected and, if they do, the worst that will happen is that they will receive an order to fix things. Or a company might continue to use cheap but hazardous substances or dangerous but fast production processes. Again, the company is betting the profit will outpace the penalty.

This is an uncharitable characterization of employers. Certainly other issues may factor into employer decisions. A company may risk its reputation by acting unsafely. It may also face higher workers' compensation premiums. And individual managers and directors may question the morality of trading their workers' health for profit. The effects of these factors are unknown, but they must be considered in the context of the capitalist social formation. Maximizing profit is widely accepted as a legitimate (and the main) goal of corporations. Where this results in the injury and death of workers, so long as you have enough money to pay the fine (if you even get one), society generally looks the other way.

Based on the evidence in Chapter 3, it is highly unlikely that employers will be caught if they violate safety standards. If they are caught, it is most likely that they will be ordered simply to remedy the violation. In effect, there is no cost to violating the law. The one exception to this is if a worker is very seriously injured or killed. In this case, an employer is likely to face an inspection that may lead to prosecution. But here, the odds of a prosecution are still relatively slim and the fines imposed — while significant in absolute value — are often small in terms of a firm's overall operating budget.

This analysis is confirmed by the research of Tompa, Trevithick, and McLeod.[6] Health and safety inspections are weakly associated with fewer or less severe injuries. There was also only mixed evidence that the prospect of being penalized for health and safety violations lead to fewer or less severe injuries. Not surprisingly, however, there is strong evidence that actually being penalized leads to fewer injuries.

This analysis simply makes sense. Employers begin

complying when there is a high probability of enforcement and penalty. This suggests that regulation can be effective — just not in its current form. Again, this should not be a surprise. Why obey the speed limit when the cops at the speed trap didn't bring their ticket books? Given this fairly commonsense conclusion, why do so few governments enforce occupational health and safety laws aggressively? And why do they, instead, focus on softer forms of regulation such as education and incentives?

Why regulate ineffectively?

Legislators and bureaucrats rarely acknowledge their systems don't work very well, let alone proclaim why they choose to regulate ineffectively. So, to understand why ineffective regulation is the norm requires some speculation. Let's begin by recalling that the state must mediate the conflicting claims of workers and employers. The resulting policy will likely be influenced (although not entirely determined) by the power each group wields.

Historically, capital has been much more powerful than labour. There are relatively few capitalists (versus many labourers), thus they are easier to organize. Capitalists have more resources. They also have clearly common interests. Consequently, they are better able to articulate what they want and apply pressure on politicians and bureaucrats. This does not mean that capital always gets what (or all that) it wants. It does, however, suggest that capital can exert significant influence on public policy.[7] Capital typically seeks to minimize state intervention, exerting pressure on the state both directly (e.g., by lobbying) and indirectly (e.g., by shaping public discourse). Capital certainly benefits from state efforts that legitimize the capitalist social formation through laws that protect workers. But any such laws must minimally impair the ability of employers to maximize productivity, either by organizing work efficiently or by externalizing costs.

By contrast, workers are more difficult to organize. To create sustained pressure on government, individual workers must create or join a mobilizing structure, must develop a shared understanding of the problem and the potential solutions. There must also be a political opportunity for workers to exert pressure. These are not insurmountable barriers, but there difficulties to overcome. Existing mobilizing structures (e.g., trade union, service, civic and cultural groups) typically already have a purpose. To re-task them requires effort, may reduce the resources available to the original and/or new task, and may meet with resistance. Further, developing a common understanding can be impeded by the illegitimacy according to worker claims by the dominant ideology (which suggests workplace injuries are normal). Political opportunities are shaped by the discourse around workplace injury. The reaction to even stark evidence that workers have been sacrificed for profit is shaped by this discourse.

How is this legitimized?

Capital is also often able to frame the debate around public policy. The importance of economic stability is often linked (or sometimes made synonymous) with the public interest. Thus, public policy options are discussed in economic terms. Consequently, an employer perspective on risk of injury (it is minimal, unavoidable, and acceptable) shapes the discussion. Narrow, technical discussions about the costs and benefits (to employers) of different approaches to injury prevention displace discussions about how employer behaviour results in injuries, which might then lead to awkward questions about why employers would allow workers to be injured. This approach falsely assumes that the major consequence of workplace injury is economic. It is not — it is the injury and death of workers.

The power of capital is increased by the nature of workplace injuries. These injuries are often hard to see. Employers and governments don't keep accurate and public counts of injuries and deaths.[8] And when injuries occur, they are widely dispersed in time and space. These factors make it hard to see the scale of the problem or patterns. Layered on top of this is the tendency to describe injuries as unusual or "freak" events.[9] This dynamic allows employers, the state, and even workers to dismiss such events as unpredictable and unpreventable. This, in turn, suggests that there is no broader problem and action is neither possible or nor required. Further, states construct data that makes the system look effective.

A further complication is how the careless worker narrative obscures the responsibility of employers for exposing workers to hazards. Worker rights under the internal responsibility system (IRS) further reinforce this narrative and get government off the hook for regulatory failure. It is up to workers to raise issues, despite their inability to compel employers to address them. And it is up to workers to refuse unsafe work, despite the risks they run by such a refusal.

This pattern of thinking around workplace injuries allows regulators to appear to be addressing workplace injuries (even though their regulatory approach is clearly ineffective) while at the same time minimally impeding employer decision making — decision making that is important in maintaining profitability and thus attracting investment. Casting discussion in economic terms also obscures that a political decision about whether profit or workers' health will be protected has been made by disguising it with quantification and technical discussion.[10] In this way, the state is able to balance the demands of the capital accumulation process and social reproduction.

INJURY IN THE NEW ECONOMY

While the purpose of employing workers — making a profit — has not changed over time, the way employers organize work and their relationships with workers have changed. These changes negatively affect injury prevention efforts. They also allow us to infer from employer behaviour how employers truly view health and safety. Two changes in particular warrant discussion: the intensification of work and the development of precarious employment.

Work intensification

The purpose of organizational restructuring is to increase the efficiency of an organization, generally with an eye to improving the bottom line. This can take a number of forms, including downsizing, outsourcing, just-in-time production, and the implementation of various quality improvement initiatives. One consequence of such changes is that workers may find themselves working harder and/or longer. More work, more complex tasks, and being responsible for multiple tasks (often eliminating "down time" on the job) or tasks over which one has little decision-making authority are all ways in which employers can intensify work. Technological change (e.g., portable computing devices and phones) also means that work can now follow some workers home or on vacation.[11]

Work intensification increases worker stress and negatively affects worker health. Among the outcomes identified by the U.S. National Institution on Occupational Safety and Health are cardiovascular disease, musculoskeletal disorders, and psychological disorders. Intensification can also increase exposure to toxic substances, accidents (due to fatigue and inexperience), impact the development of repetitive strain injuries (RSIs), and may increase the risk of experiencing workplace violence (due to working more hours and at unconventional hours). Reduction in workforce size may also result in a loss of safety knowledge and training.[12]

Darius Mehri provides a rare insider's glimpse into lean production, based on his time working in Japan for a Toyota subsidiary.[13] Fast production lines contributed to ill health, including high blood pressure, hearing problems, injuries (including amputations), and deaths. Minimizing the floor space used creates more hazards due to proximity of workers and equipment. Compelling workers to complete multiple tasks (instead of the single task typical of production line work) increases the opportunity for errors and reduces the opportunity for workers to recover or rest during work. Injuries are hidden to transfer medical costs from the employer to the state medical system. Injured workers are immediately returned to work. Those who cannot work must still come into work to sit and do nothing. Safety is framed as the responsibility of workers.

Precarious employment increases risks

Over time, Canada has also seen a shift away from standard employment relationships. In their place, many workers (disproportionately women and ethnic minorities) find themselves engaged in precarious work. Precarious work is characterized by "limited social benefits and statutory entitlements, job insecurity, low wages, and high risks of ill-health." [14] Self-employed and (notionally) independent contractors may experience precarious work. So, too, may employees whose jobs are short-term and part-time.

There is some evidence that precarious work itself leads to poorer health for workers.[15] A recent Canadian study found some job characteristics — such as scheduling uncertainty, constantly searching for work, and constant evaluation — are associated with poorer health outcomes.[16] This suggests certain employment relationships with certain characteristic appear to be associated with different health outcomes.

Precariousness can also have a direct effect on workplace injuries. Workers with less experience on the job are more likely to be injured.[17] Precarious workers appear to experience different hazards from workers with more permanent jobs.[18] Workers who fear for their jobs may have a higher rate of injury because they may ignore safety policies to maintain production levels.[19]

It appears that knowledge of safety, while important, does not by itself lead to compliance with safety rules or lower levels of injury. An important mediating factor appears to be whether workers are motivated to follow the rules based on their assessment of what behaviour is rewarded by the employer. This research — while preliminary — is consistent with evidence that lean production techniques negatively affect worker health and safety.[20]

Workers in precarious jobs may also have less access to health and safety protections. Some forms of work (e.g., self-employment) may fall outside of statutory regulation. Other sectors where precarious work is common (e.g., agriculture and domestic work) are often excluded from the ambit of legislation. When workers in precarious jobs have the right to know, participate, and refuse, their ability to exercise these rights is mediated by the increased vulnerability that their employment status creates. Precarious workers are also less likely to believe raising a health and safety issue will result in the remediation of the issue. In effect, precarious work further undermines the already weak rights to know, participate, and refuse. This should not be surprising; undermining worker power is, of course, one of the reasons employers have sought to reorganize how work is completed.

What do intensification and precarious employment tell us?

Earlier in this chapter, it was suggested that companies may choose to endanger workers in order to increase their profitability. It is difficult to prove conclusively that this occurs, outside a few well-documented cases, but this conclusion is consistent with the profit imperative that underlies capitalist social formation. It is also a plausible explanation for the many instances where employers have acted in ways that both endanger workers and maximize their profitability.

Intensifying work and altering the nature of the employment relationship provide further and contemporary evidence
that supports the conclusion that employers prioritize profit
and intentionally trade it off against workers' health. Increasing work intensity is designed to maximize profitability. And
it has clearly known (and predictable, if one takes a moment to
think about it) health consequences for workers.

Precarious employment has similar health consequences but
evidences much more elaborate and intentional employer behaviour. Reorganizing work so independent contractors and temporary employees can do it is a significant undertaking for an
employer — one that must be motivated by an expectation of a
significant return. This may come in the form of a lower wage
bill. It also comes in the form of a reduction or elimination of
statutory standards they must meet for these workers. The intentionality of these changes — that employers explicitly trade
off worker health and safety for profit — is difficult to deny.

CONCLUSION

This discussion suggests three major conclusions about injury
prevention in Canadian workplaces. The first conclusion is that
injuries occur in high numbers. This appears to represent an
intentional strategy by employers to transfer production costs
to workers in order to maximize employer profitability. Such
a strategy is consistent with the imperatives of capitalism. It
is also facilitated by the significant labour market and legal
power of employers — power that workers typically cannot
effectively challenge. It is also important to note that hundreds
of thousands of workplace injuries occur each year despite prevention efforts.

Among the factors contributing to this regulatory failure is
the long-term use by the state of demonstrably ineffective regulatory strategies. These strategies are ineffective for several
reasons. Chief among these reasons is that injury prevention

schemes channel worker energy and workplace conflict into mechanisms that manage and diffuse such conflict. For example, workers are given responsibility to police the provision of safe workplaces by their employers. But they are not given strong rights or access to an effective enforcement system. Consequently, workers must work hard and/or take significant risks to challenge unsafe work situations. This reduces the threat posed by workplace injuries to the capital accumulation and social reproduction processes — worker efforts are channelled into systems that are structurally defective and away from taking direct electoral or workplace action.

Finally, governments legitimize allowing employers to prioritize profitability over safety in three ways: (1) they blame workers for injuries, making it difficult to refocus discussion on the contribution of employers to injuries; (2) they use cost-benefit arguments, which implicitly adopt an economic perspective on workplace injury and prioritizes maximizing profit over preventing injury and death; and (3) they take advantage of the difficulty we have in "seeing" workplace injuries and, indeed, exacerbate this by manipulating injury statistics to create the appearance that workplaces are safer than they are.

— FIVE —

COMPENSATION OF WORKPLACE INJURY

In 1999, 58-year-old Shirley Zubick was injured at work by a falling shelving unit, suffering a concussion and a torn rotator cuff for which she subsequently had surgery. Prior to her injury, Zubick had received a layoff notice. Her employer did not have workers' compensation coverage. Her employer's private insurance provided 90 days of disability benefits. Zubick has not worked since and her lawsuit against her employer — which would have provided $30,000–$40,000 in compensation — was unsuccessful because she could not prove that her employer knew the shelving unit was faulty and failed to fix it. Ten years later, this matter is still not resolved. Her employer is pursuing her for approximately $120,000 in costs, which will likely mean she will lose her house.[1]

Zubick's case shows us several things. First, injured workers who are not covered by workers' compensation still face the spectre of financial ruin as a result of their injury. Canada does not have a comprehensive disability insurance system to assist those who cannot earn an income due to injury.[2] Second, suing one's employer for every-day workplace injuries remains a risky proposition for workers. For those with work-related injuries, workers' compensation is the most accessible source of financial support. Third, employers act in their own interests in cases of workplace injury — in this case, a labour union seeking to recover court costs — with seemingly little concern for the consequences of those actions for the worker.

This chapter examines why workers' compensation systems were created. We then turn to how workers' compensation serves the interests of employers, workers, and the state and the effect this has on the system's longevity. Despite providing workers with more predictable, immediate, and stable compensation, workers' compensation has many detractors. Examining the process of injury recognition reveals a pattern wherein decisions about injury recognition limit employer liability for injuries. This is particularly the case for injuries that emerge over or after a long period of time, do not demonstrate a clear pathology, tap into an existing social prejudice, and/or entail significant costs for employers.

When combined with the tendency of workers' compensation boards (WCBs) to limit benefit entitlements (as discussed in Chapter 6) and worker power (as discussed in Chapter 7), the process of injury recognition suggests that an important outcome of workers' compensation is to contain employer claim costs. One result of this behaviour is that some of the costs of work-related injuries are transferred onto workers, their families, and government-funded medical and social assistance programs.

WORKERS' COMPENSATION IN CANADA

Overview of workers' compensation

Each province and territory has established a workers' compensation system. Legislation compels certain categories of employers to pay premiums to a workers' compensation board, thereby gaining coverage for their workers.[3] Other categories of employers may be permitted to purchase voluntary coverage. Approximately 80 percent of workers are covered by workers' compensation.[4]

When a worker is injured on the job, the WCB is notified and determines whether compensation is warranted. If an injury is deemed compensable, the WCB provides benefits. Benefits can include medical aid to treat injuries and vocational rehabilitation to assist workers to recover their earning capacity. Workers who have lost earnings receive wage-loss benefits at 75–90 percent of their net loss. Workers who are killed on the job have their funeral expenses covered. Where there are dependents, the survivors may receive ongoing pensions.

Employers fund all of these benefits through premiums. The premiums are adjusted annually to ensure there are sufficient funds to cover all costs associated with workplace injuries. An employer's annual assessment is based upon its payroll, the claims record of similar employers and, in some cases, by the employer's claims record.

Development of workers' compensation in Canada

State-operated workers' compensation systems were implemented at the beginning of the twentieth century. As noted in Chapter 2, workers' compensation addressed the fact that injured workers rarely received any compensation under the common law, thereby becoming impoverished. Workers' compensation also ameliorated (to some degree) the social instability caused by such widespread and clear injustice. Although Quebec was the first province to implement workers' compensation (albeit administered by the courts until the 1930s), the principles of workers' compensation are most clearly expressed in the five principles ("the Meredith principles") contained in the report of Ontario's Royal Commission on workers' compensation.[5]

The first principle (collective liability) holds that liability for work injuries should accrue to the workers' compensation system as a whole, rather than to individual employers. This prevents a single incident from bankrupting an employer — a situation likely to deprive injured workers of compensation. In this way, collective liability displaces the tort system, leading directly to the second principle of no-fault compensation. No-fault compensation means workplace injuries are compensated regardless of fault. This makes irrelevant any attribution of blame for an incident. It also effectively removes the whole area of injury and compensation from litigation. The focus instead is on compensation and the injured worker receives benefits and services through an administrative process.

Meredith recommended that employers should fund the cost of benefits and services to injured workers, along with the expense of administering the system. Employer funding is based on the capitalized cost of the injury (i.e., the projected cost over the duration of the injury) rather than the current cost only (i.e., the annual cost). This ensures that costs are not passed between employers, as individual businesses and even whole industries open and close over time. Among other things, this was thought to create an incentive for employers to reduce injury rates by improving workplace safety.

The fourth principle (wage-loss replacement) requires workers to be compensated directly by the WCB for a portion of any wage loss attributable to an injury. The establishment of an accident fund guarantees that compensation monies are available, thus assuring injured workers of secure and prompt compensation and future benefits. Herein lies an important trade-off: workers gain stable, predictable, and immediate compensation but give up the right to sue their employers and gain compensation for non-quantifiable losses (e.g., pain and suffering).

Finally, Meredith recommended all matters related to workers' compensation be administered by an independent WCB, which operates exclusively as decision-maker and final authority for all claims and all related administrative matters. The clear intent was that the WCB should be autonomous — both politically and financially independent of government and any special interest group that may have the ear of a politician.

The activities of the WCB would be focused solely on serving the needs of workers and employers in an efficient and impartial manner.

Workers' compensation as a compromise

In the 40 years following Meredith's 1913 report, all provinces came to adopt systems founded on these principles. The resulting compromise has endured nearly a century of political and economic change. Workers' compensation has not, for example, been subject to the degree of intervention and erosion that collective bargaining has been since the 1970s.[6] This may mean that workers' compensation entails a relatively low cost on (or threat to) the capital accumulation process and thus there is relatively little for capital or the state to gain via intervention. It may also be that the political costs of meaningful change to workers' compensation are high. Examining the advantages workers' compensation provides for employers, workers, and government is instructive.[7]

Workers' compensation limits employers' liability for work-related injuries. Specifically, the tort bar eliminates the risk of employer bankruptcy, fixes the cost of injury in the short-term, and spreads the cost of injury over an entire industry group. As discussed below, the state and WCBs further reduce employer liability by limiting the acceptance of particular types of injuries as well as the level and/or duration of benefits awarded. The expectation of stable, predictable, and immediate injury compensation also lowers the cost of injury to workers. This reduces workers' motivation to seek significant changes in the labour process to reduce workplace hazards — changes that can erode employer profitability. This may be an example of the dialectic of partial conquest, whereby concessions won by workers via collective resistance raise the stakes of future resistance.[8] In these ways, workers' compensation provides employers with a significant economic advantage.

Workers' compensation also provides a political benefit for employers. The process of gaining compensation absorbs worker and trade union energy. By directing attention and energy to claims management, the compensation process reduces the resources workers have available to challenge employer control over the labour process. And the creation of a bureaucratic system of compensation frames workplace injuries as a normal and manageable outcome of work, rather than a profit-motivated transfer of cost from the employer to the worker via unsafe work practices.

For workers, predictable, immediate, and stable workers' compensation is a significant improvement over the tort system, when work-related injury, disease, or death would often catapult workers and their families into poverty. This significantly reduces pressure on trade unions and on governments to address the root issue: unsafe work practices organized by employers. Those workers not covered by workers' compensation (some 20 percent of the workforce) may work in very safe jobs or very dangerous ones.[9] Workers with safe jobs have little reason to exert pressure on the state or trade unions to improve safety. Other workers not covered by workers' compensation may work in precarious jobs and have little ability to exert pressure on the state or trade unions to improve safety.[10]

The state benefits from workers' compensation because it maintains the production process by limiting employer liability for workplace injuries. It also maintains social reproduction by partially ameliorating the consequences of work-related injuries for workers and consuming their time and energy with claims management. Further, worker attempts to introduce more fundamental change are likely to be tempered by the knowledge that workers' compensation exists only at the pleasure of the legislature. In these ways, workers' compensation reduces the likelihood of workers taking direct and collective action.

Worker and employer support for workers' compensation

also means substituting injury compensation for prevention entails a relatively low political cost to the state. In this way, the state is able to preserve the capital accumulation process against the threat of social unrest stemming from workplace injury without significantly endangering its own political legitimacy among its citizens. Making WCBs responsible for administering it deflects political pressure: compensation is the responsibility of an independent agency and its decisions are cast as technical, not political, decisions.

Finally, workers' compensation creates a framework within which employers and workers can seek to shift peripheral costs onto each other without normally risking the collapse of the entire edifice. In this way, workers' compensation acts much like Canada's laws governing unionization and collective bargaining. Employers and workers can contest with each other within a relatively stable and predictable framework.[11] This places limits on both what can be won and lost in the to and fro of lobbying.

INJURY RECOGNITION REVISITED

The Meredith principles charge WCBs with determining which injuries are compensable. While outright denials of claims are relatively uncommon, embedded in this seemingly technical process are political decisions about the scope of compensation and the types of injuries that warrant it.[12] By placing legislative and policy limits on claim acceptance, the state and WCBs have periodically extended employer liability protection. Of particular interest are instances where WCBs apply standard tests to injuries that have difficulty meeting them and where WCB apply special tests or otherwise limit compensation to injuries that are potentially very expensive to compensate.

Determining compensability

When a worker is injured, the WCB must decide whether the worker should receive compensation. Workers are normally eligible for workers' compensation when the following three conditions are met:

- the worker's employer has workers' compensation coverage,

- the worker sustains an injury compensable under the Act, and

- the injury results from employment.[13]

Determining whether an employer has workers' compensation coverage is normally a straightforward task. Rendering a judgment on the second and third conditions can be more complex. The decision begins with considering how an "accident" is defined by the applicable legislation. For example, Manitoba's *Workers' Compensation Act,* defines an "accident" as follows.

1(1) In this Act, "accident" means a chance event occasioned by a physical or natural cause; and includes

(a) a wilful and intentional act that is not the act of the worker,

(b) any

(i) event arising out of, and in the course of, employment, or

(ii) thing that is done and the doing of which arises out of, and in the course of, employment, and

(c) an occupational disease,

and as a result of which a worker is injured;

The key tests set out in statute are whether the injury arose out of and occurred in the course of employment. The definition of injury is often vague or absent. In British Columbia, a personal injury is "any physiological change arising from some cause" and includes traumatically induced psychological impairment.[14] Injuries are distinguished from diseases and only occupational diseases are compensated.

"Arises and occurs"

When deciding whether an injury resulted from employment, a WCB applies the two-part "arises and occurs" test set out in the definition of an accident. "Arises from" typically refers to the "how" of the injury, while "occurs in the course of" focuses more on the "when, where, and what" of the injury.[15] More specifically, an injury arises out of employment when it is caused by the nature, conditions, or obligations of employment (i.e., an employment hazard). An employment hazard is an employment circumstance that presents a risk of injury.[16]

The second part of the test addresses whether the injury occurred in the course of employment. This is the case when an injury happens at a time and place consistent with the obligations and expectations of employment. While time and place are not strictly limited to the normal hours of work or the employer's premises, there must be some relationship between employment expectations and the time and place of the injury.[17]

The test normally applied is that of "causative significance." This means that there must be evidence that employment contributed to the injury, but employment does not have to be the primary cause. That is to say, employment must have played more than a trivial or insignificant (*de minimus*) role but does not need be the sole, predominant, or major cause.[18] The causative significance test is well suited to traditional traumatic injuries where it is usually clear when, where, and how an injury occurred.

Balance of probabilities and presumptions

In determining causation, WCBs obtain the evidence they require to adjudicate and manage claims. In this way, workers' compensation is based on an inquiry model, rather than the adversarial model, which characterizes proceedings under tort law.[19] Nevertheless, even if the inquiry process is not explicitly adversarial, the interests of the worker and the employer are, and each side typically brings forward evidence supporting its interests.

WCBs are expected to use "the balance of probabilities" as the standard of proof in adjudication. This means the adjudicator asks: "Is it more likely than not that this worker's employment was a significant contributing factor in the development of the injury or occupational disease?" Where the evidence for or against is approximately equal in weight, the issue is resolved in favour of the worker claiming benefits.[20] This standard is different from "beyond a reasonable doubt" or scientific certitude.[21]

When it isn't possible to gather enough evidence to determine if an injury both "arises and occurs," WCBs may rely upon "statutory presumptions" about injuries. In Manitoba, these presumptions are:

> 4(5) Where the accident arises out of the employment, unless the contrary is proven, it shall be presumed that it occurred in the course of the employment; and, where the accident occurs in the course of the employment, unless the contrary is proven, it shall be presumed that it arose out of the employment.

These presumptions ensure that workers are compensated when the evidence indicates the injury either 1) arose out of **or** 2) occurred in the course of employment (i.e., where a determination can be made about one but not the other).[22]

Politics of injury recognition

As discussed in Chapter 3, defining an injury is a political process that is informed by the interests and power of the state, employers, and workers. Workers' compensation systems influence the injury-recognition process by accepting some injuries as compensable and thereby legitimizing them. The injury-recognition process also influences workers' compensation systems. For example, employers may hide information about workplace hazards, oppose the expansion of occupational health and safety (OHS) regulations and compensation plans, and game these same plans to maximize their profitability. This behaviour affects the willingness of WCBs to recognize some injuries as compensable. Governments have also at times acted to reduce employer liability by delaying recognition and limiting the acceptance of injuries. For their part, workers often seek to both maximize the compensation available as well as create safer and healthier workplaces by limiting employers' ability to organize work.

Workers' compensation systems implicitly adopt the biomedical model of injury causation that underlies Canadian approaches to occupational health and safety. As stated in Chapter 3, the three basic assumptions made about work-related injuries are:

· the mechanism of injury will be discernable, or at least mostly distinguishable from other events or disease processes,

· the injury will manifest itself at the time of or reasonably soon after the injury occurs, such that the injury can be causally related to a work-place event, and

· the course and treatment of the injury will be broadly similar from one person to the next.

These assumptions reflect the belief that illness must have a biological source (or pathology). Further, the degree of illness must be proportional to the degree of biological malfunction. Objective medical knowledge (e.g., test results, observations, functional evaluations) is more valued than patient self-reports[23]

The biomedical model plays a significant (and useful) role in workers' compensation. Medical evaluations inform decisions about injury causation and the extent of disability resulting from it. These evaluations also guide rehabilitation programs and decisions regarding when workers are employable and, thus, no longer eligible for compensation. At the time of Meredith, and for some time after, a majority of injuries considered by WCBs resulted from an acute physical injury in the workplace, reflecting the importance of resource extraction, processing, or manufacturing industries. Consequently, injuries and injury mechanisms were relatively easy to see.

As noted in Chapter 3, this model also runs afoul of recent research that suggests (1) injuries are often multi-factorial, and (2) work exerts significant effects on health and a broad range of diseases have work-related components.[24] Attempting to classify injuries as work-related and non-work-related (thereby ignoring the interactive effect between occupational and broader environmental factors) is likely an impossible task.[25] Alternatives (narrowing causation or expanding it) both have significant drawbacks. Consequently, the existing approach remains in operation — often to the disadvantage of injured workers.[26]

Work-related musculoskeletal disorders and causation

Work-related musculoskeletal disorders (WMSDs) are an example of the contested nature of injury recognition that has emerged as the type, frequency, and severity of work-related injuries has changed. Service-sector work and the growing use of technology appear to be associated with an increasing rate of non-traumatic injuries, such as cumulative injuries resulting from repetitive activity or occupational diseases.[27] Among the non-traumatic injuries associated with the service industry are WMSDs, such as strains and sprains of the back, neck, shoulder, arm, and wrist. Repetitive strain injuries (RSIs), such as carpal tunnel syndrome, develop over time, may have multiple causes, and may be difficult to link to employment. There has also been a tendency in North America to suggest WMSDs are psychological in origin.[28]

Andrew Hopkins notes that historical contingencies in Australia meant that it labelled RSIs as an "injury" instead of characterizing the condition as an "occupational neurosis" or even a "regional pain syndrome" (which was initially advocated by some medical authorities).[29] It also confronted the popular conception that the cause of RSI was somehow embedded in technology (i.e., was inevitable) by showing that the increase in RSIs was due to changes in the labour process caused by speeding-up work and staff cutbacks. In addition to allowing easy access to compensation (at least at first), the government of Australia placed limits on speed and required regular breaks. In many places, keyboard operators were reclassified as administrative assistants, assigned broader duties, and provided with ergonomically designed furniture.

This response stands in contrast to the treatment of RSI victims in the United States, where the prominent explanation of the epidemic was based on the assumption that it was essentially a form of neurosis. Psychiatrists and orthopedic surgeons reasoned that, if the symptoms were not detectable using conventional medical equipment (i.e., did not conform to the biomedical model), the pain could not have a physical basis, and must therefore be psychological in origin. Norton Hadler, for example, posits that regional musculoskeletal disorders reflect a worker's (in)ability to cope with environmental stressors rather than a definable pathology.[30] Other research suggests, however, that there are four categories of risk factors that influence the occurrence and course of WMSDs:

- individual characteristics and personality traits, such as previous WMSDs, age, obesity, smoking, and gender;

- physical (biomechanical) factors, such as vibration, lifting, and posture;

- psychophysical factors, such as one's perception of how demanding work is; and

- psychosocial factors, such as the work environment and how much control the worker has over the job.[31]

Regarding psychosocial factors, such factors as "limited job control, monotonous work, psychologically demanding work, and low workplace social support" seem to make an independent contribution to the onset of WMSDs.[32] It is not entirely clear how psychosocial factors affect injury causation. Yet, jobs without the key psychosocial risk factors seem to protect workers' health, while jobs with risk factors seem to increase the risk of injury.

The challenges WMSDs pose for causation creates an opportunity for employers to dispute these claims. Suggesting that the injury is largely psychosomatic creates a narrative that justifies denying compensation for such claims.[33] Yet, where there does appear to be a link between a WMSD and the structure of a job and/or the work environment, disallowing claims or limiting benefit entitlements without consideration of such factors allows an employer to transfer the costs of production to workers.

Occupational diseases

Occupational diseases also pose challenges to traditional approaches to causation, in part because their (typically) long latency periods and the presence of myriad other potential factors make it difficult to definitively determine that work contributed to the disease in other than a *de minimus* way.[34] As a result, there is significant under-compensation of occupational disease in Canada. For example, Allen Kraut estimated morbidity and mortality from occupational diseases in 1989.[35] Examining cancer, asthma, chronic airways disease, heart disease, and carpal tunnel syndrome, Kraut estimated that between 77,900 and 112,000 new occupational diseases arose that year. But Canadian WCBs accepted only 37,927 occupational disease claims in 1989. This suggests between 40,000 and 74,000 occupational diseases were uncompensated in 1989 alone.

As noted in Chapter 3, the state historically has been reluctant to recognize, regulate, or compensate many occupational diseases. While the complex causation of such diseases is often cited as a reason for delay or refusal, there is also evidence that governments are concerned about the economic consequences of extending employer liability. Yet, in some cases, governments have stipulated causation through a list of presumptive diseases in legislation, regulation, or Board policy.

Alberta's *Firefighters' Primary Site Cancer Regulation*, for example, stipulates certain types of cancers among firefighters are automatically compensable after a minimum period of workplace exposure. The effect of such a designation is to place the onus on the WCB or the employer to bring forward information to establish why an injured worker should not be eligible for compensation, rather than vice-versa. Yet, as noted in Chapter 3, few occupational cancers are handled in this way, the majority of which are not reported to WCBs and thus rendered invisible.

Limiting liability: Psychological injuries

In Canada, 40 percent of wage-loss insurance claims (inside and outside workers' compensation) are related to mental health problems.[36] Governments and WCBs have restricted liability for many psychological injuries, either by outright exclusion or by subjecting them to more rigorous tests of causation. Indeed, Canada's Kirby Commission report in 2002 noted that only four provinces had not excluded mental illness from coverage in their legislation.[37] Alberta's WCB requires all of the following criteria to be met for a psychological injury to be compensable:

- there is a confirmed psychological or psychiatric diagnosis as described in the DSM-IV,

- the work-related events or stresses are the predominant cause of injury,

- the work-related events are excessive or unusual in comparison to the normal pressures and tensions experienced by the average worker in similar occupations, and

- there is objective confirmation of events.[38]

This test is much more stringent than the arises-and-occurs standard applied to other types of injuries.[39] There must be a clear diagnosis by a physician, there must be some record of what event caused the psychological injury, and the event causing the injury must be both the predominant cause of the injury and extraordinary.[40]

The higher standard of causation applied to psychological injuries reflects, in part, the complexity of psychological injuries as well as the expectation that they can stem from many factors.[41] Yet, a worker will likely receive compensation for a back-pain claim (an injury that is also multi-factorial and difficult to quantify) even if the claim is the result of a non-acute event. Treating these broadly analogous injuries differently suggests an inconsistency in workers' compensation policy — an inconsistency that punishes workers who have an injury to which a social stigma is attached.

The almost wholesale exclusion of such injuries allows employers to transfer the costs of psychological injuries caused by work to workers. Indeed, in the 1990s, Saskatchewan modified its policy on accepting chronic stress claims in order to address fiscal pressures and claim proliferation.[42] Cost pressures combine with the potential for workers to fake psychological symptoms and the general social disapproval of mental illness to make these injuries easier for governments and WCBs to reject.

Chronic pain syndrome

A small percentage of injured workers develop chronic pain, as well as such closely related conditions as fibromyalgia, and claim that it is related to their work.[43] Chronic pain is difficult to cope with within the biomedical model and is vulnerable to statutory and policy efforts to limit compensability, in part because it can be labelled as a psychological problem or malingering.[44] A 2003 Supreme Court of Canada ruling on two Nova Scotia cases of chronic pain demonstrated that workers can resist employer and government efforts to limit injury recognition, although few workers are likely able and willing to fight their cases to the Supreme Court. More likely, they will end up accessing workers' compensation appeal systems (see Chapter 7).

The workers in these cases suffered work-related injuries and developed chronic pain. Nova Scotia's *Workers' Compensation Act* and regulations limited workers' compensation benefits to a four-week treatment program. The workers appealed their decisions, claiming this policy discriminated against chronic pain sufferers on the basis of disability, thereby violating s.15(1) of the *Charter of Rights and Freedoms.* The Supreme Court of Canada (SCC) agreed, noting that uniform benefit limitations ignored the needs of workers who were permanently disabled by chronic pain and made no attempt to distinguish between workers who were genuinely suffering and required compensation and those who might be abusing the system. Finally, the SCC provided some commentary on the difficult causation issues related to chronic pain cases:

Although the medical evidence before us does point to early intervention and return to work as the most promising treatment for chronic pain, it also recognizes that, in many cases, even this approach will fail. It is an unfortunate reality that, despite the best available treatment, chronic pain frequently evolves into a permanent and debilitating condition. Yet, under the Act and the FRP [Facility Response Plan] Regulations, injured workers who develop such permanent impairment as a result of chronic pain may be left with nothing: no medical aid, no permanent impairment or income replacement benefits, and no capacity to earn a living on their own. This cannot be consistent with the purpose of the Act or with the essential human dignity of these workers.[45]

New regulations were subsequently enacted to guide the handling of chronic pain cases. Compensating the approximately 4000 workers whose claims were improperly denied was estimated at $220 million with ongoing annual costs of approximately $11 million. This one liability alone resulted in a 3 percent increase in average assessments by the WCB.[46] This decision requires that all injuries must now be given similar treatment by workers' compensation systems. Whether the special treatment given to psychological injuries, for example, remains viable is unclear. This case also demonstrates how the broader web of rules governing employment can affect the operation of workers' compensation.

CONCLUSION

Workers' compensation is a useful political solution to the problems caused by workplace injury. Workers get stable and predictable compensation. Employers get a liability shield, significantly reduced worker militancy, and making predictable accident costs. Governments receive a way to reduce and manage conflicts over work-related injuries and an administrative body to deflect political pressure onto. Despite the enduring nature of this compromise, workers' compensation does not resolve the structural conflicts embedded in workplace injury. Hundreds of thousands of workers are injured and killed each year and the interests of workers and employers conflict in the adjudication and administration of resulting claims.

On the surface, claims adjudication appears neutral. Claims are decided by a neutral third party (the WCB), decisions reflect the application of complex policies to the available (often medical) evidence, and decisions are based on the individual merits of a claim. Yet looking beneath this veneer suggests injury-recognition for compensation purposes is just as politicized as it is for injury prevention. Over time, a pattern of claim denial has emerged, wherein legislatures and WCBs have made political decisions about the standard of causation used to adjudicate a claim, thereby limiting employer liability. A combination of properties appears to make some types of injuries (e.g., WMSDs, occupational diseases, psychological injuries) particularly vulnerable to such treatment. Such injuries typically exhibit one or more of the following characteristics:

- they emerge over or after a long period of time, which obscures their connection to work and also facilitates terming the injury "an ordinary disease of life,"

- they do not demonstrate a clear pathology, thus violating the biomedical approach to causation and creating an opportunity to suggest that they injury reflects psychological problems or malingering,

- they tap into an established social prejudice, thereby facilitating the marginalization of the claim and/or the claimants, and/or

- they entail a significant economic cost to employers (including an increase in workers' compensation premiums), if deemed compensable.[47]

When combined with the tendency of WCBs to limit benefit entitlements through deeming workers employable (even if they are not employed) and encouraging early return to work programs (which may or may not be in the interests of workers), it appears that workers' compensation seeks to minimize employer claim costs where politically feasible. These latter techniques are examined in Chapter 6. This tendency offloads the costs of compensating work-related injuries on workers, their families, and government-funded medical and social assistance programs. This is often justified as protecting the system from abuse (i.e., worker fraud).

The state is able to maintain its political legitimacy while doing this in several ways. By focusing on individual worker claims, workers' compensation makes it difficult to view workplace injury as a structural feature of employment that transfers production costs to workers. Where an injury can be subject to different treatment due to its inherent properties, the state may take action to limit the acceptance of such an injury. Precluding some forms of injury from compensation serves to divide workers: those who are marginalized in this process may have difficulty finding support from those who expect to receive benefits for their more "legitimate" injuries and don't care to risk the loss of such benefits through collective resistance.

—SIX—

WORKER BENEFITS AND
CLAIMS MANAGEMENT

Injured workers often suggest that the purpose of workers'
compensation systems is to deny any claim where a denial is
possible and cut off all benefits as soon as possible. In this
way, workers' compensation is less about compensation and
more about limiting employer liability for injuries. Most people dismiss such statements as hyperbole or sour grapes. Yet
this perspective is analytically useful because is highlights how
workers' compensation board (WCB) funding creates pressures
to minimize claim costs.

As we saw in Chapter 5, when WCBs determine which injuries are recognized, they are making a political choice that
allocates costs for injuries between workers and employers.
WCBs make similar choices when they manage accepted injury claims. Focusing on returning workers to employability
(instead of employment) and the growing interest in early return to work programs reduce employer liability by transferring costs to workers. The threat of having one's earnings
"deemed" (see next section) disciplines workers to accept this
treatment. This behaviour is sanctioned because workers are
assumed to be malingers, work is believed rehabilitative, and
(bizarrely) being absent from work due to injury is thought

unhealthy. The highly contestable and political nature of these beliefs tends to be lost amid the social disapprobation that surrounds malingering.

The real issue is actually an economic one. Employer premiums are the source of almost all WCB funding. Employers (understandably) seek to minimize these payments. This method of funding injury compensation creates interesting pressures and mechanisms. For example, experience-rating systems create the impression that employers are reducing the rate and/or severity of workplace injuries (while lowering their premiums) without actually achieving any such reduction. In this way, the state appears responsive to the demands of workers without significantly impacting the capital accumulation process. When the downplaying of injury levels is combined with drawing attention to worker fraud, it becomes possible to direct attention away from the core issue of unsafe work practices.

EARNINGS-LOSS BENEFITS

The majority of injured workers experience little or no loss of income from workplace accidents.[1] Those who do can have a portion of their loss offset by earnings-loss benefits.[2] In New Brunswick, workers who experience an earnings loss due to a compensable injury that extends beyond the day of injury are entitled to benefits equal to 85 percent of their estimated net loss of earnings. Most workers are subject to a three-day waiting period (during which time they are not eligible for compensation) and the disability must be medically confirmed.[3]

There are two important features of this policy. First, it compensates for a portion (85 percent) of actual net earnings losses. Second, there is a maximum level of insurable earning, which that was $54,200 in 2008.[4] In other provinces, the amount ranges between 75 percent and 90 percent of net earnings.[5] Partial compensation is said to reflect that workers' compensation was historically a system of co-insurance, designed to protect workers from ruinous loss, but not all losses.[6] A second rationale for partial compensation is that less-than-full compensation is thought to create an incentive for workers to return to work as quickly as possible.[7] Of course, it also directly saves employers money by reducing claim costs and, consequently, their premiums.

Deeming earnings

Workers experiencing a compensable wage loss receive either temporary total disability (TTD) benefits or temporary partial disability (TPD) benefits. Seriously injured workers may start out on TTD benefits and then move on to TPD as they return to part-time and/or modified work. As workers recover from their injuries, those unable (or unwilling) to obtain employment or who obtain employment that does not (in the WCB's opinion) represent their earnings capacity may have their TPD benefits based on "deemed" income rather than actual earnings. Deemed income is the earnings from a job the WCB considers the worker reasonably able to be hired to do, given any temporary work restrictions.[8]

The process of deeming turns on distinguishing returning workers to "employability" from returning workers to "employment." Workers are considered employable when suitable work has been identified that the worker is capable of performing. Suitable work is employment the worker is qualified to perform, does not endanger the worker's recovery or safety (or the safety of others) and is reasonably available in or near the worker's locale (or to a place the worker could reasonably relocate).[9] Distinguishing employability from employment is meant to reflect that workers' compensation does not compensate a worker for job loss, but rather for a reduction in employability due to a work-related injury.

Focusing on employability also addresses WCBs' lack of

control over a worker's job search effort, the availability of employment opportunities, and employers' hiring decisions.[10] Employers note that deeming motivates workers to seek employment. Critics note the underlying verve of deeming is that workers could get jobs if they wanted them. This assumption does not grapple with the impact of economic conditions and discrimination against disabled workers on a worker's job search.[11] Further, it deprives workers of compensation for economic losses that are the direct result of their workplace injury. Regardless of whether workers return to work or have their income deemed, employers' claim costs are reduced, which (as discussed below) can reduce their premiums.

Permanent disabilities and the dual-award system

Workplace injuries leave some workers with permanent disabilities. These disabilities may cause both economic losses (e.g., permanent impairment of earning capacity) and non-economic losses (e.g., a measurable clinical impairment of limb function) that negatively impact a worker's life. Over time, some jurisdictions have moved to a dual-award system for permanent disabilities that compensates workers separately for economic and non-economic losses.

Ongoing earnings-loss benefits (sometimes called a pension) for permanent disabilities are common, although the duration of this payment (e.g., lifetime, until age 65) varies between jurisdictions. This payment may also be adjusted to reflect changes in earning capacity (e.g., due to long-term improvement or deterioration). Workers may also receive a one-time, lump-sum award for non-economic loss (i.e., impact on a worker's quality of life outside the workplace). This payment is typically calculated based upon the degree of permanent impairment and may be adjusted based upon such factors as the nature of the impairment and the workers' age. In Ontario, the maximum non-economic loss was $79,623.83 in 2008.

The dual award system has an intuitive sense to it: it more closely aligns payments with earnings loss. Yet, it also has the effect of making permanently injured workers subject to WCB review and benefit changes throughout their lifetime.[12] This undermines the security of income of permanently injured workers, although the degree to which permanently disabled workers face significant alterations in wage-loss benefits over time is unstudied. Politically, this has the effect of placing injured workers on "probation" indefinitely, thereby making them less likely to resist WCB directives.

OTHER BENEFITS

The majority of compensable injuries entail little or no time lost from work and do not require rehabilitation.[13] When a work-related injury impairs a worker's employability, WCBs often provide a variety of return-to-work (RTW) services, including counselling services, job-search assistance, temporary modified work programs, training and vocational assessments, and workplace modifications.[14]

Vocational rehabilitation and early return to work

Vocational rehabilitation (VR) programs are designed to increase the probability of a worker returning to employment. Research suggests that VR tends to work better for those who were already traditionally advantaged in the labour market.[15] It is not clear whether those VR recipients who find work have a long-term attachment to the labour market. A study of Ontario workers' compensation claimants who experienced a period of work-absence found that only 40 percent of those who returned to work did so with a subsequently stable pattern of employment. The remainder had additional periods of absence — one-third eventually left employment permanently because of the effect of their injury.[16]

There has been growing interest in early return to work

(ERTW) programs. These programs see employers providing modified job duties to injured workers rather than having injured workers stay at home on TTD benefits.[17] ERTW is, in part, a response to growing concern about the cost of workers' compensation claims and their effect on employers' premiums.[18] WCB premiums are discussed below, but the short of it is that employers have periodically applied political pressure on the state and WCBs to reduce premiums. There are three ways to respond to this pressure:

Reduce injuries: WCBs and the state can provide inducements (e.g., incentives, penalties) that encourage employers to reduce work-related injuries. This approach places an onus on employers to reduce injuries and, in doing so, suggests work-related injuries are within employer control. It also requires employers spend money on workplace safety. This shifts the cost from compensation premiums to occupational health and safety budgets and may not entail any actual savings for employers.

Reduce benefits: WCBs and governments can reduce claims costs by limiting benefit access or reducing benefit levels. This carries the risk of increasing worker resistance to unsafe work practices and to the operation of the compensation system, thereby imperilling social stability.

Early return to work: Returning injured workers to work as quickly as possible reduces claim costs and means workers are contributing to the employer's operation. This approach has good optics, does not interfere with the employer's management of the workplace, and does not necessarily reduce worker benefits. ERTW also addresses the employer's obligations under the relevant human rights legislation to accommodate the needs of disabled workers.

Is early return to work a good idea?

ERTW programs are said to enhance workers' overall recovery. This claim is largely based on research about low-back pain. This research suggests activity (versus bed rest) is often beneficial in injury recovery. This has resulted in ERTW bring portrayed as a form of rehabilitation. It is not clear, however, to what degree work is analogous to the more generalized term "activity." As we saw in Chapter 1, work differs from other activities because it occurs in the context of a power relationship designed to maximize productivity. Modified work runs contrary to the organizing logic of this relationship and not all employers are willing to truly provide suitable modified work. When this occurs, employees face pressure to work in a manner that is contrary to their medical restrictions, perhaps aided by the (over) use of pain medication. This creates the risk of re-injury and, potentially, addiction. Further, in some instances, the benefits of activity for lower back pain are generalized to other types of injury, for which there is no supporting medical evidence.[19]

Workers who resist employer pressure to do things contrary to their rehabilitative best interests risk being labelled as uncooperative and having their benefits reduced or terminated. This reflects that pain is difficult to quantify and, therefore, difficult to factor into adjudicative decisions. This lack of quantification raises the spectre of moral hazard (i.e., there are incentives for workers to exaggerate the extent, nature, or duration of their injuries for financial gain). ERTW is, in fact, often offered as a remedy to moral hazard because it returns workers to work and thereby deprives them of the purported benefits of injury exaggeration. The issue of moral hazard highlights that benefit provision is significantly influenced by concerns about the economic impact of benefits on employer premiums.

ERTW also finds support in psychological theories of work and mental health. The longer workers are away from work, the less likely it is that they will return to their pre-accident job. It is not clear why this is the case. Perhaps this relationship reflects the fact that the more severely one is hurt, the longer one is off work, and the less likely one is to return to work. The lack of a clear explanation opens the door, however, to speculation about other reasons. For example, research suggests a correlation between work absence and poor mental health.[20] Some theorists also assert that being away from work causes a loss of occupational bonding and that workers begin to perceive themselves as invalids. This may be exacerbated by a desire to avoid painful activities.[21]

The relatively unstudied nature of ERTW allows proponents to argue that ERTW reduces the probability of a worker being disabled in the long term and improves the mental health of a worker. This logic of these assertions is questionable. It is unclear whether work absence (or its duration) is indeed the cause of long-term disability, poor mental health, or a loss of occupational bonding. There may be other factors at work (e.g., the severity of the injury). Further, even if work absence causes these outcomes, it is not clear that the causality works both ways. That is to say, reducing the duration of work absence may not reduce the probability of long-term disability, poor mental health, or a loss of occupational bonding.

The political economy of ERTW
What is clear about ERTW is that it reduces benefit duration and claim costs by compelling workers to return-to-work and financially punishing those who do not. This benefits employers, although they may face some additional costs due to the disruption caused by modified work. Yet even these costs can be transferred to other workers (who pick up the slack) and/or the injured worker (who may or may not experience the accommodation that was promised).

WCBs also benefit. The financial and administrative costs of a claim are transferred back to the employer and this savings, plus the reduced claims costs, can be used to reduce the premium rates charged to employers in the rate group. The state and WCBs can also reap reputational rewards from appearing to reduce the length injured workers are off work and creating the impression that workplaces are safer than they are, as discussed in Chapter 3.

Most of the costs of this strategy (e.g., less compensation, the potential for re-injury, misapprehension regarding how safe work is) are borne by workers. And these costs may be distributed in a gendered manner: injured men whose normal work might be physically demanding can often be accommodated via the provision of "light" office work. Women, whose normal work is often "light" work, have fewer options for modified work.[22] Overall, workers' experiences with ERTW are isolated and idiosyncratic and thus it is difficult for workers (and for researchers) to see commonalities and identify the root cause of them. This dynamic (discussed in Chapter 7) eliminates much of the political cost of ERTW as a strategy to manage compensation costs.

Medical services

Workers are entitled to medical aid to treat or alleviate the effects of a compensable injury. This includes a wide variety of goods and services that promote recovery from the effects of an injury. Medical aid is defined in Saskatchewan's *Workers' Compensation Act* as:

> 2(o) "medical aid" means medical and surgical aid,
> hospital and skilled nursing services, chiropractic and
> other treatment and artificial members or apparatus

There has been pressure on WCBs to expand the scope of medical aid as new technological changes and the profit motive have resulted in new diagnostic and treatment procedures. WCBs have started drawing boundaries around such treatments and diagnoses in an attempt to both limit the financial impact of such treatments on workers' compensation and protect injured workers from unnecessary and unproven techniques. For example, Alberta's policy on non-standard medical treatment prohibits payment for such aid unless it meets six stringent criteria.[23] Few treatments that aren't already standard will meet these criteria. A similar policy governs the acceptability of diagnoses reached via non-standard diagnostic techniques.

So why not just prohibit all such treatments and diagnoses? The policy rationale for this approach is that flexibility in the policy can be useful (e.g., allowing the rapid adoption of a promising new technique), but the tests minimize the potential risk to the worker. The legal reason centres on the concept of "fettering discretion." In short, WCBs are governed by the common law maxim, "(s)he who hears must decide." That is, the WCB decision maker must decide. While this decision can be guided by policy, that policy cannot be regarded as bindingly inflexible rule.[24] Thus, simply to prohibit nonstandard medical aid may well result in appeal bodies overturning the decisions because the WCB did not actually exercise its authority to decide a matter as required by statute. The result is policies with very restrictive criteria to effectively preclude nonstandard diagnostic and treatment techniques.

Fatalities

Although the rate of fatal accidents has declined as the economy has shifted towards one based on services, over 1000 workers are killed on the job every year.[25] The dependents of workers killed by compensable injuries are generally eligible to receive fatality benefits.[26] Compensation is only paid when a worker's death is a result of an accident. For example, a fatality caused by a progressive work-related disease or a workplace injury such as a fall is compensable. A fatality where, for example, a worker has a progressive, compensable disease but is killed by a fall on vacation is typically not compensable.

Fatality benefits tend to be less controversial than wage-loss benefits and ERTW services. Typically, there is little doubt as to whether the fatality is compensable and, where there is doubt, workers' compensation legislation generally gives the benefit of the doubt to the worker. One exception to this can be occupational diseases. As noted in Chapter 5, causality in these cases can be difficult to prove and employers, governments, and WCBs can be reluctant to acknowledge the work-relatedness of these diseases.

FUNDING WORKERS' COMPENSATION
Employer premiums

WCBs must maintain an accident fund that covers the projected cost of injuries and related functions by levying assessments on employers. The amounts involved can be substantial. Ontario employers paid $3.385 billion in premiums in 2006.[27] The premium paid is based upon the perceived risk of the employer, as assessed by the WCB, as well as the employer's payroll. Generally speaking, WCBs use two mechanisms to calculate an employer's assessment rate.

First, employers are placed in a rating or industry group. A rating group comprises industries or sectors of the economy that have comparable risks.[28] The base assessment rate for each member of a rating group is the same, meaning that there is relatively little relationship between an individual employer's accident record and the premiums charged. At the level of rating group or below, each group is meant to be revenue neutral so as not to transfer costs outside of the group.[29] Second, the base assessment rate for a rating group may be further adjusted up or down to reflect a particular firm's use of the compensation system (or its "accident record"). The purpose of these experience-rating programs is to encourage employers to reduce the volume and severity of accidents.[30]

The calculated assessment rate for a particular firm is applied directly to an employer's payroll (up to the "maximum insurable earnings" for each worker), and the overall premium determined.[31] These premium costs are then (in theory) passed on to the employer's customers through higher prices. While it is illegal for employers to reduce workers' salaries to pay for workers' compensation, U.S. employers appear to have done so by withholding wage increases over time.[32] The available evidence in Canada is less compelling.[33]

Employers may also seek cost relief. Cost relief means a WCB ignores some or all of a claim for the purposes of premium calculation. The cost may be transferred to another employer or distributed among all employers. For example, employers may seek relief from additional costs associated with aggravating a pre-existing condition or previous injury. This cost may be borne by the employer the worker was employed by when the original injury occurred. Employers whose workers are injured by the negligence of another employer's workers may also seek to have the costs associated with the injury transferred to the employer whose workers were negligent.[34]

Rising premiums

Employer associations routinely express concern about rising premiums, although the evidence of long-term premium increases is equivocal.[35] Premiums vary a lot from year-to-year, but real-dollar 2007 premium rates are not significantly higher than 1985 rates.[36] Similarly, the cost of individual claims has dropped from $6,054 in 1996 to $5,205 in 2007.[37] There was an increase in long-term, real-dollar cost increases of individual claims between 1960 and 1991.[38] These long-term changes have associated with a greater degree of utilization of workers' compensation.[39] These increases may reflect employees engaging in riskier behaviour, increased reporting of injuries otherwise ignored, and/or an increase in fraudulent claims. They may also reflect changes in how WCB staff adjudicate and administer claims. Further, workers often exercise a degree of discretion in how much pain and disability they will tolerate before filing a compensation claim. Expected benefits, administrative barriers, and pressures in the workplace all likely influence when a claim is filed.

It is interesting to note that discussions of rising costs are never cast in terms of a potential virtuous circle. That is to say, rising premiums are never discussed as resulting in safer workplaces and, thus, being self-limiting. Perhaps employers don't see this association, although their interest in accident-related premium rebates indicates they are aware of the putative relationship between premiums and safety. Perhaps employers don't believe premium increases will increase safety (see Experience-rating schemes below), either because there is no relationship between them or because other accident-related costs are much greater than premium increases.

Moral hazard

A recurring theme in the academic and professional literature is the potential impact of moral hazard on claim costs.[40] Moral hazard is a polite way of saying that workers have an incentive to (and some indeed do) cheat the system by incurring and/or exaggerating their injuries or delaying their returns to work. There is some evidence supporting this assertion, yet the overall incidence of such behaviour is low.[41] For example, analysis of injuries in Quebec suggests that the length of the recovery period for back-related injuries, low-back pain, and sprains (injuries where disability is difficult to quantify) increases when insurance coverage increases. This phenomenon is not evident in other types of injuries.[42] Alberta's anti-fraud work in 1995 and 1996 resulted in an estimated savings of only $7.7 million on total claims costs of $900 million.[43]

It is interesting that discussions of fraud almost always centre on workers.[44] Employers, health-care providers, insurers, and, indeed, WCB employees can defraud the system.[45] Anecdotal evidence about American workers' compensation systems suggests employer fraud is more common and of much greater magnitude than worker fraud. Injured workers certainly have an opportunity and incentive to defraud the system, although no more so than do employers, health-care providers, and WCB employees. So why, then, the focus on worker fraud?

Part of the answer is that worker fraud is easier to detect than fraud by employers or WCB staff. WCBs have greater access to worker information that would reveal fraud than they do to employer information. And WCBs can count on employers (who have an interest in limiting claims costs) to aid them in investigations of workers. Worker compliance with investigations can be gained via threatening benefit loss. And resistance to seemingly legitimate investigations is a tacit admission of guilt — a dynamic that taps into the widespread belief that workers are untrustworthy.[46] Gaining access to evidence of employer fraud is more difficult because the information is held almost entirely by the employer. It may also entail greater political risk for WCBs, depending upon the political clout of the employer being targeted.

Focusing on worker fraud directs attention to the (mis)behaviour of workers. In this way, it contributes to the negative view of workers that is common in discussions of workplace injury: not only are some workers injured through their own stupidity, but some also abuse the compensation system. In addition to having a potentially chilling effect on the willingness of workers to file claims, this narrative directs attention away from the role of employers in causing employee injuries and fatalities by organizing work in an unsafe manner.[47] And the resulting prescription (tighten claims adjudication and management) reduces claims costs without requiring employers to reduce injury rates. This, in turn, creates a disincentive for workers to file claims or resist inappropriate return-to-work offers. Focusing on worker fraud creates a political and legislative environment more willing to accept benefit reductions.[48]

Analysis of the Ontario workers' compensation system in the 1970s and '80s also suggests compensation may not always be awarded on a no-fault basis.[49] Factors such as whether an injured worker was of deserving character (often defined in Anglo and masculine terms) and exhibited good behaviour have been important mediating considerations. While overtly racist adjudication is less apparent recently, the spectre of moral hazard provides a powerful way for WCBs and employers to shape the discourse and practice of claim adjudication and administration in a way that benefits capital.

Experience-rating schemes

Experience rating is meant to encourage employers to reduce the financial costs of workplace accidents by providing premium rebates and surcharges based on employer claim costs. Proponents suggest it mitigates the key drawback of collective liability: when rates are determined by the accident record of all firms within an industry, individual employers have no incentive to improve their safety because the resulting cost savings are spread across all employers in the industry.[50] Ontario implemented voluntary experience rating in 1953 while mandatory experience rating in some industries began in 1984 and Alberta began experience rating in 1987.[51]

Experience rating means comparing employer claims to those of similar employers, often over several years. Rebates are issued for lower than average costs. Surcharges are assessed for higher than average costs.[52] In theory, this creates an economic incentive for organizations to reduce work-related injuries. It also increases the degree to which the true cost of producing goods and services will be reflected in the price of the product.[53]

Critics of experience rating suggest linking claim costs to

premium rebates creates an incentive for employers to hide accidents and pressure workers to not file claims, to contract out hazardous work, and to file legitimate and illegitimate appeals of claims in order to improve their experience rating.[54] Further, experience rating does not consider diseases with long latency periods.[55] In effect, critics suggest it is easier and cheaper for employers to game experience-rating systems than it is to lower the number and severity of their accidents.[56]

Effect of experience rating on injury frequency

The evidence that experience rating reduces the number and severity of workplace injuries is mixed. The introduction of experience rating in Ontario coincided with a reduction in fatalities by 40 percent in forestry and 20 percent in construction. The relatively dangerous nature of these industries may mean that more and/or lower cost opportunities to improve safety existed in these industries than in other industries.[57] A 2002 study of Quebec firms found experience rating lowered reported accident rates but, as the degree of experience rating rose, firms increasingly chose claims management over health and safety improvements as their strategy to address experience rating.[58] An examination of increased employer appeal activity among experience-rated firms in Ontario supports the assertion that claims management is an aspect of employer response to experience rating.[59]

Research in Quebec found employers are sensitive to the cost of work-related injuries (e.g., lost productivity, cost of replacing experienced workers). As costs rise, accident rates tend to decline. Yet the costs of accidents transmitted to employers through workers' compensation premiums do not appear to have any impact on the rate of occupational injury.[60] That is to say, the marginal extra cost from experience rating was not significant enough to spur action. This may reflect that even greater costs are associated with increasing safety.[61]

Interestingly, a similar pattern is also found for 1919, when rewarding foremen for reducing accident rates was found to yield little return—perhaps because production incentives swamped the bonus effect.[62]

This finding runs contrary to a 1994 study that suggested Ontario's experience rating encourages employers to improve safety practices.[63] Yet, this study also found experience rating had an even a greater effect on claims management, including claims monitoring and appeals, as well as interacting with adjudicators to trigger unofficial reviews of claims. Employers were less motivated to provided modified work. Overall, employers sought to minimize the number of claims accepted and the duration of benefits provided.

Effect of experience rating on injury duration
The effect of experiencing rating on claim duration is also interesting. A 1992 Quebec study found experience rating did not significantly affect the rate of reported accidents but was associated with an *increased* duration of compensation.[64] This runs contrary to the expected effect of experience rating, whereby employers are rewarded for moving injured workers off compensation and back into modified work. The study offers no explanation for this result. Research in Ontario found a similar effect, nothing that the introduction of experience rating in the construction industry resulted in an 8.4 percent increase in the duration of compensation.[65]

This counter-intuitive outcome may reflect employers acting to convert lost-time claims (which affect their experience rating) into no-lost-time claims and thereby prevent wage-loss benefits from triggering. Mild injuries are most amenable to this conversion strategy and mildly injured employees are likely provided with modified or light duties for the duration of their injury. The increased duration after the introduction of experience rating reflects that the subsequent lost-time claim population comprises more severely injured workers, who would naturally require benefits for a longer time.

Experience rating may also have other, unintended effects. A study of New Zealand experience rating found that the probability of employers asking unlawful, disability-related questions on job application forms rose 71 times for each 1 percent increase in workers' compensation premiums. With a 2 percent premium increase, firms were more likely to ask such questions than not.[66] In effect, experience rating creates a significant incentive for employers to manage claims proactively (through discriminatory hiring practices) as well as reactively.

A further criticism of experience rating is that it may not achieve a reduction in the actual incidence of accidents because experience rating is determined by claims data, not safety performance.[67] That is to say, there is little link between safety behaviour and the incentive/penalty scheme. Employers may pursue a reward through claims management rather than altering safety behaviour. When this dynamic is combined with the marginal impact of workers' compensation premiums on the overall costs of injuries for employers, some suggest by a ratio of one to four, experience rating will not elicit further health and safety investment by employers.[68] Instead, employers substitute less expensive claims management behaviour.

Rationale for experience rating

The evidence suggests experience rating has little to no demonstrable effect on workplace safety. It also suggests that experience rating generates aggressive claims management, perhaps to the detriment of injured workers. So why, beyond the financial gain employers can realize, would states continue to use experience rating? One answer is that experience rating creates the perception that WCBs and employers are seeking to reduce workplace accidents. And the data generated by experience rating and similar regulatory schemes makes it seem that there are improvements.

The fact that experience rating doesn't generally result in safer workplaces is easy to overlook. As we saw in Chapter 3, most "accident rate" data is actually claims data. Using claims data allows changes in the accident rate as well as claim management strategies to create the impression that there are fewer and/or less severe injuries.[69] The contribution of claims management activity confounds our ability to draw conclusions from the data, something rarely made clear in the presentation of the data.

This outcome is difficult to see and document or convey in easily accessible (i.e., quantitative) form. Workers' compensation claims are adjudicated and administered privately and individually. This obscures patterns in employer behaviour (e.g., systematically disputing claims, offering meaningless or false modified work). Workers who complain about this sort of employer behaviour risk be labelled malingerers, particularly given the disproportionate attention paid to worker fraud. Workers also run up against a system that is structurally unable to police employer gaming behaviour: that claim costs reflect claim management instead of safety improvements is obscured by the claims cost metric that drives experience-rating systems.

CONCLUSION

Workers' compensation systems provide significant wage-loss, medical, rehabilitative, and fatality benefits to workers. The complex and essentially private nature of benefits administration has the same illusion of impartiality as the decision about which injuries qualify for compensation. Yet claims management is a political process. Focusing on returning workers to employability and encouraging workers to make an early return to work (while workers are under threat of income deeming) is designed to reduce employer premiums by transferring costs onto workers. In this, we find some support for the notion that workers' compensation is as much about, where possible, denying claims and limiting benefits as it is about paying out claims.

This behaviour finds justification in the widely accepted view that workers will malinger. Return-to-work programs also draw on the narrative that being off work because one is sick is somehow unhealthy and that work is indeed rehabilitative. There is little evidence to suggest that this is true, but again this narrative taps into social disapprobation around malingering. That these policies further reduce employers' already limited liability for the costs associated with work-related injuries is largely ignored.

The persistence of experience rating, despite evidence that it does not reduce injury frequency or duration, suggests its real purpose is to reduce employer premiums and create the impression that employers are reducing the rate and/or severity of workplace injuries. In this way, the state can appear responsive to the demands of workers without significantly impacting the capital accumulation process. When the downplaying of injury levels is combined with drawing attention to worker fraud, it becomes possible to direct attention away from the core issue of unsafe work-practices.

When combined with the availability of stable, predictable, and immediate compensation for the majority of injured workers, benefits administration and premium collection may reduce the willingness of workers to resist workplace injury. The individualized process of adjudication and appeal discussed in Chapter 7 further reduces the potential for collective resistance.

— SEVEN —

MANAGING WORKERS
VIA INJURY COMPENSATION

On 21 October 2009, 38-year-old Patrick Clayton walked into
the main Alberta Worker's Compensation Building in Edmonton
with a rifle, fired a single shot, and took nine hostages.[1] Clayton was an injured construction worker with a long-running
claim dispute. He had been on and off benefits for the previous
six years and was cut off again the week prior to the hostage
taking. Unable to work or gain compensation and allegedly
further injured during a workers' compensation board (WCB)
medical exam, Clayton's life unravelled: bankruptcy, welfare,
living in social housing, drug addiction, domestic violence, and
a custody dispute.

"I just got sick and tired of being treated like a piece of crap
by WCB," Clayton told an interviewer from jail. "I never knew
where I was going to stand with them from one day to the next,
all that uncertainty was nerve racking and constantly wearing
me down. ... I thought that I had already lost everything including [his son] Brandon, and that I didn't have anything else
to lose except my life. ... I never had any intentions of hurting
any of those people, I just wanted for someone to listen to my
story and for someone to help me."[2]

This incident is the most recent in a series of incidents over the years. In 1991, a brain-injured steel worker killed himself in a WCB parking lot. His death resulted in two inquires, program changes, and a government apology to his family. Protestors smashed WCB windows in 1991 and 1992. In 1993, a disable construction worker used a shotgun to take hostages. Later in the 1990s, injured workers set up a small tent city on the lawn of the WCB. Staff derisively referred to them as "happy campers." Two further government reviews followed.[3] The lawn has since been re-landscaped with hills, boulders, and prickly bushes to discourage a repeat of this protest.

While it is tempting to dismiss these incidents as aberrant, the media coverage of the Clayton hostage taking caused many injured workers to speak out about their frustration. A recurring theme is that workers' compensation is coercive and unfair — that employers and the WCB appear to conspire against them. These claims deserve consideration. Like all public programs, workers' compensation is coercive — that is the point of regulation. Publicly funded medical programs mean you can't jump the queue by paying out of your own pocket. Speed limits infringe upon your ability to drive as fast as you want. The coercive nature of these programs doesn't means they are necessarily bad. The important questions to ask are who is coerced, who benefits from the coercion, and in what ways?

Workers' compensation is coercive in its decision-making and appeals processes. The discussion in Chapters 5 and 6 suggests that WCBs use claim adjudication and management to limit employer liability and the ability of workers to resist this agenda. This chapter further develops this analysis by examining how workers' compensation decision-making and appeal processes contribute to managing worker resistance to limiting employer liability.

The chapter begins by examining how the private nature of decision-making makes it difficult for workers to know what hazards exist in the workplace and develop a shared understanding of workplace injury as a class issue. We then examine how the operation of appeals pushes WCBs and employers together to counter worker opposition. These dynamics compound the effect that incentives to participate in the system and penalties for challenging it have on the ability of workers and labour to win safer workplaces or better compensation.

Worker resistance is further constrained by the discourse about privatizing or abolishing the workers' compensation. These proposals are erroneously thought to result in a cheaper system. Yet, they create pressure on workers to limit their criticisms of workers' compensation or even defend workers' compensation or risk the loss of the benefits it provides. In the meantime, employers reorganize work in ways that make workers ineligible for coverage — thereby eroding the system out from underneath workers. The effect of these changes is disproportionately borne by women and racial minorities — groups that have less ability to resist such changes.

CLAIM ADJUDICATION AND ADMINISTRATION

Workers want safe workplaces. Historically, workers have sought safer workplaces by working together. For such efforts to be successful there has to be a political opportunity to challenge existing arrangements, some sort of group structure through which individuals can mobilize, and a process that allows individuals to form a collective understanding of the problem they face and see it as amenable to change.[4] In the context of workers' compensation, individual claim adjudication and administration makes administrative sense. At the same time, it also limits workers' ability to develop a shared understanding around the political economy of claim adjudication and administration and mobilize themselves to seek changes.[5]

Impeding a shared understanding

Workers' compensation limits the ability of workers to know the hazards they face. Each claim is adjudicated individually and information about the injury is confidential. While workers may know about recent injuries within a workplace (or even small or regional industries), individual adjudication makes it hard to identify patterns of injury. Identifying patterns of injury is important because patterns are a good indicator of how the organization of work causes injury. While patterns may sometimes be self-evident, most of the time patterns are not evident because injuries are dispersed in geography and/or time. Injury causation may also be difficult to observe.

Further, individual adjudication and claims management also means injured workers have little opportunity to interact and develop a shared understanding of their injury and compensation experiences, unless they happen to meet in rehabilitation or are part of some other community.[6] By making it hard for workers to recognize and discuss patterns of injury and compensation, the adjudication and management of claims impedes collective action. Employers are, of course, much more likely to know about patterns of injury and about who is injured, as well as to have the power to reduce or eliminate the hazards that cause these injuries. But reducing hazards and putting injured workers in contact may not be in employers' best interests because it can undermine their ability to organize work in the most profitable way.

Mobilizing workers

When workers develop a collective awareness of shared interests or problems, workers' compensation can also impede their mobilization. Receipt of compensation can, for example, reduce workers' collective interest in pursuing safer workplaces by lowering the cost of injury to workers. Similarly, compensation robs workplace injuries of much of their political verve by mitigating the financial consequences of them. Finally, workers may be disinclined to mobilize for fear of being subject to administrative harassment or losing their compensation.[7]

Where workers do act collectively (e.g., by forming an injured worker group), they face two challenges. First, such groups have limited policy capacity (the ability to participate meaningfully in policy discussions) and limited policy salience (the ability to generate consequences if their demands are ignored) over the long-term. A small cadre of organizers with few resources or allies often sustains such groups.

The second challenge faced by such groups is that, by their nature, they are non-representative. That is to say, they represent the interests of their members but not a larger group (such as "all injured workers" or "all unionized workers in a province"). They may also lack the formal organizational structure found in sophisticated worker groups such as trade unions. Consequently, injured worker groups may have little legitimacy in the eyes of the state and employers — which is convenient, because they tend to carry messages that the state and employers don't want to hear.

This lack of representative capacity often results in injured worker groups being dismissed as "special interest groups." Such terminology is an interesting example of the political economy of capitalism. Employer advocacy groups are generally viewed positively (i.e., as legitimate lobbyists) while groups concerned with worker, health, or environmental issues have the negative "special interest group" label applied to them. The fundamental difference between the two groups is whom they lobby on behalf of and the implications their policy prescriptions have for the capital accumulation process.

Role of trade unions

Trade unions are another structure through which injured workers may mobilize. The ability of unions to identify patterns and to pressure the state or employers for safer workplaces is constrained by relatively low union density (although this varies by sector and province) and the availability of resources. Some labour resources are used to assist members with their individual claims and some are directed at defending the system from proposals to alter it against the interests of workers. This reduces the resources available to seek structural change in workplaces or to workers' compensation. Further, the availability of workers' compensation to many workers may limit the willingness of unions to risk existing compensation to achieve safer workplaces or more broadly distributed compensation.[8]

Should unions desire significant change, the opportunities available to them are limited. Collectively bargaining changes one unit at a time, is slow, and employers can resist it. Whether the majority of workers will sacrifice wages or risk a strike to advance the interests of the injured is unclear.[9] The ability of unions to bring political pressure on the state is limited by the existence of a compensation system and difficulty in getting reliable injury data. Should this data be available, unions must still face resistance in the political arena and the special interest group label.[10] In this way, workers' compensation diffuses worker resistance to managerial practices that result in work-related injury.

APPEALS

Every jurisdiction in Canada allows workers and employers to appeal WCB decisions. In the 1980s and 1990s, workers heralded gaining an appeal process as a victory. Yet, like other worker "victories" over the years, the appeal process has paradoxical elements. On the one hand, it allows workers access to their own workers' compensation information and gives them an opportunity to contest WCB decisions. On the other hand, the nature of the process aligns the interests of the WCB and the employer against workers. In doing so, the appeals process reintroduces an adversarial process to workers' compensation. In some jurisdictions, it can also pit workers against the combined resources of both the WCB and the employer. When this dynamic is combined with the WCB tendency to minimize employer liability by rejecting claims and limiting worker benefits, appeals clearly contribute to a pattern of behaviour that disadvantages workers.

Internal reviews and external appeals

When dissatisfied with a WCB decision, workers or employers can ask for an internal review of a decision.[11] Anyone with a direct interest in the decision is eligible to make such a request.[12] Internal reviews typically see the decision(s) in question being re-examined, often first by the original decision maker and then by an internal review body. This might entail collecting more data, performing a documentary review of the decision, and/or holding a conference with the interested parties. Eventually, an internal review decision is generated. Most workers and employers will choose to represent themselves during these proceedings, although some hire lawyers, seek help from their union, or bring other advocates into the process.[13]

A worker or employer who is dissatisfied with the outcome of an internal review can normally file an appeal.[14] This process varies by jurisdiction. In Alberta, this application goes to the external and independent Appeals Commission for Alberta Workers' Compensation. By contrast, in Saskatchewan, the Board of Directors of the WCB is the final level of appeal. A hearing conducted in-person or by teleconference usually follows, although a hearing based solely on documents may also be possible. In an in-person or teleconference hearing, a panel hears the argument made by each party. This usually means the worker and the employer. In some jurisdictions, such as

Alberta, the WCB may also be a party.[15] Following the hearing, the appeals body normally issues a written decision of the panel's decision.[16]

How appeal processes advantage employers

Injured workers and their employers do not normally participate in decision-making about claims, although both provide WCBs with information used to render a decision. This is consistent with the non-adversarial approach to workers' compensation. When a worker or employer disagrees with the decision, they must appeal it — often while living with the consequences. The consequences of an unfavourable decision are, however, of different magnitudes for workers and employers.

A decision unfavourable to an employer may affect the employer's future premiums, but the overall effect is small and is usually easily reversible. By contrast, a decision unfavourable to a worker often results in a reduction or loss of wage-loss or other benefits. As we saw with Patrick Clayton, the financial consequence of having no income is often immediate and dire. Further, the effects of being unable to make a mortgage payment or provide food for a family are difficult to reverse, particularly if the reversal comes significantly after the original decision.

In this way, workers have much more at stake in an appeal than an employer. Further, the delays inherent in appeal processes do not impact workers and employers equally. In this way, workers' compensation appeals have an effect broadly analogous to the "work now, grieve later" principle of grievance arbitration: workers who resist modified work, intrusive medical examinations, or other WCB demands and thus have their earnings deemed to benefits cut off must bear the significant costs while awaiting remedy.[17] The remedy for such a decision cannot help but affect workers' decision-making about whether to co-operate with a WCB.

Adversarialism in appeals

The appeals process can subtly align the interests of WCB adjudicators and employers against the interests of workers. When a worker disputes a claim decision, the original WCB adjudicator typically seeks to have the decision upheld during an internal review.[18] Decisions that workers appeal typically financially benefit their employer. In the internal review process, then, we see the employer's interests (i.e., minimizing claim costs) align with the adjudicator's interests (i.e., upholding a decision limiting or precluding benefits). It is often difficult for workers to pinpoint why it appears that the WCB is conspiring with their employer against them. This dynamic is at least partially responsible for that experience. This recurring alignment cannot help shape the mindset of frontline adjudicators towards employers (often allies) and injured workers (usually opponents).[19]

When disputes come before an external appeals body, the WCB itself has an interest in ensuring its interpretation of fact and policy is upheld.[20] Where the WCB can participate in the appeals process (or, indeed, the WCB is the appeals body), the WCB and employer can act in concert against the appellant. Where the WCB cannot (or does not) participate, the WCB's original decision still frames the debate and provides a compelling body of evidence. In these ways, multiple voices argue against the worker's appeal. Further, the employer (and the WCB, if present) is more likely to have or employ knowledgeable advocates who will make full use of the procedural and factual information available to them.[21] And the employer (and the WCB, if present) are also more likely to hold positions of significant social stature and are able to make appeals to "maintaining the integrity of the system," whereas an injured employer is essentially arguing in his or her own interest. That said, an injured worker can make a most sympathetic appellant.

This is not to suggest that appeals processes are necessarily or entirely a bad thing for workers. Appeals provide workers with a means by which to remedy erroneous decisions about their claims. Yet, the alignment of interests created by the internal and external appeal processes appear to run against workers, both in the immediate appeals outcomes and perhaps in the broader orientation of adjudicators towards injured workers. When combined with the tendency of WCB legislation and policy to limit employer liability (as shown in Chapters 5 and 6), a disturbing pattern of bias against workers emerges. This bias is a function of the structure of workers' compensation and may be reinforced (or mitigated) by the beliefs and behaviours of individual adjudicators.

Political economy of appeals

Independent appeal systems were developed during the 1980s in response to widespread worker dissatisfaction with seemingly arbitrary conduct by WCBs. This has resulted in significant growth in the number of appeals.[22] There are three reasons employers appeal worker claims. First, employers may be legitimately skeptical about the validity of claims. Second, claims costs directly affect an employer's premiums via the experience-rating mechanism. Appealing these claims can reduce premiums and, if the employer can find an advocate who works on a contingency basis, the appeal costs the employer nothing. Third, employers who face significant pressure to reduce accident levels (e.g., because bids on construction job may be affected by time-loss claim records) may be seeking to send a message to their workforce about how workers making claims will be treated. By subjecting claimants to repeated and stressful appeals, employers may be able to increase worker attention to safety and/or decrease injury reporting.

Appeal systems have both costs and benefits for major stakeholder groups: employers, workers, and the state. An independent appeals process works against employers by giving workers an opportunity to seek further or higher benefits from the WCB. This can increase employer premiums, although the additional costs of losing an appeal are usually small. Depending upon the jurisdiction, employers may be able to rely upon the WCB to essentially fight an appeal for them, because the WCB will seek to have its decision upheld.

An independent appeals process gives workers an opportunity to have a disinterested third party review decisions made by the WCB in light of policy and legislation. In establishing this process (which also gives workers access to their WCB files), workers gained a significant procedural improvement. Whatever the actual outcome of an appeal, this process also gives the workers a sense that they've had their "day in court."

The threat of endless appeals also places pressure on WCBs to develop more consistent and rigorous internal decision-making and review procedures. This benefits workers by yielding more consistent and timely decisions. The downside of an independent appeals body for workers is that this process effectively forecloses political lobbying to get compensation. Legislators (who hear a significant amount about workers' compensation claims from constituents) are able to direct workers to the appeals process. Workers dissatisfied with the outcome of their appeal can be characterized as having unrealistic expectations.

Finally, the state benefits in two ways from independent appeals commissions. First, legislators can direct dissatisfied claimants and employers into the appeals process rather than having to take up constituents' issues themselves. The value of this should not be underestimated. Injured workers can be very sympathetic spokespeople and no elected official wants to be seen as unresponsive to them. Further, legislators must be careful not to be seen as exerting undue influence over the workings of an independent agency such as a WCB. This constraint makes it difficult for legislators to get action (even when they want to) that will satisfy their constituents.

The second benefit independent appeals commissions provide the state is that they reinforce the legitimacy of the workers' compensation process. Dissatisfied claimants and employers have a viable and notionally neutral appeal option. This may reduce the pressure that dissatisfaction places upon the fundamental compromise: the parties may be less politically able to and likely to seek significant change to workers' compensation if it appears there is the prospect of fair treatment. Instead, disputes are channelled into a legalistic and bureaucratic process, not unlike grievance arbitration.[23]

Impact on workers

Before leaving this topic, we should consider the impact of the compensation and appeals process on workers. There is some evidence that it can retard recovery and rehabilitation. Where the work-relatedness of an injury or disability or the degree of disability is contested, determining causation can require multiple non-therapeutic medical examinations, including invasive testing that provides no medical benefit to the worker but can be emotionally taxing and delay treatment.[24] Disputes over causation may also result in stressful litigation and can negatively impact doctor–patient relationships.[25] Further, injured workers may face surveillance, which can negatively affect the quality of their life and impede their recovery.[26]

A Quebec study by Katherine Lippel identified how the compensation process (and the action of specific actors) affected the self-reported health of injured workers.[27] The process of compensation was found to have a negative effect on workers' mental health in the majority of cases. Among the effects reported were depression and suicidal thoughts. Among the causes of this negative effect was the stigmatization of injured workers, based the belief that injured workers were defrauding the system.[28] Also important was the worker perception that an imbalance of power characterized the compensation process. Workers noted that they often felt like they were fighting the compensation board, doctors, their employer, and even their union. More specifically:

> Filing a claim with the (compensation board) leads to the intervention of a number of parties, setting in motion a series of "big machines" that seek to control the injured worker, control his future, control costs, control his body, control his appeal, control the return to work process, control his behaviour at work, or at occupational therapy, or at the doctor's office, and, in the case of clandestine surveillance, control his personal life and that of his family.[29]

Many of these parties have much greater resources and access to information than the worker. Some, such as employers, also have greater power than the worker by virtue of the employment relationship. This imbalance became particularly evident when workers were denied benefits and were forced to enter the appeals process. Workers having support from a knowledgeable advocate mitigated the effects of this dynamic. Where compensation board workers were suspicious or disrespectful, workers experienced additional mental distress. These findings were broadly similar to work done in Australia.[30]

PRIVATIZATION AND ABOLISHMENT

While disputes about individual claims and the operation of the system often command our attention, lurking just offstage is the threat of privatizing or abolishing workers' compensation. This discourse is premised on the erroneous belief that privatization or abolishment will result in a cheaper system. Despite this flawed premise, the presence of this discourse may exert pressure on workers and unions to defend workers' compensation (or limit demands for change) in order to protect the rights they have gained through it.[31] In the meantime, employers have been reorganizing work in ways that make workers ineligible for coverage—thereby eroding the system out from underneath workers. The effect of these changes is disproportionately borne by women and racial minorities—groups that have less ability to resist such changes.

Argument for returning to tort

Rising claims costs are often cited as a reason for governments to abandon or radically alter workers' compensation. One option is to return to compensating injury using the tort system. This has some advantages for the state and employers. Abolishing workers' compensation would eliminate complaints to government about the operation of such systems. Investors would be able to evade most costs associated with workplace injuries because of the legal barriers to successful civil suits outlined in Chapter 5 and the liability protection offered by the corporation form.[32] Some workers may also benefit. For example, the severely injured may reasonably expect higher settlements in court than through workers' compensation.[33]

Yet there are also significant drawbacks to a return to tort. Tort-based compensation has historically resulted in the social instability and disruption, in part because it did not provide immediate, stable, and predictable compensation for injured workers. Further, it creates the potential for unpredictable injury costs and unlimited liability for employers. These political and practical benefits augur against a return to tort. A fuller consideration of the operation of a tort system reinforces this perception.

Operation of tort-based compensation

Under the tort system, workers are responsible for the cost of an injury unless they can prove someone else ought to bear the cost and succeed in getting that someone else to pay. As we saw in Chapter 5, this remains a process fraught with risk for workers. Such a system ought to result in workers demanding hazard pay for the additional risk they are assuming. As we saw in Chapter 2, workers have always had difficulty adequately assessing hazards before taking the job, particularly as employers have an interest in hiding this information. Further, it is unclear whether workers, particularly non-unionized workers, have the necessary labour market power to compel a risk-based wage premium from employers.[34] If workers did receive hazard pay, they might then use this to purchase insurance against the possibility of workplace injury. Or they might just pocket the difference and hope for the best.

Employers may also buy insurance to mitigate the risk of an injury-induced civil suit. Or they might not. In that case, an employer found responsible for an injury may simply declare bankruptcy, its investors protected by their limited liability for the actions of the corporation. This line of speculation could continue *ad nauseum*. For example, if workers do not know which employer is insured and which is not, they cannot ask for a wage premium from the uninsured to compensate them for the risk of employer bankruptcy.

In both cases, private insurers may find that the *adverse selection* effect makes offering disability insurance unprofitable. Adverse selection begins when an insurance company offers an insurance policy covering disability. Claims cause the premiums to go up in year two and each policyholder looks at whether the higher priced insurance remains worthwhile. If the employee or company expects to file a claim, they see the insurance as a bargain and buy it. Those who don't expect to file a claim may well drop it. Consequently, the insurance company is now insuring a group that has a higher risk factor and will raise the following year's premiums. As this cycle repeats, coverage becomes unaffordable and insurers stop offering it.[35]

One solution is to have the state act as the insurer of last resort but, of course, that runs contrary to the whole idea of returning to tort.

Comparing tort and workers' compensation

Setting aside the political and practical difficulties of tort, it is useful to consider how workers' compensation stacks up against civil cases. Some researchers conclude that workers' compensation awards are monetarily comparable to tort awards.[36] Douglas Hyatt and David Law note, however, that the majority of civil actions are settled out of court and, moreover, that these settlements are generally lower than settlements imposed by the courts. Furthermore, workers receive only 48 percent of court awards. Fees and litigation costs consume the rest of the money. Workers' compensation appears to provide compensation that is better and more reliable for workers without the risks involved in a civil suit. The exception may be for severely injured workers, who generally fare better under tort law.

Hyatt and Law recognize the cost of workers' compensation premiums may be rising. Yet, they noted, such calculations often do not consider how the costs of such premiums are being borne by workers through wage rates that no longer fully compensate for the risks of an occupation. There is also some evidence that significant portions of increases in workers' compensation premiums are passed along to workers over time by lower wage increases.[37] And, as noted in the Introduction, social reproduction includes developing and maintaining the skills and well being of workers such that they can perform their role in the labour process. The state contributes to social reproduction mainly through labour and social policies, of which workers' compensation is one facet. Abolishing workers' compensation shifts significant costs associated with social reproduction onto families, the gendered nature of which means these costs are borne by women.[38]

Privatization

A second set of proposals seeks to privatize workers' compensation via the provision of some or all of workers' compensation by for-profit insurance companies. What precisely is meant by "privatization" varies and can mean one or a mixture of the following:

- for-profit insurance companies competing with a non-profit WCB,

- for-profit companies assuming total responsibility for providing insurance within (or without) guidelines established by the state,

- for-profit companies providing insurance but a WCB remains as the insurer of last resort (for those companies no insurance company will take on), or

- for-profit companies performing some workers' compensation functions under contract (e.g., claims management, rehabilitation).[39]

The first three approaches form the mainstay of American workers' compensation systems, in which private companies manage claims, while the government determines such matters as eligibility for compensation and benefit levels, and provides the processes for appeals.[40] It is commonly held that competition between insurers for customers would create an incentive for insurers to reduce the costs of workers' compensation. This belief has particular appeal because of the widespread sentiment that public-sector institutions are somehow administratively inefficient (e.g., they comprise an overly large and ineffective bureaucracy). A leaner, private-sector company can be expected to avoid this, or so the argument goes.

Impact of privatization

Let's begin by analyzing the argument for privatization from a theoretical perspective.[41] Assume publicly provided workers' compensation systems have administrative costs of approximately 15 percent. This means that a private-sector company operating even 10 percent more efficiently than a public sector WCB would only see a cost savings of 1.5 percent. Private-sector companies, however, must also generate a profit for their investors, something that is sure to negate some or all of the efficiency gains that are assumed to come with privatization. To avoid increasing rates in order to make a profit (and thus invalidating the key argument for privatization — that it will be cheaper), insurers will need to find some other way to reduce costs.

Private insurance companies may try to get employers to reduce accident rates by increasing premiums for unsafe employers. As noted in Chapter 3 and 6, this approach has not been particularly successful. Consequently, insurers may turn to decreasing benefit levels, reducing the duration of claims, or shifting costs to other programs, such as health care, welfare, or the workers' families. These approaches create the appearance that private insurance is less expensive, but in fact, they represent a cost transfer from industry to workers and the state.[42] So far, privatization doesn't look too good.

Who chooses the insurer?

The question of who chooses the insurer in a privatized system with multiple potential carriers is an important one. It seems safe to assume that, in choosing an insurer, workers and employers would pursue their own interests. Furthermore, it appears fair to assert that the adjudication of claims is complex enough that each insurer must exercise some discretion in accepting and managing claims. Thus, if the employer selects the insurer, the employer would likely seek the insurer with the lowest premiums. Low premiums most likely mean the insurer is shifting costs to the injured worker or the government. This may well jeopardize social reproduction.

By the same token, if the worker selects the insurer, the worker will likely seek the insurer with the most generous track record. This would increase employer costs and thus undermines the purpose of privatization — saving money. Unless that isn't the purpose of privatization and the real intent is to open up a publicly managed system to profit-making activity. In any event, it appears that, even if privatization could be made profitable, privatization could well founder on the issue of who chooses the insurer.

It is also possible that the complexity of the tasks performed by a workers' compensation system may render the regulation of privatization by the state so complex as to minimize or even eliminate the projected cost savings.[43] With the questions about whether privatization can lower costs and maintain social stability in mind, it is useful to see what research comparing public and private systems says.

Cost savings under privatization

Terry Thomason compared the experience of per employee assessment of workers' compensation in Canada and the U.S. between 1961 and 1989.[44] Overall, the difference was small (between $2 and $50 per employee on no more than $349) with no particular pattern to the difference. This conclusion finds support in subsequent research that indicates that the costs of publicly provided workers' compensation are no higher, and may even be lower, than privately provided workers' compensation.[45] This suggests that privatization does not result in cost savings.

Thomason notes two other interesting findings. Firstly, in 1990, 41 percent of total costs in the U.S. privatized system were for medical services, versus 14 percent in Canada.

Secondly, despite similar overall costs, Canadian programs offer more generous benefits and more extensive coverage than the American system. An earlier study by Thomason also indicates that American workers' compensation systems result in much more litigation, and that administrative costs are twice as high.[46] A third study in New York State found that claim management by private insurers, and in particular the cost of disputing claims, appears to reflect economic considerations, rather than genuine concern over causation and disability.[47] Furthermore, certain claims were more likely to be disputed and/or adjusted by private insurers in this system. These included claims by non-English speakers, younger workers (whose greater life expectancy yields higher claim costs), and workers claiming occupational disease or internal injury. This also held true where the claim value was small, and not as likely to be pursued by the worker via litigation.

A further problem is that of "creaming."[48] Creaming occurs where insurers will only insure low-risk companies (i.e., the ones potentially most profitable to the insurer). Avoiding creaming requires a significant degree of government regulation. Publicly- provided workers' compensation also better allows governments to harmonize workers' compensation payments with other social programs such as taxation, the Canada and Quebec Pension Plans, welfare, and unemployment insurance, although the fragmentation of jurisdiction in Canada complicates this.[49]

Most damaging to the notion of privatization is that there appears to be no significant research that supports the proposition that privately provided workers' compensation is less expensive than its public counterpart. An analysis of workers' compensation in 48 states from 1975 to 1995 designed to determine (in part) which set of arrangements (public, private, or mixed provision) provided the most effective form of delivery concluded there were no clear differences in costs between jurisdictions with exclusively public and exclusively private systems.[50] Where there is mixed delivery (i.e., public and private providers), employer costs appear to be higher. The overall impression arising out of this research is that privatization does not yield a less costly system for employers or a more equitable system for employees.

Economic globalization as an explanation

There is no evidence that a return to tort or privatization would result in significant cost savings. There is also good reason to believe such changes would make compensation for work-related injuries less equitable. So why do these proposals recur? Some advocates may have a personal financial interest. For example, insurance companies, injury lawyers, and companies with low risks of work-related accidents may all benefit. Other proponents may be incorrectly informed about the merits of their proposals. But other, more insightful explanations centre on the neo-liberal prescription for society.

Let's begin with the role of neo-liberal beliefs about the value of a free market and the effectiveness of privatization. Workers' compensation predates the substantial expansion of social rights and programs following the Second World War, which sought to address or ameliorate a variety of social problems by transferring income within society. Yet workers' compensation is fundamentally consistent with these programs in that they all served to maintain the social reproduction by reducing social instability.[51]

A variety of factors (e.g., trade agreements, changing technology) reduced the dependency of capital on the economic conditions in individual states. At the same time, public support for the interventionist welfare state weakened beginning in the 1970s because a growing body of evidence seemed to justify growing doubt about the state's ability to secure both economic growth and continuous improvements in public services.[52] The election of right-wing governments in the 1980s and 1990s has resulted in a variety of economic and legislative reforms designed to reduce the scope and cost of the state. These changes have been justified by reference to the supposed imperatives of economic globalization wherein government should (and perhaps must) adjust the domestic economy in order to attract transnational capital.[53]

There is no universal agreement that globalization and neo-liberal policies are new or inevitable.[54] That said, Canadian government policy makers and bureaucrats appear to accept the globalization thesis and have adopted neo-liberal policies, including in labour relations.[55] Workers' compensation is an area of state activity that imposes costs on employers and has been largely protected from profit-making activity. This makes it an attractive target for market-based reform.

Managing worker demands

A second line of explanation for these proposals is that they help manage worker agitation for improved workplace safety and injury compensation. By creating the spectre of radical restructuring that imperils the existence of workers' compensation — a system that provides significant benefits for workers — employers are able to contain demands for increased safety and compensation. Such threats can also be used to make marginal changes to workers' compensation that reduce costs and/or open up parts of the system to private-sector activity.

This analysis is based on the dialectic of partial conquest.[56] In short, workers are less likely to resist employer demands if the workers credibly believe they may lose something important. We see this in collective bargaining, where trade unions are reluctant to risk illegal strikes because they fear punishment and the loss of their security or bargaining rights. This threat helps ensure unions use the grievance-arbitration process to address instances where the employer violates the collective agreement, rather than taking the much more effective (and disruptive) step of putting down their tools and stopping production.

Proposals for privatization and a return to tort have much the same effect. They require labour to spend resources defending workers' compensation.[57] This limits the practical and political ability of labour to challenge existing workers' compensation practice: How can labour support and criticize workers' compensation at the same time? And the existence of a viable threat to workers' compensation may make labour more amenable to accepting smaller changes in the hope of preventing large ones. In this way, these proposals serve much the same purpose as the focus on moral hazard discussed in Chapter 6 — they are a way for capital and the state to advance changes that further limit employer liability without triggering widespread worker resistance.

PRECARIOUS EMPLOYMENT

Neither a return to tort nor increasing privatization appears to be a viable policy option. This suggests that they may be simply political threats that have the effect of partially constraining worker demands for safer workplaces and increased injury compensation. Is this the case? This possibility needs to be evaluated in light of the effects that growing job precariousness has on workers' compensation coverage. The success of capital in evading statutory obligations linked to standard employment relations (as discussed in Chapter 4) is perhaps a much more significant threat to workers' compensation than proposals for abolition — in part because of how effectively it can diffuse resistance by dividing workers.

Precarious work
As noted in Chapter 4, most government labour and social policies are based on a standard employment relationship (SER). Standard employment relationships entail full-time, continuing

employment for a single employer, with work conducted at the employer's place of business and under the employer's supervision. While many employees do have a standard employment relationship, 37 percent of the workforce in 2003 was engaged in non-standard work.[58] This catchall category includes wildly diverging employment relationships, conditions, and forms of work: from movie stars to day labourers. Further, both SERs and non-standard employment relationships (NSERs) have faced significant downward pressures in terms of wages and working conditions as employers (with the assistance of government) have sought to reduce the cost of labour.

To reduce costs, employers have begun re-organizing employment so as to evade statutory obligations found in the floor of rights. For example, the conversion of employees into "independent" contractors may reduce an employer's obligations under employment standards and workers' compensation.[59] This shift is often obscured and/or justified by reference to flexible forms of employment as an economic requirement and by viewing self-employment through the lens of entrepreneurship. This discourse posits that workers choose risk, autonomy, and independence over stability, but ignores that the element of choice may indeed be limited, the quality of work low, and the decision influenced by the state offloading aspects of social reproduction onto women.[60]

Recent scholarship has focused on examining the issue of precarious employment. Precarious work includes standard and non-standard forms of employment characterized by varying degrees of limited social benefits and statutory entitlements, job insecurity, low wages, and high risks to health.[61] This definition notes that workers bear the financial and social consequences of changes in the structure and organization of work. The growth of precarious forms of employment is one outcome of employer attempts to increase profitability.

Precarious work and work-related injuries

The consequences to work-related injuries of changing employment relationships, conditions, and forms of work are still emerging. The growth of small business (with less internal capacity to attend to workplace safety) and a contingent workforce (with less training on specific workplace hazards) may well increase injury rates.[62] This outcome is a form of cost transfer, from capital to labour. Yet there are some contrary pressures here. Decreasing levels of unionization and pressure on government to reduce regulatory demands may be mitigated by corporations implementing new safety programs in order to reduce their workers' compensation premiums. Yet employers' response to experience rating, documented in Chapter 6, suggests aggressive claims management is an equally plausible choice for employers.

Key features of precarious work appear to correlate with poor health outcomes.[63] This builds on the existing literature that suggests, worldwide, that workers in non-standard employment relationships (some of which are precarious) are at a higher risk of injury or illness.[64] Garment workers who work from home, for example, have higher rates of injury than similar workers in factories, perhaps reflecting greater intensity of work (exacerbated by piecework payment structures) and poor working conditions.[65] The regulation of homework has proven problematic in Canada, with no jurisdiction providing effective inspections and the administrative systems tracking injury and compensation making homework invisible as a distinct class of work. Home workers may also not know about their legislative rights or may be misled by their employers as to the rights and entitlements available to them, an issue exacerbated by the marginal social position of many home workers. Further, the type of work performed, the nature of the employment relationship, or the size of employer may affect whether the worker is eligible for workers' compensation in the event of injury.[66]

Precarious work and workers' compensation

The impact of precarious work on workers' compensation is well documented in Australia. Among the key outcomes are declining coverage rates due to exclusions and/or voluntary coverage requirements for some self-employed contractors. Exacerbating this decline was a reduction in effective coverage (where injured workers made claims) due to worker ignorance and fear of employer reprisal as well as frequent job and employment status changing. Overall, fewer than half of injured workers make workers' compensation claims and part-time workers were less likely than full-time workers to make a claim.[67]

Complex work arrangements increase the administrative burden on WCBs to determine whether a claimant has workers' compensation coverage and whether an injury occurred in the course of that work.[68] The complexity of work arrangements also creates difficulties in premium collection, which is predicated upon employers registering for workers' compensation coverage and accurately reporting their payroll. There is no reason to believe these same dynamics do not occur in Canada.

Contraction in workers' compensation coverage externalizes the cost of work-related injuries to health care, unemployment insurance, and welfare systems. It also may seriously compromise "accident" statistics (which are normally based on workers' compensation claim statistics), thereby understating the level of overall injury and the industries in which it is occurring. Job churning also impedes clinical diagnoses of work-related illnesses as well as cohort and epidemiological studies.[69]

Implications of precarious work for workers' compensation

Precarious work affects a subset of all workers and has both gendered and racial aspects.[70] By disadvantaging a small (but growing) and largely marginalized segment of the workforce, employers are able to increase their profitability. The ability and willingness of other workers to oppose these changes is limited by their (un)awareness of the change, the appearance that these change are inevitable, workers' sense of their own vulnerability, the (un)availability of mobilizing structures, and the ways in which collective resistance is channelled into manageable dispute resolution mechanisms that minimize the potential for mass resistance.

Historically, the regulation of employment has both provided workers with protection and disciplined them to accept the power and decisions of employers.[71] The protection provided by workers' compensation and the implicit threat of precarious employment reduces the likelihood that workers will resist reductions in benefits or limitations in coverage. The exclusion of precarious work from workers' compensation retards our ability to know the full extent of workplace injuries. It also justifies offloading the cost of injury onto these workers by reference to the "choice" made by these workers to bear the consequences of work-related injuries themselves in exchange for whatever advantages allegedly accrue to independent contractors.

CONCLUSION

Decision-making is an exercise of power. As we saw in Chapters 5 and 6, WCBs use claims adjudication and management to limit the compensation that is paid out to injured workers. This process reinforces employer power. Individualized claims adjudication and management makes it difficult for workers to know what hazards exist and develop a shared understanding of workplace injury as a class issue. Workers also face an appeals process that can align the WCB and the employer against a worker. When these things are combined with the incentives to participate in the existing system of injury prevention and compensation as well as penalties for challenging it, the ability of workers and labour to seek safer workplaces or better compensation is constrained.

Where workers do seek changes, they must consider proposals that privatization or simple abolishment would result in a cheaper system. This is demonstrably untrue, but may pressure workers to limit their demands or defend the existing system (even thought it may run contrary to their interests) or risk the possibility of undesirable changes. Workers may even accede to reforms in the hope of maintaining the core of workers' compensation — a system that does provide them with significant benefits.

In the meantime, employers seek to circumvent their statutory obligations to enrol in workers' compensation by reorganizing work in precarious ways. The nature of precarious employment means the effect of this offloading is disproportionately borne by women and racial minorities. These workers frequently have little ability to resist such changes. And their exclusion from trade unionism means they have little ability to seek assistance from other workers, whose own "good" jobs may be predicated on the cost savings realized from precarious workers' "bad" jobs. The overall effect of this tactic is to compel workers to defend the existing system while it is eroded beneath them to the benefit of employers.

— EIGHT —

CONCLUSION

The purpose of this book was to examine how Canadian governments prevent and compensate workplace injury, who benefits from this approach, and how they benefit. The first four chapters suggest that governments do a poor job of preventing injury. The use of ineffective regulation appears to represent intentionally prioritizing profitability over safety. And the state has contained the ability of workers to resist this agenda by shaping the discourse around injury and the operation of these systems. Examining injury compensation reveals how seemingly neutral aspects of claims adjudication and management financially advantage employers and limit the ability of workers to resist unsafe work.

Together, this analysis suggests that the prevention and compensation of workplace injuries are not solely technical or legal undertakings, but intensely political ones that entail serious consequences — most often for workers. This conclusion is quite upsetting. But the facts are difficult to dispute. Whatever the drawbacks of Canadian injury statistics, they demonstrate that hundreds of thousands of workers are injured each year on the job. This raises two fundamental questions. First, why are so many seriously injured every year? And, second, why don't governments do something about it?

WHY ARE WORKERS INJURED ON THE JOB?

In Chapter 3, I suggested that our perspective on risk — whether economic or political — determines how we explain why workers are injured. Employers often discuss the risk of injury as minimal, unavoidable, and acceptable. That is to say, injury is just a normal part of work. Not everyone agrees with this explanation, in part because the evidence simply does not support this view.

For example, is the risk of injury minimal? Six hundred thousand serious injuries a year suggest not. In fact, the risk of workplace injury is significant — at least to workers. Is the risk of injury unavoidable? Again, no. Employer decisions about the what, when, where, and how of production determines who is exposed to what risks. Avoiding injuries just costs more. And employers understandably are affected by concerns about profitability, more so than safety. Is the level of risk in the workplace acceptable? That depends on who you are. Of course, risk is acceptable for employers. They aren't injured and they reap most of the benefits from unsafe (but profitable) business decisions. Workers — who are routinely maimed and killed — often disagree.

One consequence of believing workplace injury is normal is that injury prevention is really only warranted if the economic benefits exceed the cost. This prescription reflects the fact that the employers are rewarded for maximizing profitability. If employers can externalize the cost of unsafe work practices to workers (via injury) while retaining the financial benefits (such as greater profitability stemming from cheaper inputs or faster production), then the benefits of injury prevention will never outweigh the associated costs.

It may seem unkind or unfair to blame employers for worker injuries. There are certainly other factors at play. For example, workers may make mistakes. They may even act recklessly. But these causes make a relatively small contribution to overall injury rates. Further, they are secondary causes: workers are only in a position to be injured by their error or stupidity because the employer has structured work to create this opportunity. This is, in fact, implicitly recognized in law. Employers are granted vast power over the workplace and workers and thus have a corresponding duty to ensure the workplace is safe — a duty that reflects their power to make workplaces unsafe.

WHY DON'T GOVERNMENT INJURY-PREVENTION EFFORTS WORK?

The economic perspective on risk may also help explain why governments use demonstrably ineffective injury-prevention strategies. Government injury-prevention activity must result in benefits that outweigh the costs — both for the state and for the employers that the state is regulating. The key cost of workplace injury to the state is the threat injury poses to social reproduction. When someone is injured on the job — especially if the injury is horrific or the victim's life is dramatically altered — it raises questions about why the injury happened and who was responsible.

This questioning can cause workers to wonder whether the existing social formation — whereby employers organize work in ways that injure workers — is legitimate. This line of inquiry is exceptionally threatening to the government of the day, which is complicit in maintaining this relationship and thus can face electoral consequences. It also threatens the production process itself. What if workers started acting directly in the workplace to protect themselves and demand safety improvements?

One way to maintain social stability is to prevent workplace injury. To get employers to alter how they organize work requires the state to cause (or threaten to cause) additional costs to employers. This has, however, consequences for the state. Employers have historically resisted state regulatory efforts because it adds cost and reduces profitability. Alternately, governments can protect the production and social reproduction processes by managing the perceptions of workers about workplace injuries.

Perception management occurs in several ways. The worst financial effects of workplace injury are (partly) mitigated by the availability of workers' compensation. Governments give workers (weak) health and safety rights that create the appearance that workers can protect themselves. Governments (sometimes) fine and prosecute employers when there is a serious injury or fatality, thereby obscuring the lack of effective prevention strategies. And governments and employers cooperate in partnerships, which create the impression (but not the fact) of decreasing risk of workplace injury.

DO GOVERNMENTS ACTUALLY PRIORITIZE PROFIT OVER SAFETY?

Suggesting governments choose ineffective injury-prevention strategies because, at a high level, they prioritize profit over safety is a bold statement. There is, however, plenty of evidence of this when you start to look for it. Let's start with enforcement. As we saw in Chapter 3, occupational health and safety (OHS) violations attract legal sanction only when a worker has been injured or killed. Otherwise, employers who operate an unsafe workplace normally receive only a verbal or written warning. What message does this send? Perhaps this says unsafe workplaces are unacceptable. But I think the actual message is more nuanced: unsafe workplaces are unacceptable only if they result in an injury or death that threatens social stability.

Why is that placing workers at risk of injury is not a big deal? The first reason is that risk (and its mitigation) is often difficult to see — until someone is maimed or killed. Consequently, risk of injury does not have the same political verve as actual injury or death. In these ways, risk of injury poses less threat to the social formation than does the occurrence of injury. Consequently, the government benefits little from preventing

injuries by reducing risk. Conversely, the government benefits greatly from condemning injuries (via pronouncements,
fines, and prosecutions) when they occur. This condemnation
creates the appearance that the state disapproves of workplace injury when, in fact, its day-to-day injury-prevention
activities (e.g., inspections, fines) do little to reduce the risk of
injury to workers.

The second reason is the pervasive view that employers
are engaged in socially productive activities and are able to
act responsibly. Within this perspective, education, persuasion, and the occasional prosecution appear to be effective
strategies to remedy non-compliance. This view ignores the
incentives employers have to externalize production costs by
placing workers at risk of injury. This approach also entails
relatively little monetary cost to the state or employers and
can thus be justified on a cost-benefit basis. Finally, this approach entails little political cost because — despite evidence
that education and persuasion are ineffective — it is difficult
for workers to argue that the state ought not to educate and
persuade employers.

WHY DON'T WORKERS CALL "HOOEY" ON THIS APPROACH?

Workers have difficulty arguing against education and persuasion for two reasons. First, these activities have "motherhood"
qualities about them. What reasonable person is opposed to education? Or asking someone nicely to stop doing something?
Second, explaining why education and persuasion don't work
requires workers to accept (and convince others) of some awkward truths about employment. Specifically, that employment
is a relationship of power, wherein power is asymmetrically
distributed and is used by employers in ways that frequently
disadvantage and endanger workers.

Revealing the true political economy of employment —
the ways in which capital has advanced its economic goals by

shaping the political and legal landscape — is generally unwelcome. Such discussion highlights that we are dependent upon and subservient to our employers. And that our employers are rewarded when they exploit us to their own ends. Further, it suggests employers have co-opted the political and legal systems to support them in doing so. No one really wants to hear this. Consequently, it is difficult for workers to oppose the compliance orientation of government.

CAN WORKERS PROTECT THEMSELVES?

The state has granted workers three rights — to know, to participate, and to refuse. In theory, workers can protect themselves by knowing about hazards, working with the employer to remedy them and — ultimately — to refuse unsafe work. But theory and practice diverge. As we saw in Chapter 3, these weak rights are more about creating the appearance of protection than actually empowering or protecting workers.

Information about hazards is often unavailable, incorrect or simply withheld by the employer. The ability of workers to pressure employers to remedy health and safety hazards — even where there is a joint health and safety committee (JHSC) — is constrained by the limited enforcement efforts of governments in the absence of an injury or death. And the right to refuse is tempered by the potential for workers to be disciplined, penalized, and terminated for doing so.

What this system does very well is channel worker concern and energy into a process that employers control. Discussing safety on the shop floor or in the union hall appears illegitimate because there is a "proper" place to discuss it. And personal knowledge and experience is similarly delegitimized: the employer pays experts to ensure the workplace is safe. Overall, the internal responsibility system (IRS) creates the impression that workers are not as vulnerable as they really are to the health consequences of decisions made by an employer.

DO SAFETY INCENTIVES REDUCE INJURIES?

Governments and workers' compensation boards (WCBs) have created incentive schemes, whereby employers with good accident records receive a rebate on their workers' compensation premiums. These incentive schemes are designed to encourage employers to reduce the number and severity of worker injuries. These systems, however, are subject to gaming by employers, who can (and do) substitute aggressive case management in place of reducing the number and severity of workplace injuries.

These systems typically operate on the basis of numeric injury indicators, such as claim costs, lost-time claims, or claim duration. As noted in Chapter 3, this sort of injury data is misleading because it does not document the number of injuries. Rather, it documents injuries reported to and accepted by WCBs. The result is an underestimation of injury rates. Employer gaming further skews these numbers downward, increasing the degree of underestimation over time. This makes it appear that workplaces are safer than they are.

BUT HOW DOES GOVERNMENT LEGITIMIZE PRIORITIZING PROFIT OVER SAFETY?

First, governments don't describe workplace injury in accurate terms. They use terms such as *accident, tragedy,* and *unforeseen event* or *freak event.* These characterizations avoid placing blame on anyone. Further, injuries and fatalities are often not seen at all. Their geographic and temporal distribution is wide and they are often not reported. The government gets some help in this department from the media.

When a fatality is reported (because injuries almost never are), the report is usually limited to "A worker was killed 15 kilometres south of town today. Occupational health and safety is investigating." It is rarely possible to draw a conclusion about causation or responsibility at this point. And when such information is available, interest in the event has passed. In

this way, reporting portrays   ret-
table) events, a tendency th   apathy about them.

This, however, is not th   ents
have adopted three main str   The
most obvious one is blamin   This
approach has a long pedig   are-
less worker myth of the nineteenth century. It is simply updated with a more modern look. Alberta's "stupid" and "bloody
lucky" campaigns focus on worker behaviour as the root cause
of injury. They ignore the much more significant contribution
employers make to injury rates when they decide to organize
work unsafely.

Governments also make cost-benefit arguments about enforcement. It is true that inspectors cannot be everywhere all
the time. But they could be more places and act more assertively
to address the impressive body count that employers rack up
every year. That they do not do this reflects a (quiet) political
decision regarding the degree of money the government wants
to spend on protecting workers and the degree of inconvenience
and cost the government wants to cause employers. The seemingly neutral criterion of cost-benefit is, in reality, an effort to
legitimize the particular level of worker injury and death the
government is prepared to put up with.

As noted above, government and government agencies create data that says workplaces are safer than they are and are
growing safer. That this data reflects WCB claims (rather than
true injury rates) is ignored. As is the fact that this data is not
only susceptible to employer gaming, but that governments and
WCBs give employers incentives to game it — thereby making
it less accurate over time. Finally, governments have developed
injury compensation schemes that undermine the political will
and power of workers to address workplace injury.

WHO BENEFITS FROM INJURY COMPENSATION? AND HOW?

Workers' compensation provides most workers with predictable, stable, and immediate compensation. In these ways, workers' compensation is unquestionably a significant improvement for workers. Yet workers' compensation also benefits governments and employers. And it entails some difficult-to-see costs for workers. Examining these suggests that, rather than supplementing or reinforcing injury prevention efforts, workers' compensation acts as a substitute for injury prevention.

For governments, employer-funded compensation reduces the threat that the financial and social consequences of workplace injuries historically posed to the legitimacy of a capitalist social formation. Workers (mostly) no longer face (total) financial ruin when they are injured at work. Further, having something to lose makes the working class less likely to challenge the existing system. And governments are able to deflect worker demands to WCBs and their appeal mechanisms.

Employers receive three main benefits. First, employer liability for injuries is limited to wage-loss replacement, medical aid, and rehabilitation costs. And this cost is spread across an industry or rate group. In this way, the cost of injuries is limited and made more predictable than it is under tort. This mitigates a significant risk for employers. What cost is directly borne by an employer via experience rating does not appear to be significant enough to alter employer behaviour.

Second, workers' compensation operates to reduce the cost of injuries to employers in a couple of ways. Injuries that emerge over or after a long period of time, do not demonstrate a clear pathology, tap into an established social prejudice, and/or entail a significant economic cost are often found non-compensable. More commonly, workers are targeted for early return-to-work (ERTW) programs under threat of having their wage-loss compensation terminated, despite limited evidence that ERTW is advisable or effective.

Third, the provision of compensation diffuses worker pressure for safer workplaces. Compensation reduces an important source of dissatisfaction for injured workers and leverage for their advocates. And the operation of workers' compensation serves to channel worker energy into a system that focuses attention on remediating individual injuries and away from identifying patterns of injury and preventing them. This protects the ability of employers to organize work in the most profitable manner. In this way, compensation acts as a substitute for prevention.

HOW DOES COMPENSATION LEGITIMIZE LIMITING EMPLOYER LIABILITY?

Limiting employer liability by constraining the types of injuries accepted is justified by relying upon the biomedical conception of injury. That is to say, it is expected that the mechanism of injury will be discernable, the injury will manifest itself at the time of or reasonably soon after the injury occurs, and the course and treatment of the injury will be broadly similar from one person to the next. Where these assumptions are not met, additional scrutiny and barriers occur.

This scrutiny is justified by reference to the potential for moral hazard—that workers might be cheating the system. That employers, health-care providers, insurers, and WCB employees also have the opportunity to defraud the system is largely ignored. Limiting employer liability via ERTW programs is legitimized by suggesting workers will malinger, work is rehabilitative, and (bizarrely) being absent from work due to injury is unhealthy. The fundamental questions about the effectiveness of ERTW programs and the moral hazard they create for employers are largely ignored.

OCCUPATIONAL DISEASE AS A MICROCOSM

The political nature of injury recognition—in both prevention and compensation—is an important source of legitimation.

Consider occupational diseases. The effect of exposing workers to hazardous chemical or biological agents is normally slow to appear. And the relationship is often hard to see. These characteristics make it very hard for workers to know they are being put at risk and act to protect themselves. These same characteristics allow employers to pass costs to workers — by using hazardous substances and/or unsafe production techniques — in the form of disease and death.

It can be difficult to accept that employers can be so cold blooded. There is, however, ample evidence of just such behaviour with regards to asbestos, fluorspar, and uranium mining. But, as we saw in the case of young women painting radium on watches, such behaviour is not limited to any one sector. And this behaviour is widespread enough that a pattern is evident. It usually goes something like this:

1. Workers raise concerns regarding the health effects of an industrial process.

2. Employers dismiss worker claims that anything is wrong. This continues as long as possible.

3. Employers commission research into the problem. Employers may try to influence, misrepresent, minimize, undermine, or suppress unfavourable findings.

4. Employers eventually accept a substance is hazardous, focusing on controlling risk and compensating injury, rather than eliminating the hazard.

Among the strategies used by governments and employers are exposure limits. As we noted in Chapter 3, such exposure limits are typically based on inadequate evidence at levels that industry is already operating at. Further, these exposure limits are based on preventing the worst consequences of the exposure. There is little attention to difficult to substantiate concerns, the effects of long-term, low-level exposure, or the synergistic effects of multi chemical exposures.

The effect of relying on faulty exposure limits is to create the impression that work is safe, when it is not. When such limits are codified in occupational health and safety laws and regulations, these limits — which are consistently found to be too high — become essentially unassailable. They provide political and legal cover for the government and employers while continuing to expose workers to hazardous substances.

SO WHAT?

These conclusions can appear rather disheartening. Is every worker victory — gaining injury compensation, safety rights, WCB appeal processes — just a further defeat? Clearly not. Pressure brought by workers to prevent and compensate injury over the past 100 years has generated tangible improvements. The point of this analysis is that the effectiveness of these changes has been limited in ways that mean workplace injury remains commonplace and injury compensation is partial.

These limitations — and the political reasons behind them — are often absent from discussions of injury prevention and compensation. It is impolite to point out that government injury prevention efforts still allow hundreds of thousands of workers to be injured each year. And suggesting that employers cause injuries by the job design decisions they make — decisions made in the pursuit of profit — is often a conversation ender.

Yet it is precisely this sort of conversation that is necessary to increase the degree to which workers can effectively utilize their existing rights and demand increased rights. For example, while the rights to know, participate, and refuse have limitations, the strength of these rights appears to turn on how they are used by workers. Workers who adopt an overtly political approach can significantly increase their ability to gain health and safety improvements.

Educating workers is a common exhortation in the trade union movement. The degree to which such efforts result in tangible changes in the perspective of workers and willingness to mobilize is unclear. This may be affected by the approach taken to the topic: a more technical approach to labour relations issues may result in less behavioural change than a more political approach. Education regarding workplace safety seems more likely to produce results because of the significant and immediate consequences that workplace injury has for workers and their families.

This is not to say that discussion alone will bring change. The state faces powerful inducements to maintain both production and social reproduction. The current approach to injury prevention and compensation reflects a political calculation regarding the costs and benefits of workplace injury. Creating a heightened awareness of the prevalence of workplace injury and the ineffectiveness of current approaches can change the calculation. Two employer narratives are particular vulnerable to cooptation: (1) workers are our most valuable resource, and (2) there are no accidents.

ARE WORKERS OUR MOST VALUABLE RESOURCE?

Human resource managers and corporate leaders are fond of saying "workers are our most valuable resource." Everyone wants to believe this is true. Saying it provides employers with moral authority — by implication, they must be looking out for workers' best interests. This only makes sense if workers are truly an employer's most valuable resource. Yet the spilled blood of more than a half million workers each year suggests this sloganeering is largely spin, designed to increase the productivity that can be extracted from workers and stop them from considering the difficult question of why employers can expose them to hazards in the pursuit of profit.

Workers are employers' most valuable resource only in an

instrumental and ironic sense: they are treated just like any other production input and are expendable if the return is high enough. The implicit moral commitment to worker welfare is clearly absent. The narrative is highly vulnerable to being unmasked: if workers are so valuable, why is work organized in ways that resulted in widespread injury? This line of questioning naturally leads to examining the root causes of worker injury and what workers can do to reduce them.

IS THERE REALLY NO SUCH THING AS AN ACCIDENT?

Politicians and safety gurus often say there are no such things as accidents. This is indeed true. When workers are injured, for example, as a result of being exposed to chemical substances where there has been no testing of their toxicity, this is not an accident. It is a reasonably predictable outcome of employer decisions about the organization of work and state decisions about regulation. This holds true for most workplace injuries — their timing may be tricky to predict but rarely are the causes a surprise.

Again, this narrative can be used to ask hard questions of employers and the state. If there truly are no accidents, why do we continue to see so many injuries? The reason employers organize work unsafely is because they can externalize much of the cost of any resulting injuries. This process is facilitated by ineffective regulation. This line of discussion leads immediately to questioning how employers can be motivated to organize work more safety. Increasing the cost of injuries borne by employers by increasing the cost of ineffective regulation to the state is one obvious solution. It also leads to questions about why the state does not do this.

THE POLITICAL ECONOMY OF WORKPLACE INJURY

Despite the emancipatory potential of examining workplace injuries through the lens of political economy (or perhaps because of this), injury prevention and compensation are usually discussed in technical terms. The analysis presented in this book suggests that such technical discussion directs our attention away from the political nature of injury prevention and compensation — a process that distributes the costs and benefits of workplace injuries between workers and employers. Revealing the political economy of workplace injury allows us to better understand the full implications of prevention and compensation systems.

Neither the state nor employers come off looking particularly good in this analysis. It is important to keep in mind that governments are not necessarily conspiring with employers to imperil workers' health and safety. Rather, the existing system is one solution to conflicts over the prevention and compensation workplace injury that threaten production and social reproduction. Historical contingencies have influenced the options available to governments as they try to maintain both production and social reproduction.

The political economy of injury prevention and compensation appears to be broadly similar to that which is evident in the broader industrial relations system. It represents a temporary accommodation of the interests of some (predominantly white, male) workers and provides these workers with tangible benefits. At the same time, it does little to impede employers' ability to organize and direct work in a manner that is profitable, albeit unsafe. In addition to mitigating the more egregious effects of unsafe work (thereby undermining resistance), this system channels conflict and worker resources into a highly legalistic process that retards worker resistance. Further, the system is operated in a way that extends employer liability coverage as broadly as possible by limiting who is covered, what injuries are accepted, and the duration for which they are compensated.

In this way, occupational health and safety and workers' compensation are paradoxical. On the one hand, they create a higher level of protection and compensation than workers have ever had in the past. These successes obscure, however, that workers continue to be injured and killed in vast numbers. This level of injury and death reflects the limited reach of occupational health and safety. It also reflects that workers' compensation continues to be a substitute for injury prevention and a way to manage worker resistance. This is clearly an immoral and unacceptable arrangement.

NOTES

Introduction

1 K. Wilkins and S. Mackenzie, "Work Injuries," *Health Reports* 18(3) (2007): 1–18.

2 J. Komarnicki and S. Myers, "Cochrane Women Joins Farmworkers' Fight for Rights After Losing Use of Arm," *Calgary Herald*, 2 April 2009.

3 E. Mandel, *Power and Money* (New York: Verso, 1992); A. Picchio, *Social Reproduction: The Political Economy of the Labour Market* (Cambridge: Cambridge University Press, 1992).

4 V. Walters, "Occupational Health and Safety Legislation in Ontario: An Analysis of Its Origins and Content," *Canadian Review of Sociology and Anthropology* 20(4) (1983): 413–434; E. Tucker, "The Determination of Occupational Health and Safety Standards in Ontario, 1860–1982," *McGill Law Journal* 29 (1983/84): 260–311; E. Tucker, *Administering Danger in the Workplace: The Law and Politics of Occupational Health and Safety Regulation in Ontario, 1850–1914* (Toronto: University of Toronto Press, 1990).

5 A. Picchio, *Social Reproduction: The Political Economy of the Labour Market* (Cambridge: Cambridge University Press, 1992); L. Clarke, "Disparities in Wage Relations and Social Reproduction," in *The Dynamics of Wage Relations in the New Europe*, eds. L. Clarke, P. de Gijsel, and J. Janssen (London: Kluewer, 2000), 134–139.

Chapter One

1 E. Stolte, "Charges Dismissed in Alberta Bailing Co. Workers' Death," *Edmonton Journal*, 27 November 2008.

2 M. Yates, *Naming the System: Inequality and Work in the Global Economy* (New York: Monthly Review Press, 2003). Yates provides a compelling analysis of capitalist economies.

3   J. Godard, *Industrial Relations, the Economy and Society, 3rd Edition* (Concord: Captus, 2005).

4   H. Drost and R. Hird, *Introduction to the Canadian Labour Market, 2nd Edition* (Nelson: Scarborough, 2005). There are actually multiple labour markets, segmented by occupation, industry, and/or region. For the sake of convenience, we combine these and normally refer to *the labour market.*

5   Catt, J., *Northern Hiring Fairs* (Chorley, Lancashire: Countryside Publications, 1986), 27.

6   Drost and Hird, *Canadian Labour Market.*

7   The common law is a body of law based on British legal tradition of a judge deciding matters based on the doctrine of precedent (previous decisions). Essentially, judges based decisions on established customs and conventions to ensure a uniform application of the law.

8   For a fuller discussion of employer and worker common law rights and obligations, see G. England, *Individual Employment Law, 2nd Edition* (Toronto: Irwin Law, 2008).

9   H. Glasbeek, "The Contract of Employment at Common Law," in *Union–Management Relations in Canada*, eds. J.C. Anderson and M. Gunderson (Toronto: Addison-Wesley, 1982), 65. The master-and-servant tradition of employment arose in England at the end of the thirteenth century, just as the feudal system was breaking down. The state responded to a labour shortage and rising wages (i.e., the free operation of the labour market) with the *Master–Servant Act.* This law imported certain features of the old feudal relationship into the new world of employment. Workers, for example, had to obey the commands of their masters, and could not bargain for their rate of pay. Over time, some of the details have changed, but this master-and-servant approach persists in the common-law obligations of employment.

10 To trace the development of waged work in early Canada, see B. Palmer, *Working Class Experience: Rethinking the History of Canadian Labour 1800–1991* (Toronto: McClelland & Stewart, 1992). See also C. Heron, *The Canadian Labour Movement: A Short History.* (Toronto: Lorimer, 1996).

11 S. Marglin, "What Do Bosses Do? The Origins and Functions of Hierarchy in Capitalist Production," *Review of Radical Political Economy* 6 (1974): 60–112. In England, the independent commodity production and putting-out system gave way to industrial capitalism between 1780 and 1840. Canada's industrial revolution occurred later (1850–1880). The hallmark of industrialization is the factory system. There are two basic (and competing) explanations for the rise of factories:

> **Technological determination:** Machine such as the spinning jenny and water frame were more efficient at producing goods but required a greater volume of work and workspace than could be found in small workshops. Thus, the argument is that technology drove change.

> **Control of the workforce:** Factories were more efficient because employers could de mand longer and harder work from their employees since workers were economically dependent and could be closely supervised. The evidence supports the latter theory. Factories predated the introduction of power and technological change. Rather, they began as agglomerations of smaller production units with no technological superiority. Their advantage for employers was increased control over the production process and preventing embezzlement.

12 Frederick Taylor is the usual example given here. He sought to reduce the control workers exercised over production (which impeded the ability of employers to maximize productivity) by taking jobs, breaking them down into component parts (which could be timed), and reconstructing the production process to maximize productivity. This stripped workers of control over the content and pace of work. It also allowed the use of cheaper, unskilled labour. Taylorism is still evident today when you visit any fast-food restaurant, wherein job duties are regimented and timed to maximize productivity and minimize worker discretion.

13 S. Bohme, J. Zorabedian, and D. Egilman, "Maximizing Profit and Endangering Health: Corporate Strategies to Avoid Litigation and Regulation," *International Journal of Occupational and Environmental Health* 11(6) (2005): 338–348. This analysis examines how corporations seek to maximize profitability by regulation and liability for workplace and consumer deaths and injuries. Among the tactics used are conducting or commissioning research to show a process or product is "safe," generating controversy about its effects, and attacking scientists and scientific work that suggest otherwise. Support from industry-friendly "third-party" scientists can be organized for industry's scientific positions in regulation-setting, court proceedings, and the press. Similarly, industry organizations and think tanks can be created or used to create the appearance of legitimacy and sway media and public opinion.

14 J-M. Cousineau, R. Lacroix, and A-M Girard, "The Economic Determinants of the Occupational Risk of Injury," in *Research in Canadian Workers' Compensation*, eds. T. Thomason and R.P. Chaykowski (Kingston: IRC Press, 1995), 181–194.

15 D. Nelkin and M. Brown, *Workers at Risk* (Chicago: University of Chicago Press, 1984); V. Walters, "The Politics of Occupational Health and Safety: Interviews with Workers' Health and Safety Representatives and Company Doctors," *Canadian Review of Sociology and Anthropology* 22(1) (1985): 57–79.

16 R. Kostal, "Legal Justice, Social Justice: An Incursion into the Social History of Worker-Related Accident Law in Ontario," *Law and History Review* 6(1) (1988): 1–24. Kostal outlines the social and legal history of workplace accidents in Victorian Ontario. Among the changes he notes after 1850 is an increasingly impersonal employment relationship in industries such as railroading. This theme is also picked up in E. Tucker, *Administering Danger in the Workplace: The Law and Politics of Occupational Health and Safety Regulation in Ontario, 1850–1914* (Toronto: University of Toronto Press, 1990). For a more general social history of this era, see A. Finkel, *Social Policy and Practice in Canada: A History* (Waterloo: Wilfrid Laurier University Press, 2006).

17 J. Witt, *The Accidental Republic: Crippled Workingmen, Destitute Widows and the Remaking of American Law* (Cambridge: Harvard University Press, 2004) notes that "the opinion's author, Lord Abinger, had long supported reform in the English Poor Law along the lines advocated by classical economists Malthus and Ricardo,

on the theory that state-provided material support undermined the incentives to work and led to pauperism" (p. 13).

18 Similar case law developed in the United States. E. Tucker, "The determination of occupational health and safety standards in Ontario, 1860–1982," *McGill law Journal* 29 (1983/84): 260–311, notes that this approach, including the various common-law defences employers could use to avoid liability, also reflects the precepts of nineteenth-century Liberalism which sought to maximize the ability of individuals to pursue their self-interest.

19 R. Risk, "This Nuisance of Litigation: The Origins of Workers' Compensation in Ontario," in *Essays in the History of Canadian Law, Volume 2*, ed. D.H. Flaherty (Toronto: University of Toronto Press, 1983), 418–491.

20 C. Tarpley and K. Jagman, "Workers' Compensation: Third Party Actions Against Employees Under Comparable Causation," *Journal of Air Law and Commerce*, 47 (1982): 189–205.

21 J. Carr, "Workers' Compensation Systems: Purpose and Mandate," in *Occupational Medicine: State of the Art Reviews* (Philadelphia: Hanley and Belfus, 1998), 417–422, notes that employers could also employ other defences, including acts of God, acts of a third party, inevitable accident, no duty of care, no proximate cause, justification, self-defense, and limitation of action.

22 Risk, "This nuisance of litigation."

23 M. Gunderson and D. Hyatt, "Foundations for Workers' Compensation Reform: Overview and Summary," in *Workers' Compensation: Foundations for Reform*, eds. M. Gunderson and D. Hyatt (Toronto: University of Toronto Press, 2000), 3–26. Kostal, *Legal Justice, Social Justice* notes that of the 20 work-related injury cases litigated and reported in Ontario before 1886, only three (15 percent) were successful. While the success rate is interesting, the key finding here is the small absolute number of litigated and reported cases. An 85 percent failure rate for civil suits is also reported in the American literature, but again substantiation is elusive. See: M. Aldrich, *Safety First: Technology, Labor and Business in the Building of American Work Safety, 1870–1939* (Baltimore: Johns Hopkins University Press, 1997).

24 Witt, *The Accidental Republic,* discusses cooperative insurance and the reasons it gave way to state-run workers' compensation.

25 Witt, *The Accidental Republic,* discusses the operation of such benefit plans in the United States. He also provides a compelling discussion of the tensions facing unions that operated insurance schemes.

26 A. Derickson, "To Be His Own Benefactor: The Founding of the Coeur d'Alene Miners' Union Hospital, 1891," in *Dying for a Living: Workers' Safety and Health in Twentieth-Century America,* eds. D. Rosner and G. Markowitz (Bloomington: Indiana University Press, 1989), 3–18. These worker-run plans reduced the power employers could wield over workers via the administration of employer-run benefit plans. Some workers were forced to strike for the right to control medical plans financed by their own money.

27 Aldrich, *Safety First.*

28 R. Asher, "The Limits of Big Business Paternalism: Relief for Injured Workers in the Years Before Workmen's Compensation," in *Dying for a Living: Workers' Safety and Health in Twentieth-Century America* (Bloomington: Indiana University Press, 1989), 19–33. For example, employers might require workers to sign away their right to sue in order to access employer-provided benefits in the event of a workplace injury.

Chapter Two

1 S. Hilgartner, "The Political Language of Risk: Defining Occupational Health," in *The Language of Risk: Conflicting Perspectives on Occupational Health,* ed. D. Nelkin (Beverly Hills: Sage, 1985), 25–65. Hilgartner examines this economic perspective as it affects chemical exposures in the workplace.

2 R. Iverson and J. Barling, "The Current Culture of Workplace Injury," paper presented at the Association of Workers' Compensation Boards of Canada public forum, July 2005, Ottawa, Canada.

3 For example, M. Brown, "Setting Occupational Health Standards: The Vinyl Chloride Case," in *Controversy: Politics of technical decisions, 3rd Edition,* ed. D. Nelkin (Newbury Park: Sage, 1992), 130–146, examines the establishment of exposure levels for vinyl chloride in the 1970s, noting the pressure exerted by manufacturers to set exposure limits based on what was (in the employers' view) economically feasible. Brown notes the difficulty regulators had disentangling economic and technical feasibility and that regulation was impeded both by a lack of reliable data on exposure effects and the regulator's reliance entirely on industry for information about the feasibility of standards.

4 Tucker, "The Determination of Occupational Health and Safety Standards in Ontario"; H. Glasbeek and E. Tucker, "Death by Consensus: The Westray Story," *New Solutions* 3 (1993): 14–41. This market-based approach requires employers and workers to know enough about health to make a rational choice and for all of the costs of ill health to be borne by the firm. As shown below, these assumptions do not hold up to scrutiny.

5 E. Tucker, "And the Defeat Goes On: An Assessment of Third-Wave Health and Safety Regulation," in *Corporate Crime: Contemporary Debates*, ed. F. Pearce (Toronto: University of Toronto Press, 1995), 245–267; Witt, *The Accidental Republic.*

6 J. Robinson, *Toil and Toxins: Workplace Struggles and Political Strategies for Occupational Health* (Berkeley: University of California Press, 1991), provides a detailed discussion of the hazard pay and the practicalities of exit as a worker option.

7 Risk, "This Nuisance of Litigation."

8 Kostal, "Legal Justice, Social Justice." A lawsuit gave workers a chance to resist their employer's will without fundamentally threatening the existing social structure — a structure that many workers no doubt believed was beneficial to them in many ways.

9 Aldrich, *Safety First,* exhaustively traces the use of this narrative in America to legitimize workplace injury. C. Reasons, L. Ross, and P. Paterson, *Assault on the Worker: Occupational Health and Safety in Canada* (Toronto: Butterworth and Co., 1981) examine this theme in Canada.

10 Iverson and Barling, "The Current Culture of Workplace Injury." There were differences by size of firm: 81 percent of small businesses, 79 percent of medium businesses, and 60 percent of large businesses agreed with this statement.

11 Iverson and Barling's "The Current Culture of Workplace Injury" survey of Canadians found that 61 percent of respondents
thought that workplace accidents and injuries were inevitable.
At the same time, 68 percent believed that the right amount of
attention was being paid to injury prevention.

12 D. Rosner and G. Markowitz, "A Gift of God? The Public Health
Controversy over Leaded Gasoline during the 1920s," in *Dying for
a Living: Workers' Safety and Health in Twentieth-Century America*,
eds. D. Rosner and G. Markowitz (Bloomington: Indiana University Press, 1989), 121–139. A modern twist on the carelessness narrative is that of hyper-susceptibility. Again, workers are
blamed for their injuries instead of examining the impact of job
design on exposing them to toxins. Framing injury as a result
of susceptibility leads one to removing the worker for the workplace, rather than removing the hazard.

13 For example, N. Ashford, *Crisis in the Workplace: Occupational Disease and Injury* (Cambridge: MIT Press, 1976), found that more
than half of injuries and deaths were caused by unsafe working
conditions, while less than a third were caused by unsafe acts. It
is also important to be mindful that unsafe acts may be triggered
by unsafe working conditions. Falling off a building may be due
to not wearing fall protection. But was such protection available?
Was the worker trained to use it? Was the worker pressured not
to use it? All of these explanations are difficult to see but suggest
some unsafe acts actually reflect working conditions.

14 Canadian Agricultural Injury Surveillance Program, *Agricultural injuries in Canada for 1990–2000* (Kingston: Author, 2003).

15 Aldrich, *Safety First* notes that blaming the worker suggests that
the remedy lies in worker training, supervision, and discipline.
This is a much less expensive remedy than re-engineering workplaces to eliminate hazards.

16 A similar effect can be seen in the adoption of the metric system in the 1970s. Despite 30 years of indoctrination, the only
area where the metric system has clearly displaced the imperial
system is in speed and distance measures. And this reflects that
the state has mandated metric speedometers and changed road
signs. The imperial system continues to dominant our concep

tions of weights and measures (e.g., I'm six-foot-three and I'd like a pound of butter, please).

17 Tucker, "And the Defeat Goes On." This includes the cost of civil settlements and corporate benefit plans. More recently, these costs have included workers' compensation premiums and occupational health and safety fines.

18 Tucker, *Administering Danger in the Workplace*, traces the effect of industrialization on injuries in Ontario between 1850 and 1914. Among his conclusions are that workplace injury must be understood in terms of the prevailing relations of production. A pre-industrial, pre-capitalist social formation allowed workers to determine their own work process and working pace. Industrial capitalism sees employers determining the duration of the workday and the pace and design of work. Workers have less ability to organize work in ways that are safe. Further, the nature of Taylorist job design entails long periods of monotonous work, often in close proximity to hazardous equipment. Finally, the integration of workers also meant workers could be injured through the (in)action of other workers.

19 Witt, *The Accidental Republic*, provides a thorough discussion of the American evidence regarding increasing injury rates. While some historians have suggested that injury rates (as measured by fatalities) remained stable through the late nineteenth century, Witt provides a compelling case that fatalities are a poor measure of injury rates. The assertion that injury rates increased during this period is corroborated by British injury data.

20 D. Rosner and G. Markowitz, "Safety and Health as a Class Issue: The Workers' Health Bureau of America during the 1920s," in *Dying for a Living: Workers' Safety and Health in Twentieth-century America*, eds. D. Rosner and G. Markowitz (Bloomington: Indiana University Press, 1989), 53–66. This example is American but nicely illustrates how health and safety is interrelated with the issue of productivity and job design.

21 Palmer, *Working Class Experience*.

22 A. Bale, "America's First Compensation Crisis: Conflict over Value and Meaning of Workplace Injuries under the Employer Liability System," in *Dying for a Living: Workers' Safety and Health in*

Twentieth-Century America, eds. D. Rosner and G. Markowitz (Bloomington: Indiana University Press, 1989), 34–64, traces a similar pattern in the United States.

23 Tucker, "The Determinants of Occupational Health and Safety Standards in Ontario" asserts that the addition of an income franchise in 1824, which was extended to a full male suffrage in 1888, increased the political power of the working class. Among the outcomes of these changes in Ontario were legislative changes designed to address objectionable working conditions and alter employer liability rules.

24 E. Lorentsen and E. Woolner, *Fifty Years of Labour Legislation in Canada* (Ottawa: Department of Labour, 1950); Finkel, *Social Policy and Practice in Canada*; Palmer, *Working Class Experience.*

25 E. Tucker, "Making the Workplace 'Safe' in Capitalism," *Labour/ Le Travail* 21 (1988): 45–85.

26 Tucker, "The Determination of Occupational Health and Safety Standards in Ontario" notes that legislation in 1874 addressed threshing and other machines. This was followed in 1881 by legislation addressing safety on railroads. The former was enforced via private prosecution while the latter allowed workers to sue as if they were not workers if the employer failed to comply with the Act.

27 Tucker, "Making the Workplace 'Safe' in Capitalism" notes that both employers and workers sought more inspectors. Workers sought additional inspectors to ensure increased regulation. Employers sought more than a single inspector with the expectation that multiple inspectors would result in some inspectors being drawn from industry.

28 Tucker, "Making the Workplace 'Safe' in Capitalism" and Tucker, *Administering Danger in the Workplace* document how inspectors approached compliance in ways that did not impair the employer's right to organize work in the most profitable manner. Further, compliance was sought via persuasion, rather than prosecution. This reflected the view that injuries were neutral events, unrelated to any relationship of power or the pursuit of advantage. Conflict over health and safety was also hived off from mainstream labour relations, thereby reducing the risk of social instability, particularly when combined with workers' compensation.

29   Lorentsen and Woolner, *Fifty Years of Labour Legislation in Canada*. This included Quebec (1886), Manitoba (1900), Nova Scotia (1901), New Brunswick (1905), British Columbia (1908), Saskatchewan (1909), and Alberta (1917).

30   Tucker, "Making the Workplace 'Safe' in Canada" also suggests that compliance was constructed in such as way as to exclude requiring employers to incur substantial costs in preventing injury. This reflects that inspectors accepted the view that there are no fundamental conflicts between the interests of workers and employers when it comes to health and safety.

31   Tucker, "The Determination of Occupational Health and Safety Standards in Ontario" notes that state regulation introduces an overtly political element into the regulation of safety. Among the consequences of this change is that the strength of different social classes will significantly influence the content of the regulation. One outcome is that, as the state begins regulating the economy, it must grapple with the fact that private investment decisions determine economic performance (unless the state plans to challenge private property) and thus the state must regulate with an eye to encouraging private investing. This situation often results in a confounding of the private interests of employers with the public interest.

32   Bale, "America's First Compensation Crisis" discusses this dynamic in depth as it occurred in America. Overall, the American literature on this topic is better developed than the Canadian is and can provide useful insight into the Canadian experience.

33   Carr, "Workers' Compensation Systems." In spite of this change, courts could still only award compensation in the event of employer negligence—which still had to be proven in a system of tort law. Changes in Canadian legislation followed, as set out in Tucker, "Making the Workplace 'Safe' in Canada."

34   R. Chaykowski and T. Thomason, "Canadian Workers' Compensation: Institutions and Economics," in *Research in Canadian Workers' Compensation*, eds. T. Thomason and R. Chaykowski (Kingston: IRC Press, 1995), 1–42; R. Babcock, "Blood on the Factory Floor: The Workers' Compensation Movement in Canada and the United States," in *Social Fabric or Patchwork Quilt: The Development of So*

cial Policy in Canada, eds. R. Blake and J. Keshan (Peterborough: Broadview Press, 2006), 45–58.

35 Workers' compensation was part of a broad package of social policies intended to provide a complete network of social security to German citizens.

36 Witt, *The Accidental Republic* notes that programs for veterans of America's civil war were important precursors to programs designed to compensate work-related injuries.

37 Witt, *The Accidental Republic*; H. Armstrong, *Blood on the Coal: The Origins and Future of New Zealand's Accident Compensation Scheme* (Wellington: Trade Union History Project, 2008).

38 Palmer, *Working Class Experience.*

39 Babcock, "The Workers' Compensation Movement in Canada and the United States"; A. Stritch, "Power, Resources, Institutions and Policy Learning: The Origins of Workers' Compensation in Quebec," *Canadian Journal of Political Science* 38 (2005): 549–579.

40 Stritch, "Power, Resources, Institutions and Policy Learning" notes that no-fault compensation first emerged in Quebec where the labour movement was too weak and divided to force such a concession. Witt, *The Accidental Republic* traces the development of workers' compensation in the U.S. and concludes the ability of workers' compensation to offer all stakeholders something (if only notionally) helps explain its rapid adoption.

41 Witt, *The Accidental Republic.* The most famous of these is C. Eastman, *Work Accidents and the Law* (Brookhaven Press, 1999), which is Eastman's 1910 study of workplace injury in Pittsburgh. It concluded that only 44 percent of injuries could be partially blamed on worker or co-worker error. Employer error was responsible for 30 percent. But the working conditions created by the employer contributed to a great many more injuries by placing workers in positions of heightened or constant risk. Aldrich, *Safety First* notes that, as worker carelessness lost its legal importance in America, it became less important in the discourse around injury.

42 Risk, "This Nuisance of Litigation."

43 Tucker, "The Determination of Occupational Health and Safety in

Ontario" examines Ontario's approach to employer liability and suggests that state-managed compensation would be ideologically more palatable than additional state-regulation because it is less an impediment to employers' operating their businesses as they saw fit. In this way, compensation is more consistent with the principles of classical Liberalism than additional regulation.

44   W. Meredith, *Final Report on Laws Relating to the Liability of Employers to Make Compensation to Their Employees for Injuries Received in the Course of their Employment Which are in Force in Other Countries* (Toronto: L.K. Cameron, 1913).

45   Meredith, *Final Report*, 13.

46   Risk, "This Nuisance of Litigation": 472.

47   Lorentsen and Woolner, *Fifty Years of Labour Legislation in Canada.*

48   Palmer, *Working Class Experience.* Significant strike activity and a tight labour market led the federal government to enact PC 1003. This framework was based on the U.S. *Wagner Act* and set the pattern for post-war labour relations legislation. Workers traded union recognition and a promise to bargain in good faith in exchange for not striking during the term of a collective agreement. Opinions about the long-term utility of this compromise vary significantly. For example, see the contrasting views of L. Sefton MacDowell, "The Formation of the Canadian Industrial Relations System during World War Two," *Labour/Le Travail* 3 (1978): 175–196, and A. Finkel, "The Cold War, Alberta Labour and the Social Credit Regime, *Labour/Le Travail* 21 (1988): 123–152.

49   Tucker, "The Determination of Occupational Health and Safety Standards in Ontario."

50   M. Nash, *Canadian Occupational Health and Safety Law Handbook* (Don Mills: CCH Canadian, 1983).

51   R. Storey, "From the Environment to the Workplace… and Back Again? Occupational Health and Safety Activism in Ontario, 1970s–2000+," *Canadian Review of Sociology and Anthropology* 41(4) (2004): 419–447, among others, notes the importance of northern Ontario miners in kick starting the Canadian occupational health and safety movement. Storey also helpfully explores

the interactions between the development of the health and safety and environmental movements.

52 Storey, "From the Environment to the Workplace." R. Storey, "Activism and the Making of Occupational Health and Safety Law in Ontario, 1960s–1980," *Policy and Practice in Occupational Health and Safety* 1 (2005): 41–68, traces the development of occupational health and safety in Ontario. Among his findings are that occupational health and safety reform was driven by activists at the periphery of the trade union movement, concern centred on exposures to toxic substances, and the movement was strongest in unionized and male-dominated sectors.

53 Walters, "Occupational Health and Safety Legislation in Ontario" traces these pressures and convincingly links them to Ontario's move towards the internal responsibility system in the 1970s. She suggests that worker pressure was less important in the enactment of legislation than were the financial pressures caused by workplace injury on employers and the state.

54 *Toronto Daily Star* (1960).

55 B. Walker, "Government Regulation of Health Hazards in the Ontario Uranium Mining Industry, 1955–1976," in *At the End of the Shift: Mines and Single-Industry Towns in Northern Ontario,* eds. R. Bray and A. Thomson (Toronto: Dundurn, 1992), 130–139. Levels of radiation and silica were both above industry-recommended safety levels. Rank-and-file activism was muted, however, in part because of concerns about the financial viability of uranium mines. Ineffective federal regulation of radiation levels reflected the federal government's interest in expanding Canada's nuclear industry. Similarly, Ontario's Department of Mines was focused on promoting and expanding the mining industry, not addressing workplace safety issues.

56 This can be seen in Ontario's Ham Commission (1974), Alberta's Gale Commission (1975), and Quebec's Beaudry Commission (1977).

57 Nash, *Canadian Occupational Health and Safety Law Handbook.* Saskatchewan began this trend with new legislation in 1972. Ontario, Alberta, and New Brunswick followed in 1976, Newfoundland and the federal jurisdiction in 1978, and Quebec in 1979. British Columbia, Prince Edward Island, and the Yukon enacted

occupational health and safety regulations under existing workers' compensation legislation.

58   D. Verma, "Occupational Health and Safety Trends in Canada, Particularly in Ontario." *Annals of Occupational Hygiene* 40(4) (1995): 477–485.

59   *The Occupational Health and Safety Act*, s.3(a).

60   For example, s.4(1)(a) of Manitoba's *The Workplace Health and Safety Act*. Similarly, s.25(2)(h) of Ontario's legislation requires employers "take every precaution reasonable in the circumstances for the protection of a worker."

61   P. Schmidt, *Lawyers and Regulation: The Politics of the Administrative Process* (Cambridge, UK: Cambridge University Press, 2005).

62   Neo-liberalism is the political expression of economic globalization. Among its prescriptions are for a smaller and less active state. This reduces taxation, which, along with costs savings associated with weaker labour and environmental laws, is supposed to prevent capital flight by transnational employers. This ideology had a significant impact on Canadian governments during the 1990s. R. Storey and E. Tucker, "All That is Solid Melts into Air: Worker Participation and Occupational Health and Safety Regulation in Ontario, 1970–2000," in *Worker Safety Under Siege: Labor, Capital and the Politics of Workplace Safety in a Deregulated World*, ed. V. Mogensen (Armonk: M.E. Sharpe, 2006), 157–185, examine the impact of neo-liberalism on OHS in Ontario between 1970 and 2000. Costs associated with workplace injury were managed in a variety of ways, including emphasizing early return to work programs. Government emphasis shifted to increasing the number of inspections but at a reduction in quality. Among the changes were having OHS inspectors mediate work refusals over the phone. In effect, external regulation is limited to instances of injury or death when prosecution is required. Changes in the labour market and the nature of employment undermined the internal responsibility system (an issue further discussed in Chapter 3).

63   Storey and Tucker, *Worker Safety Under Siege*, note that in Ontario, short-lived bipartite governance of health and safety reduced shop-floor activism over health and safety, thereby reducing the ability of organized labour to respond to its exclusion. Other

jurisdictions (e.g., Alberta) never saw the degree of shop floor activism around health and safety and thus the movement towards government–employer partnerships occurred without any intervening depoliticization.

64 Storey and Tucker, *Worker Safety Under Siege*, E. Tucker, "Remapping Worker Citizenship in Contemporary Occupational Health and Safety Regimes," *International Journal of Health Services* 37(1) (2007): 145–170; Lewchuk, Clarke, and de Wolff (forthcoming); R. Haddow and T. Klassen, *Partisanship, Globalization and Canadian Labour Market Policy* (Toronto: University of Toronto Press, 2006) provide a very useful overview of labour market policy in Ontario, Quebec, Alberta, and British Columbia, including discussion of occupational health and safety and workers' compensation.

65 Law Reform Commission of Canada, *Workplace Pollution* (Ottawa: Author, 1986).

66 As noted in Tucker, "Remapping Worker Citizenship," the level and degree of state enforcement is subject to significant changes in response to political pressure. Crude indicators of enforcement (such as field activity by inspectors) show a long-term downward trend between 1970 and 2005, although other indicators (such as prosecutions) show more variability.

67 In the word of Ontario's Ham Report, "Since both parties desire the good of the individual worker, confrontation can and must be set aside with respect both to accidents and to health-impairing environmental exposures." Ontario. *Report of the Royal Commission on the Health and Safety of Workers in Mines* (Toronto: Ministry of the Attorney-General, 1976), 121.

68 K. Kelloway, and L. Francis, *Management of Occupational Health and Safety* (Toronto: Nelson, 2008), provide a useful summary.

69 There are several types of exposure limits, including time-weighted average limits, short-term exposure limits (which are 15-minute exposures that should not be repeated more than a few times per day), and exposure ceilings (levels above which no one should be exposed).

70 After the WHMIS system was implemented, R. Sass, "The Limits of Workplace Health and Safety Reforms in Liberal Economics,"

New Solutions 3(1) (1992): 31–40 notes Saskatchewan's government removed a regulatory clause from provincial legislation that prohibited employers from refusing information demands based on trade secrets.

71 As Schmidt, *Lawyers and Regulation* notes, enforcing the law requires inspectors to use their discretion because the generalities of formal law can be applied to specific factual cases without some interpretation. That said, trends in the application of discretion can reveal various things, such as unworkable laws, emerging circumstances not well addressed by the law, and patterns of influence and power.

72 G. Gray, "The Responsibilization Strategy of Health and Safety: Neoliberalism and the Reconfiguration of Individual Responsibility for Risk," *British Journal of Criminology* 49(3) (2009): 326–342, notes that workers are the target of 37 percent of ticketable offenses, supervisors 38.3 percent, and employers only 24.7 percent. Gray advances the argument that this distribution reflects a growing "blame the workers" approach to occupational health and safety.

73 The basis of a refusal could be a genuine belief that the work was hazardous, having a reasonable cause to believe that the work was hazardous, or having objective evidence of a hazard. The second standard is the norm in Canada. Some legislation and arbitrators have qualified this by requiring the danger be out of the ordinary for the work or the harm imminent and thus inescapable except through work refusal.

74 In Chapter 3, we will examine the use of informal refusals.

75 G. Gray, "A Socio-legal Ethnography of the Right to Refuse Dangerous Work," *Studies in Law, Politics and Society* 24 (2002): 133–169.

76 This incentive system was built upon a government–industry partnership (Partnership in Health and Safety) that began in 1989. This partnership sought to reduce work-related injuries and illnesses by encouraging employers and workers to develop OHS management systems (AEII, 2007b). Employers who passed an audit of their health and safety management system (performed by certified auditor, generally from a safety association) received a Certificate of Recognition (COR).

77 WCB, "Partners in Injury Reduction" Brochure (Edmonton: Alberta Workers' Compensation Board, 2007). Under the PIR program, first-time COR recipients receive a 10 percent reduction in their WCB industry rate during their first year. Further, by reducing WCB claim costs or maintaining claim costs at least 50 percent lower than the industry average for two consecutive years, employers can receive further discounts up to a 20 percent discount.

Chapter Three

1 *Edmonton Journal* (29 July 2009). Father of five killed in Alberta work accident. http://www.edmontonjournal.com/business/Father+five+killed+Alberta+work+accident/1838940/story.html. Accessed 29 July 2009.

2 Internationally, the International Labour Organization (ILO), *Facts on Safety* (Geneva: Author, 2004) reports 270 million workplace accidents and 160 million occupational diseases each year. L. Osberg and A. Sharpe, *An Index of Labour Market Well Being for OECD Countries* (Ottawa: Canadian Centre for the Study of Living Standards, 2003), compared fatality rates among OECD countries and noted that Canada tied with Italy for having the highest rate of fatalities per 100,000 workers in 2001. Canada also had the smallest reduction in the rate of fatal injuries between 1980 and 2001.

3 Wilkins and Mackenzie, "Work Injuries."

4 T. Ison, "The Significance of Experience Rating," *Osgoode Hall Law Journal* 24(4) (1986): 723–742.

5 H. Shannon and G. Lowe, "How Many Injured Workers do not File Claims for Workers' Compensation Benefits?" *American Journal of Industrial Medicine* 42(6) (2002): 467–473 found that 40 percent of eligible injured workers did not submit a workers' compensation claim, although there was a positive relationship between increasing injury seriousness and the likelihood of filing a claim. Even so, 30 percent of injuries resulting in lost-time that would be eligible for compensation were not reported to a WCB.

Brickey and K. Grant, "An Empirical Study of Work-Related Accidents and Illnesses in Winnipeg," (Winnipeg: Unpublished,

1992), studied injuries in Winnipeg and found that fewer than half of workers who had been injured filed a claim with workers' compensation. In the UK, B. Reilly, P. Paci, and P. Holl, "Unions, Safety Committees and Workplace Injuries," British Journal of Industrial Relations 33(2) (1995): 275–288, noted that only 30 percent of workplace injuries were reported under the Reporting of Injuries, Diseases and Dangerous Occurrences Regulations in 1990.

6   Association of Workers' Compensation Boards of Canada, "Summary Table of Accepted Time-Loss Injuries/Diseases and Fatalities by Jurisdiction," http://www.awcbc.org/en/national-workinjuriesstatisticsprogramnwisp.asp#Stats.

7   A. Dembe, *Occupational and Disease: How Social Factors Affect the Conception of Work-Related Disorders* (New Haven: Yale University Press, 1996), examines the history and recognition of RSIs at length.

8   When you look for this, it becomes easy to see. For example, job postings for building supervisors (a predominantly male occupation) frequently list as a requirement the ability to periodically lift heavy weights. By contrast, job postings for nurses and health care aides (a predominantly female occupation) frequently contain no information about lifting requirements, even though these workers routinely lift patients. In this way, the physical demands of female work are hidden. K. Messing, *One-Eyed Science: Occupational Health and Women Workers* (Philadelphia: Temple University Press, 1998), discusses the issue of women's occupational health and the relative invisibility of non-reproductive issues at length in her excellent book on the topic.

9   L. Elinson, "The Compensation of Occupational Disease in Ontario," in *Research in Canadian Workers' Compensation*, eds. T. Thomason and R. Chaykowski (Kingston: IRC Press, 1995), 195–209; T. Ison, "Recognition of Occupational Disease in Workers' Compensation," (paper presented at the CCOHS Conference on the Recognition and Prevention of Occupational Disease, Toronto, Canada, 3–4 March 2005).

10   R. Rennie, "'All Part of the Game': The Recognition of and Response to an Industrial Disaster at the Fluorspar Mines, St. Lawrence, Newfoundland, 1933–1978," in *Working Disasters: The*

Politics of Response and Recognition, ed. E. Tucker (Amityville: Baywood Publishing, 2006), 77–102.

11 M. Firth, J. Brophy, and M. Keith, *Workplace Roulette: Gambling with Cancer* (Toronto: Between the Lines, 1997).

12 J. Brophy, M. Keith, and J. Schieman, "Canada's Asbestos Legacy at Home and Abroad," *International Journal of Occupational and Environmental Health* 13 (2007): 235–242; S. Epstein, *The Politics of Cancer Revisited* (USA: East Ridge Press, 1998).

13 R. Storey and W. Lewchuk, "From Dust to DUST to Dust: Asbestos and the Struggle for Worker Health and Safety at Bendix Automotive," *Labour/Le Travail* 45 (2000): 103–140.

14 A particularly chilling account of the corporate cover-up can be found in D. Kotelchuck, "Asbestos: The Funeral Dress of Kings — and Others," in *Dying for a Living: Workers' Safety and Health in Twentieth-Century America*, eds. D. Rosner and G. Markowitz (Bloomington: Indiana University Press, 1989), 192–207. One interviewee recalls a lunch meeting in 1942 or 1943 where he asked one of the Brown brothers whether he would withhold information about asbestosis from afflicted workers, to which the brother responded, "Yes. We save a lot of money that way" (p. 202). This attitude is consistent with the mass of documentation about corporate behaviour that has been uncovered during asbestos lawsuits.

15 D. Dewees, "Paying for Asbestos-Related Diseases under Workers' Compensation," in *New Perspectives in Workers' Compensation*, ed. J. F. Burton (Ithaca: ILR Press, 1988), 45–70.

16 E. Tucker, "Introduction: The Politics of Recognition and Response," in *Working Disasters: The Politics of Response and Recognition*, ed. E. Tucker (Amityville: Baywood Publishing, 2006), 1–18.

17 A. Nugent, "The Power to Define a New Disease: Epidemiological Politics and Radium Poisoning," in *Dying for a Living: Workers' Safety and Health in Twentieth-Century America*, eds. D. Rosner and G. Markowitz (Bloomington: Indiana University Press, 1989), 177–191.

18 Variations on this pattern are evident in many instances of occupational hazards, including lead (Rosner and Markowitz, "Safety and Health as a Class Issue") and asbestos (Kotelchuck, "Asbestos";

Storey and Lewchuk, "From Dust to DUST to Dust"). The creation of employer-favourable science is documented in W. Graebner, "Hegemony Through Science: Information Engineering and Lead Toxicology, 1925–1965," in *Dying for a Living: Workers' Safety and Health in Twentieth-Century America*, eds. D. Rosner and G. Markowitz (Bloomington: Indiana University Press, 1989), 140–159. This pattern very similar to what Bohme, Zorabedian, and Egilman, "Maximizing Profit and Endangering Health" describe in their analysis of corporate efforts to evade regulation and liability for consumer and worker injuries and fatalities.

19 M. Quinlain, C. Mayhew, and R. Johnstone, "Trucking Tragedies: The Hidden Disaster of Mass Death in the Long-Haul Road Transportation Industry," in *Working Disasters: The Politics of Response and Recognition*, ed. E. Tucker (Amityville: Baywood Publishing, 2006), 19–64.

20 Alberta has a long history of this behaviour. Reasons, Ross, and Paterson, "Assault on the Worker," note that Alberta used blame the worker approaches as far back as 1979's "Alive" campaign and documents the then-CEO of Alberta's health and safety programming as stating that 70–80 percent of injuries and fatalities were caused by careless workers.

21 www.bloodylucky.ca.

22 AEII, "Occupational fatalities in Alberta, 1997–2006" (Edmonton: Alberta Employment, Immigration and Industry, 2007).

23 This bias recurs through discussion of cancer and reflects the importance of treatment to patients and the "cure" orientation of health care, although other motives (including the profitability of cancer treatment) also appear to play a role. See D. Davis, *The Secret History of the War on Cancer* (New York: Basic Books, 2007).

24 Epstein, *The Politics of Cancer Revisited*; Firth, Brophy, and Keith, *Workplace Roulette*.

25 Epstein, *ibid*; R. Proctor, *Cancer Wars* (New York: Basic Books, 1995); European Agency for Health and Safety at Work, *Work-Related cancer* http://osha.europa.eu/en/OSH_world_day/occupational_cancer; K. Steenland, C. Burnett, N. Lalich, E. Ward, and J. Hurrell, "Dying for Work: The Magnitude of U.S. Mor-

tality from Selected Causes of Death Associated with Occupation," *American Journal of Industrial Medicine* 43(5) (2003): 461–82.

26 Firth, Brophy, and Keith, *Workplace Roulette*.

27 Canadian Cancer Society/National Cancer Institute of Canada, *Canadian Cancer Statistics 2005* (Toronto: Author, 2005).

28 Alberta Cancer Foundation, *Cancer and the Workplace: An Overview for Workers and Employers* (Edmonton: Author, 2005).

29 Alberta Workers' Compensation Board, *Cancers and Respiratory Diseases, Number of Newly Reported Claims and Accepted Claims (by Detailed Description), Transaction Year: 1991–2005* (Edmonton: Author, 2005).

30 Exposure limits are discussed at length below — for now suffice to say that the reliability of these levels of exposure is the subject of significant question.

31 Alberta Cancer Foundation, *Cancer and the Workplace*.

32 Alberta Cancer Foundation, *Cancer and the Workplace*, 14.

33 Asbestos-related diseases, for example, demonstrate that workers can pressure the state and employers to recognize, address, and compensate some forms of occupational diseases. Yet the number of diseases so recognized is few and updated infrequently. In Alberta, there is statutory recognition of 11 major forms of occupational disease or conditions.

34 I. Schultz, J. Crook, K. Fraser, and P. Joy, "Models of Diagnosis and Rehabilitation in Musculoskeletal Pain-related Occupational Disability," *Journal of Occupational Rehabilitation* 10(4) (2000): 271–293.

35 E. Shainblum, T. Sullivan, and J. Frank, "Multicausality, Non-traditional Injury and the Future of Workers' Compensation," in *Workers' Compensation: Foundations for Reform* eds. M. Gunderson and D. Hyatt (Toronto: University of Toronto Press, 2000), 58–95.

36 R. Storey, "From the Environment to the Workplace... and Back Again? Occupational Health and Safety Activism in Ontario, 1970s–2000+," *Canadian Review of Sociology and Anthropology* 41(4) (2004): 419–447 examines the interaction of occupational health and safety and the environmental movement.

37 K. Lippel, "Workers' Compensation and Controversial Illnesses," in *Contesting Illness: Process and Practices*, eds. P. Moss and K. Teghtsoonian (Toronto: University of Toronto Press, 2008), 47–68, traces the use of this model in cases where illness is contested.

38 V. Walters and T. Haines, "Workers' Use and Knowledge of the Internal Responsibility System: Limits to Participation in Occupational Health and Safety," *Canadian Public Policy* 14(4) (1988): 411–423, found that 49 percent of workers used their own experience as their main source of information about the presence or absence of a health effect. The experience of co-workers was the main source for 30 percent of workers, and personal feelings (i.e., lacking any evidentiary basis) was the main source for 20 percent. Employers and health and safety representatives each comprised the main source for 7 percent of workers. Interestingly, relying on self-knowledge (as opposed to "medical knowledge") about workplace hazards to trigger action is broadly consistent with the recent recommendation of Bob Sass, the creator of the three rights that came to define OHS in the 1970s. See: D. Smith, *Consulted to Death: How Canada's Workplace Health and Safety System Fails Workers* (Winnipeg: Arbeiter Ring, 2000).

39 This raises interesting questions. Should workers be educated so they can better act within the dominant paradigm? Or should workers be taught how to express their concerns, thereby bringing these to concerns into the mainstream of debate?

40 V. Walters, and T. Haines, "Workers' Perceptions, Knowledge and Responses Regarding Occupational Health and Safety: A Report on a Canadian Study," *Social Science and Medicine* 27(11) (1988): 1189–1196.

41 L. McDonnell, "Assessment Policy as Persuasion and Regulation," *American Journal of Education* 102 (1994): 394–420; A. Schneider and H. Ingram, "Behavioural Assumptions of Policy Tools," paper presented at the 39th Annual AIR Forum, 1990, Seattle, United States; L. McDonnell, and R. Elmore, *Alternative Policy Instruments* (Santa Monica, CA: The RAND Corporation, 1987).

42 For example, http://www.ama.ab.ca/cps/rde/xchg/ama/web/advocacy_safety_1898.htm

43 http://employment.alberta.ca/whs/learning/ergonomics/data/ergonomics.html

44 Gray, "The Responsibilization Strategy of Health and Safety."

45 B. Doern, "The Political Economy of Regulating Occupational Health: The Ham and Beaudry Reports," *Canadian Public Administration* 20(1) (1978): 1–35.

46 W. Lewchuck, M. Clarke, and A. de Wolff, "Precarious Employment and the Internal Responsibility System: Some Canadian Experiences," Working paper 2008-02 (Hamilton: McMaster University, 2008).

47 Work refusals are an indicator of workers exercising their rights. Renaud and St-Jacques (1988) found non-union workers accounted for only 2.9 percent of work refusals even though they accounted for 72.2 percent of the workforce.

48 Walters and Haines, "Workers Use and Knowledge of the Internal Responsibility System."

49 Walters and Haines, "Workers' Perceptions, Knowledge and Responses Regarding Occupational Health and Safety."

50 V. Walters and M. Denton, "Workers' Knowledge of their Legal Rights and Resistance to Hazardous Work," *Relations Industrielles/Industrial Relations* 45(3) (1990): 531–547. This broadly replicates Nelkin and Brown's, *Workers at Risk*, findings although the important variable is knowledge, not gender, education, or unionization.

51 P. Smith and C. Mustard, "How Many Employees Receive Safety Training During Their First Year of a New Job?" *Injury Prevention* 13 (2007): 37–41.

52 Smith, *Consulted to Death*, attributes this quote to Saskatchewan's Bob Sass.

53 This point is made in Sass, "The Limits of Workplace Health and Safety Reforms in Liberal Economics." I have extended his discussion in a manner with which he may not agree with.

54 Reilly, Paci and Holl, "Unions, Safety Committees and Workplace Injuries"; W. Lewchuck, L. Robb and V. Walters, "The Effectiveness of Bill 70 and Joint Health and Safety Committee

in Reducing Injuries in the Workplace: The Case of Ontario,"
Canadian Public Policy 22(3) (1996): 225–243; J. O'Grady, "Joint
Health and Safety Committees: Finding a Balance," in *Injury and
the New World of Work*, ed. T. Sullivan (Vancouver: University of
British Columbia Press, 2000), 162–197; C. Tuohy and M. Simard,
"The Impact of Joint Health and Safety Committees in Ontario
and Quebec," Unpublished manuscript (Canadian Association of
Labour Law, 1993).

55 E. Bernard, "Canada: Joint Committees on Occupational Health
and Safety," in *Work Councils: Consultation Representation and
Cooperation in Industrial Relations*, eds. J. Rogers and W. Streeck
(Chicago: University of Chicago Press, 1995), 351–374; A. Eaton,
"Factors Contributing to the Survival of Employee Participation
Programs in Unionized Settings," *Industrial and Labor Relations
Review* 47(3) (1994): 371–389; A. Eaton and P. Voos, "Productiv-
ity-Enhancing Innovations in Work Organization, Compensation
and Employee Participation in Union vs. Non-union Sectors," *Ad-
vances in Industrial and Labor Relations* 6 (1994): 63–109; A. Hall,
"The Corporate Approach to Occupational Health and Safety:
A Labour Process Analysis," *Canadian Journal of Sociology* 18(2)
(1993): 1–20; T. Kochan, L. Dyer and D. Lipsky, *The Effectiveness of Union Management Safety and Health Committees* (Kalamazoo: Upjohn Institute for Employment Research, 1977); N.
Milgate, E. Innes and K. O'Loughlin, "Examining the Effectiveness of Health and Safety Committees and Representatives:
A Review," *Work: Journal of Prevention, Assessment and Rehabilitation* 19(3) (2002): 281–290; Tuohy and Simard, ibid; Tucker,
"And the Defeat Goes On"; D. Walters, "Trade Unions and the
Effectiveness of Worker Representation in Health and Safety
in Britain," *International Journal of Health Services* 26(4) (1996):
625–641; Walters and Haines, "Workers' Use and Knowledge
of the Internal Responsibility System"; D. Weil, "Are Mandated
Health and Safety Committees Substitutes for or Supplements
to Labor Unions?" *Industrial and Labor Relations Review*, 52(3)
(1999): 339–360.

56 R. Fidler, "The Occupational Health and Safety Act and the Internal Responsibility System." *Osgood Hall Law Journal* 24(2)
(1985): 315–352.

57 Lewchuk, Robb and Walters, "The Effectiveness of Bill 70 and Joint Health and Safety Committee in Reducing Injuries in the Workplace" found that Ontario workplaces where JHSCs were struck before or soon after such committees were legislatively required saw a meaningful reduction in lost-time injuries (as much as 18 percent). Where committees were slow to develop, there was little or no improvement in safety performance. This may suggest that JHSC have difficulty overcoming employer resistance and/or worker apathy.

58 A. Hall, A. Forrest, A. Sears and N. Carlan, "Making a Difference: Knowledge Activism and Worker Representation in Joint OHS Committees," *Relations Industrielles/Industrial Relations* 64(3) (2006): 408–436.

59 The most effective politically active representatives exhibited significant self-learning and access of wide-ranging information sources. They tended to use and promote the knowledge of workers about unsafe working conditions, rather than relying solely upon scientific knowledge. They also tended to focus on the underlying causes of issues and present managers with solutions.

60 Hall, Forrest, Sears, and Carlan, "Making a Difference: Knowledge Activism and Worker Representation in Joint OHS Committees." These workers did not appear to recognize that their ability to achieve improved health and safety turned on their individual power and political influence.

61 Walters, "The Politics of Occupational Health and Safety"; Walters and Haines, "Workers' Use and Knowledge of the Internal Responsibility System"; V. Walters, W. Lewchuk, J. Richardson, L. Moran, T. Haines and D. Verma, "Judgments of Legitimacy Regarding Occupational Health and Safety. Regulating capitalism," in *Corporate Crime: Contemporary Debates*, ed. F. Pearce (Toronto: University of Toronto Press, 1995), 284–303.

62 The calculation of 321,000 injuries is based on Alberta WCB claims data, which has been modified to account for the at least 10 percent of workers outside the ambit of workers' compensation and that reported claims account for only 60 percent of all injuries.

63 AEII, *Joint Worksite Health and Safety Committee Handbook* (Edmonton: Alberta Employment, Immigration and Industry, 2006).

64 Several case studies demonstrate workers accepting extremely hazardous condition even while fully aware of them: Glasbeek and Tucker, "Death by Consensus"; A. Hall, "Understanding the Impact of Mine Health and Safety Programs," *Labour Studies Journal* 23(4) (1999): 51–76; Storey and Lewchuck, "From Dust to DUST to Dust."

65 Walters and Haines, "Workers' Use and Knowledge of the Internal Responsibility System."

66 Gray, "A Socio-legal Ethnography of the Right to Refuse Dangerous Work" notes that informal refusals may include altering the process or pace of work as well as refusing overtime on unsafe jobs, calling in sick and seeking transfers. These non-confrontational strategies may reflect a workers' calculus about the risk and reward of a formal refusal.

67 R. Hebdon and D. Hyatt, "The Effects of Industrial Factors on Health and Safety Conflict," *Industrial and Labor Relations Review* 51(4) (1998): 579–593 found no evidence that work refusals or health and safety complaints were used by workers to harass employers or increase worker bargaining power. Rather, they found that workplaces characterized by industrial relations conflict (e.g., strikes, arbitrations, grievances) are also characterized by conflict over health and safety matters.

68 Gray, "A Socio-legal Ethnography of the Right to Refuse Dangerous Work."

69 Gray, "A Socio-legal Ethnography of the Right to Refuse Dangerous Work" suggests that informal refusals outpace formal refuses because workers recognize that conflict with their employer may be a greater risk than the unsafe work they are concerned about.

70 M. Harcourt and S. Harcourt, "When Can an Employee Refuse Unsafe Work and Expect to be Protected from Discipline? Evidence from Canada," *Industrial and Labor Relations Review* 53(4) (2000): 684–703, analyzed 272 arbitration and labour board decisions about the right to refuse. Among their findings are that boards often look beyond the work refusal to examine the worker's general behaviour towards the employer. Dutiful workers and those with good work records are more likely to be treated less harshly than workers who were unruly. This is broadly consistent with other studies in the area: V. Walters, "State Mediation of Conflict Over Work Refusals: The Role of the Ontario Labour Relations Board," *International Journal of Health Services* 21(4) (1991): 717–729; G. Leslie, "The Statutory Right to Refuse Unsafe Work: A Comparison of Saskatchewan, Ontario and the Federal jurisdiction," *Saskatchewan Law Review* 46(2) (1982): 234–270; J. Gross and P. Greenfield, "Arbitral Value Judgments in Health and Safety Disputes: Management Rights Over Workers' Rights," *Buffalo Law Review* 34 (1985): 645–691; K. Thornicroft, "Do Lawyers Affect Grievance Arbitration Outcomes? The Newfoundland Experience," *Relations Industrielles/Industrial Relations* 49(2) (1994): 356–371; K. Thornicroft, "Gender Effects in Grievance Arbitration… Revisited," *Labor Studies Journal* 19(4) (1995): 35–44.

71 R. Hyman, *The Political Economy of Industrial Relations: Theory and Practice in a Cold Climate* (MacMillan: Wiltshire, 1989).

72 Bob Sass, the father of the three rights in Canada, himself characterized these rights as weak in Smith, *Consulted to Death*. Sass also suggests he no longer subscribes to the three rights.

73 Sass, "The Limits of Workplace Health and Safety Reforms in Liberal Economics" notes that this limitation exists even in seemingly favourable circumstances, such as in during a pilot program in a crown corporation under a New Democrat government in Saskatchewan.

74 Tucker, "And the Defeat Goes On."

75 S. Geldart, H. Shannon, and L. Lohfeld, "Have Companies Improved Their Health and Safety Approaches over the Last Decade? A Longitudinal Study," *American Journal of Industrial Medicine* 47(3) (2005): 227–36, suggest managers were less likely to view worker participation as important in improving safety between 1990 and 2001. For their part, workers felt employers were less likely to cooperate on safety.

76 WSIB, *Annual Report* (Toronto: Workplace Safety and Insurance Board, 2000).

77 CDC, *Preventing Lead Poisoning in Young Children* (Atlanta: Centres for Disease Control and Prevention, 1991). Even low levels of lead appear to have negative effects on intelligence and neuro-behavioural development

78   G. Ziem and B. Castleman, "Threshold Limit Values: Historical Perspectives and Current Practice," in *Illness and the Environment*, eds. S. Kroll-Smith, P. Brown and V. Gunter (New York: New York University Press, 2000), 120–134, trace the history of TLVs. When TLVs were first developed by the American Conference of Government Industrial Hygienists (ACGIH) in 1942, the ACGIH noted that TVL were not safe levels of exposure. By 1953, the ACGIH was indicating that TLV were a guide to safe daily levels of exposure, although there is no basis to believe that any sort of review or scientific breakthrough addressed the uncertainty about what a safe level of exposure was. There appears to be little scientific support for the levels that were set and there has been constant revision downwards as previously "safe" levels of exposure are found not to be safe after all.

79   R. Heifetz, "Women, Lead and Reproductive Hazards. Defining a New Risk," in *Dying for a Living: Workers' Safety and Health in Twentieth-Century America*, eds. D. Rosner and G. Markowitz (Bloomington: Indiana University Press, 1989), 160–176, notes that, when gender is considered, it is usually in the context of female reproduction. The solution is often to move women out of hazardous jobs (to lower-pay jobs or by firing them) rather than remove the hazard.

80   Firth, Brophy and Keith, *Workplace roulette*. Further, as precarious work results in many workers have multiple employers, there is potential for multiple exposures or unanticipated interactive effects from exposures to different chemicals.

81   B. Castleman and G. Ziem, "Corporate Influence on Threshold Limit Values," *American Journal of Industrial Medicine*, 13 (188): 531–559. Indeed, many scientists dispute the notion that there is any safe level of exposure for carcinogens and reproductive hazards. These "safe" levels reflects simply the point below which they are (at present) unable to detect ill effects.

82   Alberta Workers' Compensation Board, "Policy 02-01 'Arises out of and occurs in the course of employment'" *Policies and Information Manual* (Edmonton: Alberta Workers' Compensation Board, 1996).

83 Ziem and Castleman, "Threshold Limit Values." Animal studies contain several deficiencies such as an inability to elicit a medical history, assess the effects of exposure on cognition, or register symptoms that do not result in gross physical reactions. There is also little attention to pulmonary functioning in many of these studies — obviously an issue of concern to workers!

84 P. Dorman, "Is Expert Paternalism the Answer to Worker Irrationality?" in *Worker Safety Under Siege: Labor, Capital and the Politics of Workplace Safety in a Deregulated World*, ed. V. Mogensen (Armonk: M.E. Sharpe, 2006), 34–57.

85 This dynamic is well established. Examples include corporate obfuscation of the cancer risk associated with smoking (Davis, *The Secret History of the War on Cancer*) and the occupational risks associated with asbestos (Epstein, *The Politics of Cancer Revisited*).

86 S. Roach and S. Rappaport, "But They Are Not Thresholds: A Critical Analysis of the Documentation of Threshold Limit Values," *American Journal of Industrial Medicine* 17 (1990): 728–753.

87 Law Reform Commission of Canada, *Workplace Pollution.*

88 Alberta, "Report to the Minister of Justice and Attorney General: Public Fatality Inquiry," (Okotoks: Justice and Attorney General, 2008).

89 CBC, "Out of sync with today's changing workplace" 2007. http://www.cbc.ca/news/background/workplace-safety/outofsync.html

90 Ontario, "Report Card: Health and Safety Statistics," (Toronto: Ministry of Labour, 2008). A field visit includes inspections, investigations, and consultations. The majority of the increase comes from an increase in inspections, which Ontario terms as proactive visits (as contrasted with investigations of complaints).

This data needs to be considered in the long-term. E. Tucker, "Diverging Trends in Worker Health and Safety Protection and Participation in Canada, 1985–2000," Relations Industrielles/ Industrial Relations 58(3) (2003): 395–424, notes that there were over 70,000 field activities in 1970/71, with a long-term decline that bottomed out in 1994/95.

91 Storey and Tucker, "All That Is Solid Melts into Air." It is not clear the degree to which the doubling of orders and stop work orders between 2004/05 and 2007/08 undermines this critique.

92 CBC, "Weekend inspection rates," 2007, http://www.cbc.ca/news/background/workplace-safety/pdf/weekendvisits.pdf. This number of inspections is about average for the early 2000s. This number is based on information received under freedom of information legislation and conflicts with the 13,000 inspections claimed by the government in the press: see S. Harris, "The boom is a bust for workplace safety" *The Vue Weekly*. 27 April 2006. Tucker, "Diverging Trends in Worker Health and Safety Protection and Participation in Canada" notes this is a decline from inspections levels in the 1980s.

93 Association of Workers' Compensation Boards of Canada, "Summary Table of Accepted Time-Loss Injuries/Diseases and Fatalities by Jurisdiction"; Association of Workers' Compensation Boards of Canada. "Key Statistical Measures for 2007" http://www.awcbc.org/common/assets/ksms/2007ksms.pdf. As discussed in earlier, these workers' compensation claim statistics significantly understate the actual rate of injury.

94 CBC, "Out of sync with today's changing workplace."

95 To be fair, the number of injuries per workplace or employer might still be higher in traditionally inspected workplaces. The CBC story suggests that claim rates in health care are the equivalent of those in construction, manufacturing, and forestry.

96 CBC, "Weekend inspection rates." By contrast, Alberta had the highest rate with 14 percent of inspections occurring on a weekend in 2005.

97 CCPA, "Shifting Times: The Perils of shiftwork." (Regina: Canadian Centre for policy Alternatives. 2007) http://www.policyalternatives.ca/documents/Saskatchewan_Pubs/2007/Shifting_Times_The_Perils_of_Shift_Work.pdf.

98 Schmidt, *Lawyers and Regulation*, notes that good relationships can be important because the OHS is characterized by highly interdependent relationships. An inspector taking a hard line may be able to create consequences for an employer. But the employer,

using political connections or the press, can also create consequences for the inspector.

99   Law Reform Commission of Canada, *Workplace Pollution.*

100 Fidler, "The Occupational Health and Safety Act and the Internal Responsibility System" details the case of Stan Gray, an Ontario worker who faced seemingly endless resistance from a provincial occupational health and safety officer when he sought remedy for hazards that the employer would not address.

101 T. Ison, "The Uses and Limits of Sanctions in Industrial Health and Safety," *Workers' Compensation Reporter (BC)* 2 (1975): 203. In a partial reversal of this tendency, the Criminal Code was amended in the wake of the Westray Mine disaster.

102 "Due diligence" can be used to defend and employer charged under occupational health and safety legislation. If the employer can prove it/she/he took all precautions to protect the health and safety of worker that were reasonable under the circumstance, then the employer can be found not guilty.

103 CBC, "Out of sync with today's changing workplace."

104 Ontario, "Report Card: Health and Safety Statistics." These changes followed the election of a liberal government to replace the previous progressive conservative one.

105 AEI, "Alberta imposes record penalties for occupational health and safety violations," (Press release, 29 December 2008. Edmonton: Employment and Immigration). To be fair, prosecutions for some of these fatalities may be ongoing or previously concluded. .

106 E. Tompa, S. Trevithick and C. McLeod, "Systematic Review of the Prevention Incentives of Insurance and Regulatory Mechanisms for Occupational Health and Safety," *Scandinavian Journal of Work, Environment and Health* 33(2) (2007): 85–95.

107 The authors did not, however, provide any data about the cost-effectiveness of enforcement (i.e., it may be less financially or politically expensive to compensate injury than prevent it). The authors also note that, over time, the effectiveness of enforcement appears to have declined. This may reflect changes in the nature of work and injury.

108 Tucker, "Making the Workplace 'Safe' in Capitalism."

109 Glasbeek and Tucker, "Death by Consensus."

110 Iverson and Barling, "The Current Culture of Workplace Injury" found that 98 percent of 600 employers surveyed agreed that providing a safe working environment increased profitability.

111 A variation on "safety pays" is that safety provides strategic advantages to employers, such as customer satisfaction, worker motivation, and corporate reputation.

112 Health and Safety Executive, *The Cost of Accidents at Work.* (London: HMSO, 1993).

113 During the study no firms experienced fatalities, prosecutions or civil claims — all events that would drive up costs.

114 For example, T. Cutler and P. James, "Does Safety Pay? A Critical Account of the Health and Safety Executive Document: 'The Cost of Accidents'," *Work, Employment and Society* 10(4) (1996): 755–765.

115 No information is provided about what threshold was used or whether it was used consistently. It is also unclear if there is any sort of pattern to the accidents that were excluded.

116 Industrial Commission, "Work, health and safety, Vol. 2." (AGPS. Canberra: Author, 1995).

117 A. Hopkins, "For Whom Does Safety Pay? The Case of Major Accidents," *Safety Science* 32 (1999): 143–153. If injury costs were reduced by $2 billion, the net benefit would only be $0.34 billion. In effect, every dollar of reduced cost only results in net benefit of 17 cents. See: Industrial Commission, "Work, health and safety."

118 W. Lepkowski, "The Restructuring of Union Carbide," in *Learning from Disaster: Risk Management after Bhopal* (Philadelphia: University of Pennsylvania, 1996), 22–43.

119 R. Knight and D. Pretty, "The impact of Catastrophes on shareholder value" (Oxford University Business School, Executive Research Briefings, 1998), examined the effect of major catastrophes on 15 corporations. While all saw short-term drops in shareholder value, some corporations saw a net gain after 50 trading days.

120 Health and Safety Executive, *The Role of Managerial Leadership in Determining Workplace Safety Outcomes* (London: HMSO, 2003).

121 Health and Safety Executive, *The Role of Managerial Leadership in Determining Workplace Safety Outcomes*, 19.

122 There is growing evidence that lost-time claims are also in decline in British Columbia and Ontario. Yet these studies do not fully grapple with whether there is an actual reduction in injury or simply a reduction in reporting. C. Mustard, D. Cole, H. Shannon, J. Pole, T. Sullivan and R. Allingham, "Declining Trends in Work-Related Morbidity and Disability, 1993–1998: A Comparison of Survey Estimates and Compensation Insurance Claims," *American Journal of Public Health* 93(8) (2003): 1283–1286, found a 22.3 percent decline in Ontario LTC between 1993 and 1998. Similar reductions in lost-time injuries were reported during this period on two other panel surveys (one measuring work-related injuries and illnesses restricting activity and other addressing work-related injuries causing absences of one-week or more from work).

Overall, there appears to be a general downwards trend in reported injuries during this period. The downward slope of LTCs is steeper than those of other measures. That is to say, LTCs have been decreasing faster than then other indicators of injury. Both the LTC measure and the measure of work-related injuries causing absences of one-week or more from work can be affected by employer claims management behaviour (see the discussion of experience-rating schemes in Chapter 5), thus may overstate the reduction in actual injuries. Further, the claims systems may be less sensitive to the development of chronic injuries, where workers may exercise a degree of discretion in when they file a claim. The measure examining work-related injuries and illnesses restricting activity shows a decline over time. In theory, this measure ought to control for employer claims management techniques. The large variations in reported restrictions in this study suggest it may not be particularly reliable.

More recently, F. Breslin, E. Tompa, C. Mustard, R. Zhao, P. Smith and S. Hogg-Johnson, "Association Between the Decline in Workers' Compensation Claims and Workforce Composition and Job Characteristics in Ontario, Canada," American Journal of Public Health 97 (2007): 453–455, examined lost-time claims in Ontario between 1990 and 2003. They noted a decline on lost-time claims over time, with the proportion of manual jobs in each industry being associated with the claim rate. This decrease may reflect the export of hazardous jobs overseas and/or improvements in technology. The impact of claims management on lost-time claim prevalence was not addressed. See also C. Breslin, P. Smith, M. Koehoorn, and H. Lee, "Is the Workplace Becoming Safer?" *Perspectives on Labour and Income 18*(3) (2006): 36–42.

123 Drawn from AHRE, *Ministry Annual Report 2003–04*. (Edmonton. Alberta Human Resources and Employment, 2004); AHRE, *Ministry Annual Report 2004–2005*. (Edmonton. Alberta Human Resources and Employment; AHRE 2005); AHRE, *Ministry Annual Report 2005–2006*. (Edmonton. Alberta Human Resources and Employment, 2006); AEII. *Occupational Injuries and Diseases in Alberta: Lost-time Claims, Disabling Injury Rates and Claim Rates.* (Edmonton: Alberta Employment, Immigration and Industry, 2007); AEII, *Ministry Annual Report 2006–07.* (Edmonton: Alberta Employment, Immigration and Industry, 2007); AEI, *Annual Workplace Safety Statistics Provide Mixed Results.* (Edmonton: Alberta Employment and Immigration, 2008); AEI, *Annual Workplace Safety Statistics Show Mixed Results* (Edmonton: Alberta Employment and Immigration, 2009); AEI, *Annual report, 2008/09.* (Edmonton: Alberta Employment and Immigration, 2009).

124 For a fuller analysis of Alberta's performance measurement system, see B. Barnetson, "Performance Measures in Alberta's Labour Programming," *Canadian Political Science Review*, 2(1) (2008): 35–50.

125 E. Soderstrom and J. Stewart, "Adjudicating claims," in *Occupational Medicine: State of the Art Reviews*, eds. T. Guidotti and J. Cowell (Philadelphia: Hanley and Belfus, 1998) 273–278; Alberta Workers' Compensation Board, *Workers' Compensation Board – Alberta 2008 Annual Report* (Edmonton: Workers' Compensation Board, 2009).

126 Alberta Workers' Compensation Board, "2008 Premium Rate." (Edmonton: Workers' Compensation Board, 2008).

127 W. Baer, "Workplace health and safety update," presentation at the Petroleum industry Annual Safety Seminar. Edmonton, 3 May 2006.

128 AEII, "Work Safe Alberta News, May/June" (Edmonton: Alberta Employment, Immigration and Industry, 2007), 2.

129 Drawn from AEII. *Occupational Injuries and Diseases in Alberta: Lost-time Claims, Disabling Injury Rates and Claim Rates.* (Edmonton: Alberta Employment, Immigration and Industry, 2007); AEII, *Ministry Annual Report 2006–07.* (Edmonton: Alberta Employment, Immigration and Industry, 2007); AEI, *Annual Workplace Safety Statistics Provide Mixed Results.* (Edmonton: Alberta Employment and Immigration, 2008); AEI, *Annual Workplace Safety Statistics Show Mixed Results.* (Edmonton: Alberta Employment and Immigration, 2009); AEI, *Annual Report, 2008/09.* (Edmonton: Alberta Employment and Immigration, 2009); WCB, *Workers' Compensation Board – Alberta 2008 Annual Report.* (Edmonton: Workers' Compensation Board, 2009).

130 Alberta Workers' Compensation Board, *Workers' Compensation Board – Alberta 2007 Annual Report* (Edmonton: Workers' Compensation Board, 2008); AEI, "Annual workplace safety statistics show mixed results" (Edmonton: Alberta Employment and Immigration, 2009). As U. Bültmann, R-L. Franche, S. Hogg-Johnson, P. Côté, H. Lee, C. Severin, M. Vidmar, and N. Carnide, "Health Status, Work Limitations, and Return-to-Work Trajectories in Injured Workers with Musculoskeletal Disorders," *Quality of Life* 16(7) (2007): 1167–1178 note, a return to work does not mean the end of symptoms or complications for workers. Pain, depressive symptoms, and work limitations continue for workers with WMSDs even after they returned to work.

131 AHRE, *Ministry Annual Report 2005–2006.* (Edmonton. Human Resources and Employment, 2006); AEI, *Annual Workplace Safety Statistics Show Mixed Results.*

132 There has also been an increase in the workforce. The rate of occupational fatality (fatalities per 1 million person years worked) has remained stable over time. See: AEI, *Annual Report, 2008/09* (Edmonton: Alberta Employment and Immigration, 2009).

133 AEII, "About Worksafe Alberta: Fact Sheet," (Edmonton: Alberta Employment, Immigration and Industry, 2007). In that occupational disease fatalities often involve a time lag and the types of fatalities accepted by the WCB may be affected by changing

policies, it is difficult to accurately assessment the level of ultimately fatal occupational diseases being acquired today.

134 T. Ison, "The Significance of Experience Rating."

135 As we saw earlier in this chapter, Shannon and Lowe, "How Many Injured Workers do not File Claims for Workers' Compensation Benefits?" found 40 percent of eligible injured workers in their Canada-wide sample did not submit a workers' compensation claim (with a much higher proportion in Alberta), although there was a positive relationship between increasing injury seriousness and likelihood of filing a claim. Even so, 30 percent of injuries resulting in lost-time that would be eligible for compensation were not reported to a WCB.

136 Ison, "The Significance of Experience Rating."

137 Barnetson, "Performance Measures in Alberta's Labour Programming"; B. Barnetson and M. Cutright, "Performance Indicators as Conceptual Technologies," *Higher Education* 40(3) (2000): 277–292.

138 Breslin, Tompa, Mustard, Zhao, Smith and Hogg-Johnson, "Association Between the Decline in Workers' Compensation Claims and Workforce Composition and Job Characteristics in Ontario, Canada," note that changes in the number of workers employed in manual jobs appears to affect lost time claim numbers in Ontario.

139 J. Foster, Personal Communication. (Director of Policy, Alberta Federation of Labour, 15 September 2008).

140 C. Zwerling, "Salem Sarcoid: The Origins of Beryllium Disease," in *Dying for a Living: Workers' Safety and Health in Twentieth-Century America*, eds. D. Rosner and G. Markowitz (Bloomington: Indiana University Press, 1989), 103–118.

141 Storey, "From the Environment to the Workplace… and Back Again?" notes that this may simply shift exposures away from workers and onto the general population. For example, the International Nickel Company (INCO) in Sudbury reduced gas and dust concentrations in the Sudbury area by spreading them over a large area via a tall smoke stack.

142 M. Kaminski, "Unintended Consequences: Organizational Practices and Their Impact on Workplace Safety and Productivity," *Journal of Occupational Health Psychology* 6(2) (2001): 127–138,

notes that PPE is less effective because of the potential for mis-
or non-use. While writing this section of the book, I watched a
roofer working from my window. He was wearing a safety harness and had a rope. But he didn't hook the rope up to his harness while working at the edge of the building (where there was
a 20-foot drop). Oddly, he did hook on when he was working in
the middle of the flat roof (where there was no chance of falling).
At this point, it became apparent that he had nearly 30 feet of
safety line anchored at the building edge. So even had he been
wearing the harness while working at the edge of the roof, its
sole effect would have been to make retrieving his body easier.

143 G. Gray, "The Regulation of Corporate Violations: Punishment,
Compliance, and the Blurring of Responsibility," *British Journal
of Criminology* 46(5) (2006): 875–892.

Chapter Four

1 The following discussion is derived from the insightful approach
to understanding state regulation of the workplace set out in
Tucker, "The determination of occupational health and safety
standards in Ontario," Tucker, "Making the Workplace 'Safe' in
Capitalism," and Tucker, *Administering Danger in the Workplace.*

2 In this, we see a very traditionally Liberal approach to the role
of the state. Private investors, of course, may be both an investor
and a worker and thus hold moderated (or conflicting!) views on
the desirability of state interventions. The traditional Liberal
conception of the state's role has certainly been evident in Canadian neoliberal politics of the 1990s.

3 On the effectiveness of child labour laws at precluding illegal
employment in Canada, see B. Barnetson, "The Regulation of
Child and Adolescent Labour in Alberta," *Just labour.* 13 (2009):
29–47, and B. Barnetson and J. Foster, "Child and Adolescent
Employment in Alberta," forthcoming.

4 Glasbeek and Tucker, "Death by Consensus." These differences
can be difficult to see. And, faced with such stark inequality,
workers may simply accept that this is their lot in life under a
capitalist system and get on with what must be done to pay the
rent. The spectre of striking it rich or even just retiring may be
enough to make this palatable.

5 H. Glasbeek, *Wealth by Stealth* (Toronto: Between the Lines, 2002).

6 Tompa, Trevithick and McLeod, "Systematic Review of the Prevention Incentives of Insurance and Regulatory Mechanisms for Occupational Health and Safety"

7 Yates, *Naming the System.*

8 Even accessing national data on workers' compensation claims now requires that one purchase that data from the Association of Workers' Compensation Boards of Canada. Such data used to be freely available from Statistics Canada.

9 J. Barab, "The Invisibility of Workplace Death," in *Worker Safety under Siege: Labor, Capital and the Politics of Workplace Safety in a Deregulated World*, ed. V. Mogensen (Armonk: M.E. Sharpe, 2006), 3–16, notes that even clusters of deaths from the same hazard can be described as "freak" accidents — even though the hazard is well known and the accidents occur in close geographic and temporal proximity.

10 Tucker, "The determination of occupational health and safety standards in Ontario."

11 P. Landsbergis, "The Changing Organization of Work and the Safety and Health of Working People: A Commentary," *Journal of Environmental Medicine* 45(1) (2003): 61–72, examines American and European evidence regarding work intensification and its effect on occupational health and safety.

12 See Landsbergis, The Changing Organization of Work and the Safety and Health of Working People" and NIOSH, *The Changing Organization of Work and the Safety and Health of Working People*, (Cincinnati: National Institute for Occupational Safety and Health, 2002) for a summary of the literature.

13 D. Mehri, D. "The Darker Side of Lean: An Insider's Perspective on the Realities of the Toyota Production System," *Academy of Management Perspectives* May (2006): 21–42.

14 L. Vosko, "Precarious Employment: Towards an Improved Understanding of Labour Market Insecurity," in *Precarious Employment: Understanding Labour Market Insecurity in Canada*, ed. L. Vosko (Montreal: McGill-Queen's University Press, 2006), 11.

15   M. Sverke, J. Hellgren and K. Naswall, "No Security: A Meta-
     analysis and Review of Job Insecurity and its Consequences,"
     Journal of Occupational Health Psychology 7(3) (2006): 242–64; M.
     Virtanen, M. Kivimaki, M. Joensuu, P. Virtanen, M. Elovainio
     and J. Vahtera, "Temporary Employment and Health: A Review,"
     International Journal of Epidemiology 34(3) (2005): 610–22; and J.
     Ferrie, H. Westerlund, M. Virtanen, J. Vahtera and M. Kivimaki,
     "Flexible Labor Markets and Employee Health," *Scandinavian
     Journal of Work, Environment and Health* 6 (2008): 98–110, pro-
     vide a comprehensive overview of the literature. In Australia, R.
     D'Souza, L. Strazdins, L. Lim, D. Broom and B. Rodgers, "Work
     and Health in a Contemporary Society: Demands, Control, and In-
     security," *Journal of Epidemiology and Community Health* 57 (2003):
     849–54, noted high job insecurity was associated with increased
     self-rating of poor health, anxiety and depression. A similar pat-
     tern was found in the UK by J. Ferrie, M. Shipley, K. Newman,
     S. Stansfeld and M. Marmot, "Self-reported Job Insecurity and
     Health in the Whitehall II Study: Potential Explanations of the
     Relationship," *Social Science and Medicine* 60 (2005): 1593–1602.

16   W. Lewchuck, M. Clarke and A. de Wolff, "Working With-
     out Commitments: Precarious Employment and Health," *Work,
     Employment and Society* 22(3) (2008): 387–406.

17   Tuohy and Simmard, "The Impact of Joint Health and Safety
     Committees in Ontario and Quebec," O'Grady, "Joint Health and
     Safety Committees: Finding a Balance" and Lewchuk, Clarke and
     de Wolff, "Precarious Employment and the Internal Responsibil-
     ity System" note that workers in less permanent positions are less
     likely than full-time, permanent workers to receive health and
     safety training or information about toxic substances.

18   Lewchuk, Clarke, and de Wolff "Precarious Employment and the
     Internal Responsibility System" found that men in less perma-
     nent jobs were more likely to report working with toxic substan-
     ces, in noisy environments and in uncomfortable temperatures.
     Self-employed men were more likely to report working with toxic
     substances. Both men and women in less permanent jobs were
     more likely to report working in pain than men and women in
     permanent full-time employment or who were self-employed.

These finding mostly held even controlling for the effect of age, sex, and race — they are characteristics of precarious employment relationships. These findings are broadly consistent with M. Quinlan, C. Mayhew and P. Bohle, "The Global Expansion of Precarious Employment, Work Disorganisation, and Consequences for Occupational Health: A Review of Recent Research," *International Journal of Health Services* 31(2) (2001a): 335–414, research in Australia.

19   T. Probst and T. Brubaker, "The Effects of Job Insecurity on Employee Safety Outcomes: Cross-sectional and Longitudinal Explorations," *Journal of Occupational Health and Psychology* 6(2) (2001): 139–159; T. Probst, "Layoffs and Tradeoffs: Production, Quality and Safety Demands Under the Threat of Job Loss," *Journal of Occupational Health Psychology*, 7(3) (2002): 211–220. But see S. Parker, C. Axtell and N. Turner, "Designing a Safer Workplace: Importance of Job Autonomy, Communication Quality, and Supportive Supervisors," *Journal of Occupational Health Psychology* 6 (2001): 211–228, and T. Probst, "Safety and Insecurity: Exploring the Moderating Effect of Organizational Safety Climate," *Journal of Occupational Health Psychology* 9(1) (2004): 3–10. Organizational cues about the relative importance of safety and productivity may be an important influence on worker behaviour, although workers may not believe employers when they say safety is a priority. See D. Zohar, "Safety Climate: Conceptual and Measurement Issues," in *Handbook of Occupational Health Psychology*, eds. J. Campbell and L. Tetrick (Washington: American Psychological Association, 2003), 123–142, and T. Probst and T. Brubaker, "Organizational Safety Climate and Supervisory Layoff Decisions: Preferences versus Predictions," *Journal of Applied Social Psychology* 37(7) (2007): 1630–1648.

20   P. Landsbergis, J. Cahill and P. Schnall, "The Impact of Lean Production and Related New Systems of Work Organization on Worker Health," *Journal of Occupational Health Psychology* 4 (1999): 108–130.

Chapter Five

1   P. Simons, "Injured Worker, ATA Locked in Lose-Lose Situation," (*Edmonton Journal*, 3 October 2009).

2 Lippel "Workers' Compensation and Controversial Illnesses." Those who are temporarily disabled may be eligible for financial benefits through Employment Insurance. Long-term disability may allow individuals to access benefits under the Canada/Quebec Pension Plan. Some workers also have access to employer-sponsored benefit plans.

3 A government-appointed Board of Directors manages the Board's operations, and normally comprises representatives who are themselves (and in varying proportions) representative of employers, workers and the public (Stritch, 1995). In accordance with the powers granted to it in legislation, this Board typically sets policy, reviews and approves operational and financial plans, and employs a CEO and staff to administer the system. Boards typically have comprehensive and complex policy manuals that define to a high degree of specificity how they adjudicate claims, administer benefits, and collect employer premiums.

4 Gunderson and Hyatt, "Foundations for Workers' Compensation Reform." S. Bernstein, K. Lippel and L. Lemarche, *Women and Homework: The Canadian Legislative Framework* (Ottawa: Status of Women in Canada, 2001), note there are gaps in the scope of this legislation. For example, workers in non-standard employment relationships, such as unincorporated self-employed workers in New Brunswick or self-employed workers in industries excluded from mandatory coverage in Ontario, may be unable to acquire even voluntary personal coverage

5 Babcock, "Blood on the Factory Floor"; Risk, "This Nuisance of Litigation."

6 L. Panitch and D. Swartz, *From Consent to Coercion: The Assault on Trade Union Freedoms, 3rd Edition* (Aurora: Garamond, 2003).

7 The high-level discussion that follows obscures important differences over time and between the jurisdictions as well as within each of the groups. Yet concisely outlining the benefits of compensation is a useful first step in appreciating the political and economic dynamics of the compromise.

8 Mandel, *Power and Money*, discusses this dynamic. In short, workers may choose to limit activity to secure future gains because they fear that such resistance might result in the loss of past

gains. In this way, worker resistance is lessened or, perhaps, channelled into processes where it can be effectively managed by employers and the state.

An example might be the grievance process in collective bargaining legislation. Instead of putting down their tools to protest a violation of the agreement (a highly effective tactic), workers continue to work while their complaint makes its way through a lengthy grievance process. Work continues as directed by the employer until there is a resolution, by which time the issue may no longer matter.

Workers largely abide by the grievance process (despite the availability of the more effective mid-term strike) because they fear the sanctions that can occur as a result of a wildcat strike. They are often pressured by their unions to remain on the job because unions fear the potential repressive action of the employer and state if the union cannot manage their membership's behaviour.

9   Jobs where workers' compensation is not mandatory are a curious mix. They include very safe jobs (e.g., accountancy). They also include very unsafe jobs (e.g., agriculture, prostitution). The underlying rationale(s) or principle(s) for exclusions is elusive.

10 Vosko, "Precarious Employment." Precarious workers are often employed in non-standard employment relationships that (intentionally) fail to qualify for statutory protections (Bernstein, Lippel, Tucker, and Vosko, *Women and Homework*). The marginal position of precarious workers, due to their social and labour market location or the nature of their injury, limits the costs of ignoring these workers to unions.

11 For example, the unwillingness of employers to agree to proposals significantly limiting managerial authority pushes unions to monetize member demands during collective bargaining because unions have a much better chance of achieving monetary gains. While not an ideal outcome, accepting this outcome reduces the chance that employers will reject the legitimacy of trade unions and seek their destruction.

12 Soderstrom and Stewart, "Adjudicating Claims" note that, in 1996, Alberta denied only 2.3 percent of time-loss claims. In 2008, this percentage was 7.8 percent of lost-time claims (Alberta Workers'

Compensation Board, *Workers' Compensation Board – Alberta 2008 Annual Report*). These numbers do not address the containment of claim costs through benefit reductions, denials, and terminations. They also do not consider claims not filed due to an expectation of denial or for other reasons. As Shannon and Lowe, "How Many Injured Workers do not File Claims for Workers' Compensation Benefits?" note, up to 40 percent of potentially compensable injuries are not reported to WCBs.

More recent data on claims denial rates in British Columbia's health care system (H. Alamgir, S. Siow, S. Yu, K. Ngan and J. Guzman, "Compensation Patterns for Health Care Workers in British Columbia, Canada," *Journal of Occupational Environmental Medicine*," 66 (2009): 381–387, found an average of 82 percent of workers' compensation claims were accepted. Acceptance rates varied from 79 percent in community care and corporate offices to 85 percent in long-term care. There was also significant variation by type of injury. Only 46 percent of allergy/irritation claims were accepted while 98 percent of cuts and puncture wounds claims were accepted. There was also occupational variation in acceptance rates and workers with greater seniority faced lower odds of claim rejection.

13 T. Ison, *Workers' Compensation in Canada, 2nd Ed.* (Toronto: Butterworths, 1989).

14 Workers' Compensation Board of British Columbia, "Policy 14.00, 14.10 and 14.20, 'Arising out of and in the course of employment'," *Rehabilitation Services and Claims Manual*, Volume I. (Vancouver: Workers' Compensation Board of British Columbia).

15 D. Gilbert and A. Liversidge, *Workers' Compensation in Ontario: A Guide to the Workplace Safety and Insurance Act, 3rd Edition* (Aurora: Canada Law Book, 2001).

16 A hazard may be directly related to work (e.g., chemicals, machinery) or indirectly (e.g., weather conditions, insect bites, third-party vehicles). This typically excludes risks that are personal to the worker (e.g., physical condition or personal relationships) unless employment factors contributed to the occurrence of the injury.

17 Alberta Workers' Compensation Board, "Policy 02-01 'Arises out of and occurs in the course of employment'"

18 Royal Commission on Workers' Compensation in British Columbia. *For the Common Good: Final Report of the Royal Commission on Workers' Compensation in British Columbia* (Vancouver: Queen's Printer, 1999).

19 Carr, "Workers' Compensation Systems: Purpose and Mandate."

20 Workers' Safety and Compensation Commission, Northwest Territories and Nunavut, "Policy 03.04 'Decision-making'."

21 Lippel, "Workers' Compensation and Controversial Illnesses" notes that there is often a conflict between the legal requirement to prove compensability based on the balance of probabilities and the tendency for medical and scientific experts to rely upon scientific certitude. This bias towards a much more stringent test can creep into workers' compensation adjudication in medical and scientific opinions about causation. This is particularly the case when claims for controversial injuries are filed.

22 That said, there are two circumstances when an injury that arises and occurs may still be deemed non-compensable. Section 24 of Alberta's *Workers' Compensation Act* provides a limited exception to the general no-fault rule by introducing the concept of "serious and willful misconduct":

> 24(1) Subject to the Act, compensation under the Act is payable
>
> > (a) to a worker who suffers personal injury by an accident unless the injury is attributable primarily to the serious and willful misconduct of the worker, and
> >
> > (b) to the dependents of a worker who dies as a result of an accident,
>
> (2) The Board shall pay compensation under this Act to a worker who is seriously disabled as a result of an accident notwithstanding that the injury is attributable primarily to the serious and willful misconduct of the worker.

Serious and wilful misconduct refers to a deliberate and unreasonable breach of a law or rule designed for safety, well known to the worker, and enforced. The serious and wilful misconduct exception is a significant departure from the no-fault principle and, therefore, must meet a very high standard. Its use is very rare and, as s.24(2) of the Alberta Act states, it cannot be used if the worker is seriously disabled or killed. This exception is not present in all Canadian workers' compensation legislation and may entail a delay in, rather than a denial of, compensation.

A second instance in which compensation will not be payable is when the worker's actions at the time of the injury are a substantial deviation from the expectations and conditions of employment. That is to say, the worker's actions are tantamount to the worker removing him or herself from the course of employment. Among the kinds of behaviour that can take a worker out of the course of employment include a criminal act with gainful intent, intoxication where drinking is not permitted or condoned by the employer and intoxication is the sole cause of the accident, an intentional, self-inflicted injury, or actions that are exclusively personal and have no direct or indirect relationship to the worker's employment duties or the employer's operations (Alberta Workers' Compensation Board, "Policy 02-01 'Arises out of and occurs in the course of employment'").

23 Schultz, Crook, Fraser and Joy, "Models of Diagnosis and Rehabilitation in Musculoskeletal Pain-related Occupational Disability."

24 Shainblum, Sullivan and Frank, "Multicausality, Non-traditional Injury and the Future of Workers' Compensation."

25 Storey, "From the Environment to the Workplace... and Back Again" examines the interaction of occupational health and safety and the environmental movement.

26 Lippel, "Workers' Compensation and Controversial Illnesses" notes that denying workers' compensation for certain types of injury does not make the injury go away. It simply transfers the cost from one party to another.

27 J. Plumb and J. Cowell, "An Overview of Workers' Compensation," in *Occupational Medicine: State of the Art Reviews*, eds. T. Guidotti and J. Cowell (Philadelphia: Hanley and Belfus, 1998), 241–272;

A. Ostry, "From Chainsaws to Keyboards: Injury and Industrial Disease in British Columbia," in *Injury and the New World of Work*, ed. T. Sullivan (Vancouver: UBC Press, 2000), 27–45.

28 P. Kome, *Wounded Workers: The Politics of Musculoskeletal Injuries* (Toronto: University of Toronto Press, 1998).

29 A. Hopkins, "The Australian Epidemic of Repetitive Strain Injury: A Sociological Perspective," in *Working Disasters: The Politics of Response and Recognition*, ed. E. Tucker (Amityville: Baywood Publishing, 2006), 65–76.

30 N. Hadler, "The Ergonomic Injury as Social Construction," (paper presented at the workers' compensation policy review, Edmonton, Canada, October 2001).

31 M. Kerr, "The Importance of Psychosocial Risk Factors in Injury," in *Injury and the New World of Work*, ed. T. Sullivan (Vancouver: UBC Press, 2000), 93–114.

32 Kerr, "The Importance of Psychosocial Risk Factors in Injury," 103.

33 Kome, *Wounded Workers.*

34 Elinson, "The Compensation of Occupational Disease in Ontario"; Ison, "Recognition of Occupational Disease in Workers' Compensation."

35 A. Kraut, "Estimates of the Extent of Morbidity and Mortality Due to Occupational Disease in Canada," *American Journal of Industrial Medicine* 25(2) (1994): 267–278.

36 T. Stephens and N. Joubert, "The Economic Burden of Mental Health Problems in Canada," *Chronic Diseases in Canada.* 22(1) (2001): 18–23.

37 W. Gnam, "Psychiatric Disability and Workers' Compensation," in *Injury and the New World of Work*, ed. T. Sullivan (Vancouver: UBC Press, 2000), 305–328 notes that, while there has been some acceptance of "physical-mental" claims (whereby a physical event causes a mental disorder) and "mental-physical" claims (where mental stimulus causes a physical injury), so-called "mental-mental" claims (whereby mental stimulus causes a mental disorder) are often excluded from compensation. Physical-mental claims

pose the least problems because compensability has already been determined. Mental-physical claims are more difficult but the resulting physical ailments are subject to verification. Mental-mental claims pose evidentiary difficulties and the discourse is overlain with concerns about moral hazard. The overall claims are also difficult to predict.

38   Alberta Workers' Compensation Board, "Policy 03-01 'Injuries'," *Policies and Information Manual* (Edmonton: Alberta Workers' Compensation Board, 1996).

39   As noted R. U'Ren and M. U'Ren, "Workers' Compensation, Mental Health Claims and Political Economy," *International Journal of Law and Psychiatry* 22(5–6) (1999): 451–471, requiring work-related events to be excessive or unusual in comparison to normal tensions creates a situation where workers with difficult work circumstances (e.g., long or irregular hours, intense production pressures, unpleasant interactions) must experience truly exceptional events in order to qualify for compensation for psychological injuries. To the degree that those holding these positions are otherwise disadvantaged (which perhaps explains why they hold such jobs), concerns about systemic disadvantage on the basis of age or race come to the fore. In this way, the broader dynamics of employment (e.g., greater employer power, efforts to intensify and re-organize work to avoid statutory obligations) impact upon workers' compensation.

40   K. Lippel, "Workers' Compensation and Stress: Gender and Access to Compensation," *International Journal of Law and Psychiatry*, 22(1) (1999b): 79–89, study of Quebec appeal decisions also notes important gender-based differences in access to compensation for psychological injuries by gender. Among the explanatory factors are the gender of decision-makers and their interpretation of vague concepts, which appears influenced by gender in a way that benefits men.

41   S. Adler and R. Schoctet, "Workers' Compensation and Psychiatric Injury Definition," *International Journal of Law and Psychiatry* 22(5–6) (1999): 603–616, propose one approach to improve how WCBs handle causation, suggesting industrial psychiatric injuries must be (1) psychiatric injuries (2) which is work-related and

(3) which precludes employment. Their approach to causation is not significantly different from the Alberta example, excepting it requires prompt diagnosis and claim filing.

42 Gnam, "Psychiatric Disability and Workers' Compensation."

43 J. Murray, *Chronic pain study* (Halifax: Workers' Compensation Board of Nova Scotia, 1999). Chronic pain syndrome is a condition of pain that continues beyond the normal healing time for an injury or is disproportionate to the nature of the injury. It may lack an identifiable explanation and is resistant to treatment. Chronic pain is often associated with soft-tissue injuries such as strains, sprains and contusions, and can be accompanied by related symptoms such as depression, sleep disorders and fatigue. As a result of the pain and lack of success in treatment, individuals will often adopt 'pain behaviours', such as limiting their motion to a greater degree that strictly necessary. This may physically and psychologically reinforce the effect of the chronic pain, and lead to long-term debilitation and significant claim costs.

44 E. Tunks, J. Crook and M. Crook, "Chronic Pain from Musculoskeletal Injury," in *Injury and the New World of Work*, ed. T. Sullivan (Vancouver: UBC Press, 2000), 219–45. Such cases also entail using significant amounts of scientific and medical opinion, wherein conclusions and recommendations may be driven by scientific certitude, rather than the balance of probabilities test. See: Lippel, "Workers' Compensation and Controversial Illnesses."

45 *Nova Scotia (*WCB*) v Martin; Nova Scotia (*WCB*) v. Laseur,* 2003 SCC 54.

46 Workers' Compensation Board of Nova Scotia, *Adjudicating Claims Involving Chronic Pain,* (Halifax: Author, 2004).

47 M. McCluskey, "The Illusion of Efficiency in Workers' Compensation Reform," *Rutgers Law Journal* 50(3) (1998): 657–856, notes that it is possible to view these sorts of injuries as expanding workers' compensation in an unsustainable manner, imposing costs on employers that are unrelated to work. Yet she also perceptively notes that an alternative approach would be to view the expansion of workers' compensation to embrace the full range of work-related injuries as the long-delayed fulfillment of the

original purpose of workers' compensation. That these injuries may drive up employer premiums reflects that employers have historically transferred costs to workers, their families, and the state in the form of injury that is just now becoming recognized.

Chapter Six

1 For example, of the 184,248 claims reported in Alberta in 2008, 135,648 were for medical aid costs only.

2 Over time, the degree of earnings lost that is replaced has increased, clearly benefiting injured workers. Yet this is contested terrain and the direction of change has not always been upwards. For example, Newfoundland reduced the replacement rate from 90 percent of net earnings to 75 percent for accidents occurring after 1 January 1993. At that time, New Brunswick also reduced the replacement rate from 90 percent to 80 percent of net earnings for the first 39 days and 85 percent thereafter. A three-day waiting period was also introduced.

3 Workplace Health, Safety and Compensation Commission, New Brunswick, "Policy 21-210.01 'Calculation of Benefits'," Policy Manual. (Fredericton: Author).

4 Half of Canada's jurisdictions also have minimum compensation rates or levels. In Manitoba, for example, s.39(6) of the *Workers' Compensation Act* states that, if a worker's average earnings before the accident, are less than or equal to the minimum annual earnings ($17,220 in 2008), the worker will receive 100 percent of the worker's loss in earnings capacity, rather than the 90 percent normally allowed.

5 Net earnings may be based on an amount that fairly represents the worker's income, not just the income on the date of accident (DOA). This prevents workers from being unfairly advantaged or disadvantaged by a fluke of timing (e.g., income being unrepresentatively high or low because the worker was injured while working an unusual amount of overtime or an unusually few number of hours).

   With some exceptions (such as apprentices), net earnings are usually calculated retrospectively. This can mean permanently injured workers who were injured while working part-time or when they were young (and typically receiving lower pay levels) will face low levels of compensation for their entire life.

6 T. Thomason, The Escalating Costs of Workers' Compensation in Canada: Causes and Cures," in *Chronic Stress: Workers' Compensation in the 1990s*, eds. T. Thomason, F. Vaillancourt, T. Bogyo, and A. Stritch (Toronto: C.D. Howe Institute, 1995), 23–65.

7 Carr, "Workers' Compensation Systems: Purpose and Mandate."

8 For a full explanation, see P. Kichchuk, "Yukon Workers' Compensation Act Subsection 105(1) Research Series: Use of Deeming," (Whitehorse: Yukon Workers' Compensation, Health and Safety Board, 2003).

9 There are some regional differences. In Ontario, "available" means that employment must exist in the labour market to the extent that the worker has a reasonable prospect of actually acquiring the job. By contrast, Alberta requires only that the work is reasonably available in a location to which the worker may reasonably commute or relocate. There is no consideration of whether the worker has any realistic chance to obtain such work.

10 N. Keith and A. Neave, *A Practical Guide to Occupational Health and Safety and Workers' Compensation Compliance in Alberta* (Aurora: Canada Law Book, 2007).

11 A. Stritch, "Homage to Catatonia: Bipartite Governance and Workers' Compensation in Ontario," in *Chronic Stress: Workers' Compensation in the 1990s*, eds. T. Thomason, F. Vaillancourt, T. Bogyo and A. Stritch (Toronto: C.D. Howe Institute, 2005), 136–172.

12 R. Storey, "Social Assistance or a Workers' Right: Workmen's Compensation and the Struggle of Injured Workers in Ontario, 1970–1985," *Studies in Political Economy* 78. (2006): 67–91.

13 T. Ison, *Workers' Compensation in Canada, 2nd Edition* (Toronto: Butterworths, 1989).

14 Normally, workers undergo an assessment of their injuries and these assessments are used to determine the nature of the RTW services they're eligible for. Once the worker has completed RTW services (e.g., physical therapy, training, job search assistance), the worker is expected to return to work to the degree possible

given the worker's abilities. As noted above, workers may be deemed to have achieved earnings consistent with their level of employability and have their benefits reduced accordingly, even if they are not employed at this level.

15 R. Allingham and D. Hyatt, "Measuring the Impact of Vocational Rehabilitation on the Probability of Post-injury Return to Work," in *Research in Canadian Workers' Compensation*, eds. T. Thomason and R. Chaykowski (Kingston: IRC Press, 1995), 158–180, note that VR recipients with higher pre-accident wages, men, married men, and native English speakers were more likely to return to work than VR recipients with lower pre-accident wages, women, unmarried men and those for whom English is not their native language respectively. A worker's specific injury may also be an important mediating factor.

A six-country study of the effectiveness of measures designed to reduce long-term work incapacity among workers with back disorders provides further insight (Bloch and Prins, 2001). Workers scoring higher on indicators of good health (less pain, better back function) were found more likely to RTW after two years than those with poorer scores, and that better health status was correlated with personal characteristics (specifically younger age). The correlation of other characteristics (gender, education, job type) with RTW varied by country (Cuelenaere and Prins, 2001). Consistent with B. Badura, T. Schott and M. Waltz's, *Work Incapacity and Reintegration, Proposal for a Cross-national Research Study on Return to Work (RTW) After Coronary Heart Disease in the European Region* (Bielefeld: Universität Bielefeld, 1993) identification of a discrepancy between medical expectations of work resumption and actual levels of work resumption, this study found no significant correlation between medical treatment and RTW. That said, persons of similar health status had significantly different probability of RTW between countries, suggesting national differences in benefit provision and employment protection may be important factors. And many workers returned to work with no change in their health status. The success of vocational rehabilitation was mediated by other factors, such as education level and duration of training (B. Cuelenaere and R. Prins, "Factors Influencing Work Resumption: A Summary of Major Findings," in *Who*

Returns to Work and Why? A Six-Country Study on Work Incapacity and Reintegration, eds. F. Bloch and R. Prins (New Brunswick: Transaction Publishers, 2001), 273–286.

16 W. Johnson, R. Butler and M. Baldwin, "First Spell of Work Absences Among Ontario Workers," in *Research in Canadian Workers' Compensation*, eds. T. Thomason and R. Chaykowski (Kingston: IRC Press, 1995), 72–84.

17 WCBs normally provide parameters that define "suitable" modified work, such as accommodating medical work restrictions, contributing to rehabilitation, and not creating hardships for the worker. This may include changes to specific job tasks or functions, hours of work or schedule, the work environment, or equipment.

18 Keith and Neave, *A Practical Guide to Occupational Health and Safety and Workers' Compensation Compliance in Alberta*.

19 E. MacEachen, S. Ferrier, A. Kosny, and L. Chambers, "A Deliberation on 'Hurt versus Harm' in Early-Return-to-Work Policy," *Policy and Practice in Health and Safety*. 5(2) (2007): 41–62.

20 Again, it is not clear if the work absence causes the poor mental health or if poor mental health causes the work absence. Possibly, one may reinforce the other in a viscous cycle.

21 MacEachen, Ferrier, Kosny, and Chambers, "A Deliberation on 'Hurt versus Harm' in Early-Return-to-Work Policy."

22 Kome, *Wounded Workers*. This deserves some qualification. As pointed out by Messing, *One-Eyed Science*, female work is often incorrectly deemed "light" work when its demands are equal to (albeit somewhat different) or greater than male work.

23 Alberta Workers' Compensation Board, "Policy 04-06 'Health Care, General'," *Policies and Information Manual* (Edmonton: Alberta Workers' Compensation Board, 1996)

24 Workers' Compensation Review Board, *Policies and Procedures*. (Vancouver, Author, 2004).

25 Ostry, "From Chainsaws to Keyboards"; A. Sharpe and J. Hardt, *Five Deaths a Day: Workplace Fatalities in Canada, 1992–2005* (Ottawa: Centre for the Study of Living Standards, 2006). This number is based on WCB claims statistics and thus under-reports

the actual level of work-related fatalities, perhaps by as much as an order of magnitude when deaths from occupational diseases are included.

26 The level of benefits varies. Usually, WCBs pay reasonable funeral expenses. Earnings-loss benefits for survivors are also common and based upon a worker's income (just like other workers' compensation benefits). Some jurisdictions also provide other services (e.g., re-employment services for dependent spouses) and may limit the duration of benefits. To receive fatality benefits, one must have some sort of relationship (normally a family relationship) to the worker and one must be financially dependent upon the worker. Most often, benefits are provided to a spouse/partner and/or minor children. But some jurisdictions and circumstances may allow grandchildren, parents, in-laws, siblings and others to receive benefits, although normally compensation is only payable to one recipient. And, normally, if no one is eligible, no long-term compensation is paid, although funeral expenses would still be covered (Thomason, 2000).

27 WSIB, *Annual Report* (Toronto: Workplace Safety and Insurance Board, 2006).

28 The composition of industry groups varies between provinces and territories. Consequently, the number of groups rages from approximately 50 to upwards of 300. Each group needs to be large enough to adequately spread risk among members and provide premium stability. The more ratings groups there are, the more homogeneous is the composition of each of group regarding its accident risks and costs.

29 Plumb and Cowell, "An Overview of Workers' Compensation"; D. Brunsch, "Employer Services," in *Occupational Medicine: State of the Art Reviews*, eds. T. Guidotti and J. Cowell (Philadelphia: Hanley and Belfus, 1998), 345–355; T. Bogyo, "Workers' Compensation: Updating the Historic Compromise," in *Chronic Stress: Workers' Compensation in the 1990s*, eds. T. Thomason, F. Vaillancourt, T. Bogyo and A. Stritch (Toronto: C.D. Howe Institute, 1995): 92–135.

30 Sometimes called merit programs, experience-rating programs also vary between provinces. Some programs are balanced (i.e., discounts and surcharges that are awarded balance each other

out), while others do not contain this requirement. Normally, provinces with more ratings groups have less complex experience-rating systems and vice versa (F. Vaillancourt, "The Financing of Pricing of WCBs in Canada: Existing Arrangements, Possible Changes," in *Chronic Stress: Workers' Compensation in the 1990s*, eds. T. Thomason, F. Vaillancourt, T. Bogyo and A. Stritch (Toronto: C.D. Howe Institute, 1995), 66–91.

Some very large employers (mostly governments) do not pay premiums. Instead, they pay the full cost of accidents plus an administrative fee to a WCB (i.e., they are self-insured). The WCB administers these claims on these employers' behalves, making the appropriate payments and providing services. In this way, these employers are said to be perfectly experience rated through this form of self-insurance (Bogyo, "Workers' Compensation").

31 For example, if an employer has three workers, each earning $30,000 per year and has an assessment rate of $0.97/$100 of payroll, this means the employer will pay $291 per employee.

32 M. Moore and W. Viscusi, *Compensation Mechanisms for Job Risks: Wages, Workers' Compensation and Product Liability* (Princeton: Princeton University Press, 1990); J. Gruber and A. Kreuger, "The Incidence of Mandated Employer-Provided Insurance: Lessons from Workers' Compensation Insurance," in *Tax Policy and the Economy*, ed. D. Bradford (Cambridge: MIT Press and NBER, 1991), 111–143; P. Fishback and S. Kantor, "Did Workers Pay for the Passage of Workers' Compensation Laws?," *The Quarterly Journal of Economics* 110(3) (1995): 713–742.

33 M. Gunderson and D. Hyatt, "Do Injured Workers Pay for Reasonable Accommodation?" *Industrial and Labor Relations Review* 50(1) (1996): 92–104, for example, found costs of accommodation for work-related injuries were transferred in a small way to employees when an employee changed employers following an accident.

34 Keith and Neave, *A Practical Guide to Occupational Health and Safety and Workers' Compensation Compliance in Alberta*.

35 CBC, "WCB premiums on the rise says lobby group," (6 June 2001); CFIB, "WCB in crisis says Saskatchewan business community," (Canadian Federation of Independent Business, 2003).

36 Association of Workers' Compensation Boards of Canada, "Average Assessment Rates per $100.00 Payroll, 1985–2008," http://www.awcbc.org/common/assets/assessment/avg_rates_history.pdf. In 2007, the average assessment rate varied between $1.32 per $100 of payroll in Alberta and $2.75/$100 in Newfoundland. Individual jurisdictions have seen significant year-to-year variation, perhaps reflecting work by WCBs and employers to lower premiums.

37 Derived from Association of Workers' Compensation Boards of Canada, "Summary Table of Accepted Time-Loss Injuries/Diseases and Fatalities by Jurisdiction" and "Key Statistical Measures for 2007." The benefit costs incurred include short-term disability, long-term disability, survivors' benefits, healthcare, and rehabilitation services but excluded administrative costs. Averages, of course, can be deceptive and some types of claims have even higher costs. For example, in Alberta, an average lost-time claim cost $23,700 in 2005 (Keith and Neave, *A Practical Guide to Occupational Health and Safety and Workers' Compensation Compliance in Alberta*).

38 Chaykowski and Thomason, "Canadian Workers' Compensation" note that real-dollar claims costs rose from $1222 per claim in 1960 to $5179 in 1991. M. Campolieti and J. Lavis, "In Workers' Compensation, Higher Benefits Mean Lengthier Claims," *Policy Options* 20(10) (1999): 45–48, provide an interesting discussion of this trend. One explanation for long-term increases in claim costs appears to be changes in benefit levels. Some commentators argue this "benefit liberalization" includes an increase in the maximum dollar value of compensation, reductions in the wait time for compensation to kick in, and an increasing proportion of jurisdictions providing income replacement at 90 percent of net earnings. There have also been small increases in the costs associated with medical aid and vocational rehabilitation.

39 Thomason, "The Escalating Costs of Workers' Compensation in Canada" For example, a 10 percent increase in workers' compensation benefits appears to increase the probability of a claim being filed by 4 to 6 percent and the duration of a claim by 20 percent. It also increases the likelihood of awards of permanent partial disability payments.

40 H. Levitt, "Time to level WCB playing field. (Saskatoon Star-Phoenix, 4 November 2009) provides a particularly asinine example of the tendency to call injured workers lazy.

41 R. Smith, "Mostly on Mondays: Is Workers' Compensation Covering Off-the-Job Injuries? in *Benefits, Costs and Cycles in Workers' Compensation*, eds. P. Borba and D. Appel (Boston: Kluwer, 1990); R. Butler and J. Worrall, "Claims Reporting and Risk Bearing Moral Hazard in Workers' Compensation," *Journal of Risk and Insurance* 58 (1990): 191–209.

42 G. Dionne, P. St-Michel and C. Vanasse, "Moral Hazard, Optimal Auditing and Workers' Compensation," in *Research in Canadian Workers' Compensation*, eds. T. Thomason and R. Chaykowski (Kingston: IRC Press, 1995), 85–105.

43 D. Mah, "Reducing Workers' Compensation Fraud: A Deterrent Approach," in *Occupational Medicine: State of the Art Reviews*, eds. T. Guidotti and J. Cowell (Philadelphia: Hanley and Belfus, 1998), 429–438.

44 D. Michaels, "Fraud in the Workers' Compensation System: Origins and Magnitude," in *Occupational Medicine: State of the Art Reviews*, eds. T. Guidotti and J. Cowell (Philadelphia: Hanley and Belfus, 1998), 439–442.

45 For example, J. O'Grady, "When the Playing Field Isn't Level: The Underground Economy in Ontario," (paper delivered at the 33rd Canadian Construction Association Labour Relations Conference, Montreal, 5 November 2004) notes some 98,000 construction businesses existed in Ontario in 2003, of which 50,000 were not registered with the WSIB. Changes requiring mandatory personal coverage for independent construction contractors is expected to bring in an addition $511 million in revenue in 2009 (Daily Commercial News, "CFIB warns WSIB's Bill 119 will put contractors out of business" (27 November 2008).

46 While many of these same levers can be used to facilitate investigations of WCB employees, the opportunity for employee fraud is lesser due to procedural safeguards. Further, overly enthusiastic surveillance of staff may negatively affect employee relations and productivity.

47 There is little empirical evidence to substantiate this possibility. The argument has roots in the notion that workers will be less likely to file claims if they know the claim will be disputed, their credibility impugned, and that they risk employer harassment or discipline. T. Scherzer, R. Rugulies, and N. Krause, "Work-related Pain and Injury and Barriers to Workers' Compensation Among Las Vegas Hotel Room Cleaners," *American Journal of Public Health* 95(1) (2005): 483–488, found approximately one-quarter of U.S. hotel cleaners cited fear of a disciplinary or punitive reaction from their employer as a reason for not making a claim.

48 Michaels, "Fraud in the Workers' Compensation System."

49 Storey, "Social Assistance or a Workers' Right"; R. Storey, "Their Only Power was Moral: The Injured Workers' Movement in Toronto," *Histoire sociale-social history* 41(81) (2008): 99–131.

50 B. Kralj, "Occupational Health and Safety: Effectiveness of Economic and Regulatory Mechanisms," in *Workers' Compensation: Foundations for Reform*, eds. M. Gunderson and D. Hyatt (Toronto: University of Toronto Press, 2000), 187–218.

51 D. Hyatt and B. Kralj, "The Impact of Workers' Compensation Experience Rating on Employer Appeals Activity," *Industrial relations* 34(1) (1995): 95–106; C. Bruce and F. Atkins, "Efficiency Effects of Premium Setting Regimes under Workers' Compensation: Canada and the United States," *Journal of Labor Economics* 11(1–2) (1993): 38–61.

52 There is significant variation between jurisdictions and rate groups. Further, some programs to differentiate based on the size of an employer's annual assessment, perhaps reducing the degree or speed with which experience rating affects employers with lower assessments. Plans may also have caps such that the effect of a single large claim is moderated.

53 Vaillancourt, "The Financing and Pricing of WCBs in Canada." A further benefit of experience rating is that, despite the proliferation of rating groups, there are still differences within a rating group (e.g., considering types of employees, their production processes) for which experience rating accounts.

54 B. Kralj, "Employer Responses to Workers' Compensation Insurance Experience Rating," *Relations Industrielles/Industrial Relations* 49(1) (1994): 41–59; B. Kralj, "Experience Rating of Workers' Compensation Insurance Premiums and the Duration of Workplace Injuries," in *Research in Canadian Workers' Compensation*, eds. T. Thomason and R. Chaykowski (Kingston: IRC Press, 1995), 106–122.

55 Stritch, "Homage to Catatonia."

56 E. MacEachen, "The Mundane Administration of Worker Bodies: From Welfarism to Neoliberalism," *Health, Risk and Society* 2(3) (2001): 316–327. Whether employers see this as "gaming" behaviour or simply as a legitimate response to a system that imposes seemingly onerous costs upon them is legitimately open to debate. Regardless, the effect of such behaviour on workers is negative.

57 Bruce and Atkins," Efficiency Effects of Premium Setting Regimes Under Workers' Compensation."

58 T. Thomason and S. Pozzebon, "Determinants of Firm Workplace Health and Safety and Claims Management Practices," *Industrial and Labor Relations Review* 55(2) (2002): 286–307. This included having an in-house claims manager, an increasing incidence of cost-relief applications, the use of temporary modified work to reduce benefit duration and more frequent appeal activity. This suggests reactive claims management may act as a substitute for improved workplace safety, although this was more evident in low-wage firms than in high-wage firms.

59 Hyatt and Kralj, "The Impact of Workers' Compensation Experience Rating on Employer Appeals Activity." That said, not all appeal activity can be dismissed solely as gaming behaviour.

60 Cousineau, Lacroix, and Girard, "The Economic Determinants of the Occupational Risk of Injury."

61 Increasing the costs triggered by experience rating might affect employer behaviour, however, doing so takes WCBs further away from the principle of collective liability.

62 Aldrich, *Safety First.*

63 Kralj, "Employer Responses to Workers' Compensation Insurance Experience Rating."

64 P. Lanoie, "The Impact of Occupational Safety and Health Regulation on the Risk of Workplace Accidents: Quebec, 1983–87," *Journal of Human Resources* 27(4) (1992): 643–660.

65 Kralj, "Experience Rating of Workers' Compensation Insurance Premiums and the Duration of Workplace Injuries."

66 M. Harcourt, H. Lam, and S. Harcourt, "The Impact of Workers' Compensation Experience-Rating on Discriminatory Hiring Practices," *Journal of Economic Issues* 16(3) (2007): 681–700.

67 Ison, "The Significance of Experience Rating."

68 Brody, Letourneau, and Poirier (1990) in Hyatt and Krajl, "The Impact of Workers' Compensation Experience Rating on Employer Appeals Activity." The 4:1 ratio of indirect to direct costs appears to originate with a 1926 study by Herbert Heinrich. Although this number has wide currency, it appears based on faulty accounting (Aldrich, *Safety First*), thus the precision of this ratio ought to be considered speculative.

69 Ison, "The Significance of Experience Rating."

Chapter Seven

1 Edmonton Journal, (22 October 2009). WCB hostage taking ends peacefully.

2 W. Day, "Patrick Clayton Interview" (2009). http://groups. google.com/group/nf.general/browse_thread/thread/6819 e44d58477009?pli=1

3 Haddow and Klassen, *Partisanship, Globalization and Canadian Labour Market Policy.*

4 Social movement theory posits that successful social movements can be understood by examining the interplay between: (1) the structure of political opportunities, (2) the mobilization structure via which individuals can pursue their collective interests, and (3) the framing process which allows individuals to form a collective understanding of the problem(s) they face and see it as amenable to change (D. McAdam, J. McCarthy and M. Zaid, "Introduction: Opportunities, Mobilizing Structures and Framing Processes — Towards a Synthetic, Comparative Perspective in Social Movements," in *Comparative Perspectives on Social*

Movements, eds. D. McAdam, J. McCarthy and M. Zaid [New York: Cambridge University Press, 1996], 1–20.)

5 Storey, "Social Assistance or a Workers' Right" and "Their Only Power was Moral."

6 For example, ethnic communities may create a means by which injured workers can interact. See: Storey, "Their Only Power was Moral."

7 There is little research on this topic. The creation of injured worker groups suggests mobilization is not entirely impeded. Yet, these groups are often populated (at least in part) by workers who have been denied compensation and thus have little further to lose.

8 This is consistent with Mandel's *Power and Money* dialectic of partial conquest and mirrors the effect critics of grievance arbitration suggest that highly legalistic process has on collective worker resistance to unacceptable employer demands and orders. See D. Drache and H. Glasbeek, *The Changing Workplace: Reshaping Canada's Industrial Relations System* (Toronto: Lorimar, 1992).

9 The willingness of workers to sacrifice wages or risk a strike is likely affected by the degree to which injury is viewed as a class-based issue. As noted earlier, the operation of workers' compensation retards the ability of workers to see the degree and nature of injuries. This in turn reduces the political salience of safety within trade unions.

10 Unions, of course, could force the issue via direct action such a strike. Whether there is the appetite for such action and whether union leaders are prepared to violate the peace obligation found in labour legislation is unclear. Unions, in fact, are expected to ensure their members don't take direct action in this way (Hyman, *The Political Economy of Industrial Relations*).

11 In 2008, Alberta saw 2620 requests for a decision review brought forward to its internal appeals body on 211,737 active claims (*Workers' Compensation Board – Alberta 2008 Annual Report*).

12 For benefit decisions, the parties will typically be the worker or the worker's dependant (if the worker was killed) and the employer. Employers can likewise seek a review of decisions made

about their premium assessment. Typically, reviews must be sought with a specified time. See: D. Harte and D. Smith, "Workers' Compensation Appeal Systems in Canada and the United States," in *Occupational Medicine: State of the Art Reviews*, eds. T. Guidotti and J. Cowell (Philadelphia: Hanley and Belfus, 1998), 423–427. The vast majority of appeals are regarding worker benefits (e.g., Workers' Compensation Appeal Tribunal, *Workers' Compensation Appeal Tribunal 2008 Annual Report* (Vancouver: Author, 2008).

13 Some jurisdictions may provide workers with access to WCB appeals advisors.

14 Alberta's Appeal Commission received 879 appeals in 2007/08. Of the 2074 issues resolved (a single appeal may contain multiple issues) in 2007/08, it upheld the WCB decision on 833 issues, overturned/partially supported or created an alternative resolution on 781 issues, and reached another conclusion on 460 issues (ACAWC, "2008 presentation to the annual general meeting," (Edmonton: Appeals Commission for Alberta Workers' Compensation, 2008).). A similar pattern of upholding/varying is evident in BC (Workers' Compensation Appeal Tribunal, *Workers' Compensation Appeal Tribunal 2008 Annual Report*).

15 Evidence can include a summary of the facts, testimony by witnesses, and discussion of key legislative or policy provisions. Although broadly similar to a civil court case, it is often structured in a manner that is less overtly adversarial. For example, questions for a witness may be provided to and asked by the hearing chair, rather than directly by a party.

16 An appeal body's decision is normally considered final. For example in Alberta, s.13.4 of the Alberta Act limits the right of appeal to the courts to questions of law or jurisdiction. What this privative clause means is that an appeal decision may be quashed by a court only for such reasons as a breach of natural justice, significant error of fact or law, or a jurisdictional error — limitations typical for a quasi-administrative tribunal (England, *Individual Employment Law, 2nd Edition*). Simple dissatisfaction with the decision or a difference in reasoning will not be considered grounds for judicial review.

17   In Alberta, appeals filed with the Appeals Commission were on average completed in 144 days in 2007/08. Complex appeals were completed in 182 days on average (ACAWC, "2008 presentation to the annual general meeting,"). Such appeals typically have a longer history of adjudication and review prior to entering the appeals process.

18   There is little study of the internal workers of workers' compensation adjudication and review processes. I draw this conclusion based on my experience working for a WCB and from discussions with other WCB staff (in both Alberta and elsewhere). I also find the internal logic of this behaviour compelling: absent very good reason (which typically results in a reconsideration of the decision by the adjudicator), adjudicators seek to have their decisions (which they made in good faith) upheld because a reversal may negatively affect the adjudicator's status among his or her peers as well as the adjudicator's self-perception. The involvement of other WCB staff during an internal review can limit the influence of the adjudicator can exert on this process, although the shared experiences of adjudicators and policy restrictions in effect means that the original adjudicator's opinion and rationale may be persuasive.

19   Again, I base this on my experience in the Alberta WCB and discussions I've had with others. While few adjudicators are openly or irrationally hostile to workers, many rely upon employer evidence over worker evidence based on the supposition that employers have less at stake than workers do. On any individual claim, that is likely true. But the incremental value of being relied upon by WCB adjudicators over a large number of claims is clearly present and well known to employer representatives.

20   The right of a WCB to participate in a hearing varies between jurisdictions. In Alberta, WCBs are given notice of appeals and may request status as an affected party. In Ontario, the Workplace Safety and Insurance Board is not generally allowed to participate in appeals.

21   K. Lippel, "Workers Describe the Effect of the Workers' Compensation Process on Their Health: A Quebec Study," *International Journal of Law and Psychiatry* 30 (2007): 427–443.

22 For example, a variety of changes in Ontario's compensation system (including the creation of an independent appeals tribunal) resulted in a substantial growth of appeals. D. Law, "Appeals Litigation: Pricing the Workplace Injury," in *Workers' Compensation: Foundations for Reform*, eds. M. Gunderson and D. Hyatt (Toronto: University of Toronto Press, 2000), 299–326, asserts that the rise in appeal activity in Ontario was in large part due to a deliberate opening of a previously 'insulated' compensation decision process.

Further, changes in the type and frequency of injuries can pose challenges in determining whether and what compensation ought to be granted. The perception that the changing nature of injury has increased the potential for adjudicative error may augur in favour of greater independence in the appeals system. It is also important to consider how creation of additional appeal activity may affect the interests of the parties.

23 Independent appeals commissions create both benefits and costs for WCBs. This arrangement splits responsibility for a claim between the WCB (which administers claims and sets policy) and the appeals body (which interprets policy and determines the final disposition of claims) (Chaykowski and Thomason, "Canadian Workers' Compensation"). The result is conflicting interpretations of WCB policy and intermittent legal wrangling between WCBs and their appeal bodies. Further, WCBs almost always end up arguing "against" workers at appeals commission hearings when they defend their interpretation of policy, which is a difficult public relations issue for WCBs.

That said, appeals commissions externalize the difficulties of contentious claims. If the employer walks away dissatisfied from an appeal about a worker claim, responsibility is shifted from the WCB to the appeals commission. Similarly, if a worker walks away dissatisfied, responsibility is (at minimum) now shared between the WCB and the appeals commission. This also provides WCBs with political cover: legislators face less overall pressure from constituents and those legislators seeking to intervene can be passed off to the appeals commission. Finally, appeals commissions restore some of the legitimacy to workers' compensation systems because the WCB isn't compelled to both make the initial decision and final appeals decision on a claim — a fundamental conflict of interest.

24 T. Ison, *Compensation Systems for Injury and Disease: The Policy Choices* (Toronto: Butterworths, 1994).

25 K. Lippel, "Therapeutic and Anti-therapeutic Consequences of Workers' Compensation," *International Journal of Law and Psychiatry* 22(5–6) (1999a): 521–546.

26 K. Lippel, "Private Policing of Injured Workers: Legitimate Management Practices or Human Rights Violations?" *Policy and Practice in Health and Safety* 1(2) (2003): 97–118. This surveillance may reflect a welfarization of workers' compensation, whereby injured workers are stigmatized for making claims. This may be exacerbated by the financial incentives created for employers by experience rating.

27 Lippel, "Workers Describe the Effect of the Workers' Compensation Process on Their Health."

28 Stigmatization is a recurring theme in worker experiences (B. Beardwood, B. Kirsh, and N. Clark, "Victims Twice Over: Perceptions and Experiences of Injured Workers," *Qualitative Health Research* 15(1) (2005): 30–48; J. Eakin, "The Discourse of Abuse in Return to Work: A Hidden Epidemic of Suffering," in *Occupational Health and Safety: International Influences and the New Epidemics,* eds. C. Peterson, and C. Mayhew (Amityville, New York: Baywood Publishing, 2005), 159–174; J. Eakin, E. MacEachen and J. Clarke, "'Playing it Smart' with Return to Work: Small Workplace Experiences Under Ontario's Policy of Self-reliance and Early Return," *Policy and Practice in Health and Safety* 1(2) (2003): 19–42. This can be enhanced where the employer's fault for the accident is ignored while the worker's contribution can be used as the basis for disputing a claim.

29 Lippel, "Workers Describe the Effect of the Workers' Compensation Process on Their Health," 435.

30 C. Roberts-Yates, "The Concerns and Issues of Injured Workers in Relation to Claims/Injury Management and Rehabilitation: The Need for New Operational Frameworks," *Disability and Rehabilitation* 25(16) (2003): 898–907.

31 McCluskey, "The Illusion of Efficiency in Workers' Compensation Reform" provides an extensive analysis of U.S. workers' compensation reform efforts. She argues that reforms aimed at improving "efficiency" mask efforts to shift costs towards injured workers and away from employers and insurers by obscuring the purpose of reform. My argument is broadly similar in that it suggests privatization and abolish are rhetorical devices designed to constrain worker demands (or resistance to employer demands) by creating a threatening alternative.

32 Glasbeek, *Wealth by Stealth*.

33 Yet even moderately injured workers may find themselves disenchanted if either (or both) the level or probability of compensation declines (D. Hyatt and D. Law, "Should Workers' Compensation Continue to Imbibe at the Tort Bar?" in *Workers' Compensation: Foundations for Reform*, eds. M. Gunderson and D. Hyatt [Toronto: University of Toronto Press, 2000], 327–360.)

34 Thomason, "The Escalating Costs of Workers' Compensation in Canada."

35 Bogyo, "Workers' Compensation."

36 Hyatt and Law, "Should Workers' Compensation Continue to Imbibe at the Tort Bar?"

37 J. Chelius and J. Burton, "Who Actually Pays for Workers' Compensation? The Empirical Evidence," in *Workers' Compensation Year Book: 1995*, ed. J. F. Burton (Horsham: LRP Publications, 1995), 153–159.

38 Vosko, "Precarious Employment"

39 Ontario has experimented with private delivery of vocational rehabilitation. Trade unions assert this has resulted in delays in accessing services, higher costs and longer claim duration, but such claims are difficult to substantiate.

40 Thomason, "The Escalating Costs of Workers' Compensation in Canada"; D. Dewees, "Private Participation in Workers' Compensation," in *Workers' Compensation: Foundations for Reform*, eds. M. Gunderson and D. Hyatt (Toronto: University of Toronto Press, 2000), 219–260.

41 This discussion draws directly on Dewees, "Private Participation in Workers' Compensation."

42 Privatization can also have other costs, such as agency costs. An agency cost is an additional cost generated because the process of delegating authority requires that contracts be structured and enforced, and because the interests of the agent (i.e., private insurer seeking profit) and the principal (i.e., government seeking equitable compensation objectives) are not perfectly aligned. These costs tend to rise over time as the relationship between the agent and the principal loosens.

43 Dewees, "Private Participation in Workers' Compensation" also notes a key risk that accompanies privatization: what would happen to injured workers and their claims if an insurance company goes bankrupt?

44 Thomason, "The Escalating Costs of Workers' Compensation in Canada."

45 T. Thomason and J. Burton "The Cost of Workers' Compensation in Ontario and BC," in *Workers' Compensation: Foundations for Reform*, eds. M. Gunderson and D. Hyatt (Toronto: University of Toronto Press, 2000), 261–298.

46 Thomason (1992) in Thomason "The Escalating Costs of Workers' Compensation in Canada."

47 T. Thomason, "Workers' Compensation Claims Adjustment: Determinants and the Cost of Claims," Working Paper Series QPIR 1992–96 (Kingston: Queen's University School of Industrial Relations, 1991).

48 Bogyo, "Workers' Compensation."

49 Bogyo, "Workers' Compensation"; Thomason, "The Escalating Costs of Workers' Compensation in Canada."

50 T. Thomason, T. Schmidle, and J. Burton, *Workers' compensation: Benefits, costs and safety under alternative insurance arrangements.* (Kalamazoo: Updike Institute, 2001). It is important to be mindful of the data limitations they note.

51 G. Teeple, *Globalization and the decline of social reform* (Toronto: Garamond, 1995); B. Jessop, "Towards a Schumpeterian Work

fare State? Remarks on Post-Fordist Political Economy," *Studies in Political Economy* 40 (1993): 7–39.

52 P. Aucoin, "Politicians, Public Servants and Public Management: Getting Government Right," in *Governance in a Changing Environment*, eds. B.G. Peters and D.J. Savoie (Montreal: Canadian Centre for Management Development and McGill-Queen's University Press, 1995), 113–137.

53 F. Castles, "On the Credulity of Capital: Or Why Globalization Does not Prevent Variations in Domestic Policy Making," *Australian Quarterly* 68(2) (1996): 65–74.

54 For example, see G. Albo, "Neoliberalism and the Discontented," Debate and Theory: The socialist project website. 2008. http://www.socialistproject.ca/theory; G. Skogstad, "Globalization and Public Policy: Situating Canadian Analyses," *Canadian Journal of Political Science* 33(4) (2000): 805–824; W. Tabb, "Globalization is an Issue, the Power of Capital is The Issue," *Monthly Review.* 49(2). http://www.monthlyreview.org/697tabb.htm.

55 J. Peters, *A Fine Balance: Canadian Unions Confront Globalization* (Ottawa: The Canadian Centre for Policy Alternatives, 2002; L. Panitch and D. Swartz, *From Consent to Coercion: The Assault on Trade Union Freedoms, 3rd Edition* (Aurora: Garamond. 2003). This includes labour law amendments designed to weaken unions and make certification more difficult, instances of legislating workers back to work and imposing provisions into collective bargaining agreements, enacting mandatory wage freezes, rollbacks, or days off without pay, and calculated efforts to decrease workers' bargaining power via changes in the eligibility and benefit levels of social assistance programs.

56 Mandel, *Power and Money.*

57 There is no empirical research on this dynamic. I base this assertion on my conversations with trade unionists in Alberta and elsewhere. The logic is compelling though: criticizing workers' compensation creates an opportunity for change. The power of capital to shape the nature of any change makes trade unionists somewhat reluctant to criticize workers' compensation as a structure. Criticism about individual cases has less potential to upset

the apple cart and more directly addresses the concerns of members. Consequently, much energy is directed into individual case management rather than seeking structural reform.

58 C. Cranford and L. Vosko, "Conceptualizing Precarious Employment: Mapping Wage Work across Social Location and Occupational Context," in *Precarious Employment: Understanding Labour Market Insecurity in Canada*, ed. L. Vosko (Montreal: McGill-Queen's University Press, 2006), 43–66.

59 That said, there are indications that this trend is not entirely one way. In late 2008, Ontario's Liberal government proclaimed Bill 119, which required most small construction contractors to purchase personal WSIB coverage.

60 L. Vosko and N. Zukewich, "Precarious by Choice: Gender and Self-employment," in *Precarious Employment: Understanding Labour Market Insecurity in Canada*, ed. L. Vosko (Montreal: McGill-Queen's University Press, 2006), 67–89.

61 L. Vosko (ed.), *Precarious Employment: Understanding Labour Market Insecurity in Canada* (Montreal: McGill-Queen's University Press, 2006).

62 M. Gunderson and D. Hyatt, "Workforce and Workplace Change: Implications for Injury and Compensation," in *Injury and the New World of Work* (Vancouver: UBC Press, 2000), 46–68.

63 W. Lewchuk, A. de Wolff, A. King and M. Polyani, M. "The Hidden Costs of Precarious Employment: Health and the Employment Relationship," in *Precarious Employment: Understanding Labour Market Insecurity in Canada*, ed. L. Vosko (Montreal: McGill-Queen's University Press, 2006), 241–262.

64 M. Quinlan, "The Implications of Labour Market Restructuring in Industrialized Societies for Occupational Health and Safety," *Economic and Industrial Democracy* 20 (1999): 427–460; M. Quinlan and C. Mayhew, "Precarious Employment and Workers' Compensation," *International Journal of Law and Psychiatry* 22(5–6) (1999): 491–520; P. Bohle, M. Quinlan and C. Mayhew, "The Health and Safety Effects of Job Insecurity: An Evaluation of the Evidence," *Economic and Labour Relations Review* 12(1) (2001): 32–60; Quinlan, Mayhew and Bohle, "The Global Expansion

of Precarious Employment, Work Disorganisation, and Consequences for Occupational Health"; M. Quinlan, C. Mayhew and
P. Bohle, "The Global Expansion of Precarious Employment,
Work Disorganisation and Occupational Health: Placing the Debate in a Comparative Historical Context," *International Journal
of Health Services* 31(3) (2001): 507–536; B. Cameron, *The Occupational Health and Safety Implications of Non-standard Employment.* (Toronto: Workplace Safety and Insurance Board, 2001);
M. Quinlan, "The Global Expansion of Precarious Employment:
Meeting the Regulatory Challenge," 2003. http://www.actu.asn.
au/public/ohs/quinlan.html.

65 Quinlan and Mayhew, "Precarious Employment and Workers'
Compensation."

66 Berstein, Lippel, and Lamarche, *Women and Homework.*

67 Quinlan, "The Global Expansion of Precarious Employment,"
uses part-time workers as a proxy for contingent workers.

68 Royal Commission on Workers' Compensation in British Columbia, *For the Common Good.*

69 Quinlan, "The Global Expansion of Precarious Employment."

70 Vosko, "Precarious Employment."

71 S. Bernstein, K. Lippel, E. Tucker, and L. Vosko, "Precarious Employment and the Law's Flaws: Identifying Regulatory Failure
and Securing Effective Protection for Workers," in *Precarious
Employment: Understanding Labour Market Insecurity in Canada,*
ed. L. Vosko (Montreal: McGill-Queen's University Press, 2006),
203–220.

Select Bibliography

Aldrich, M. *Safety First: Technology, Labor and Business in the Building of American Work Safety, 1870–1939*. Baltimore: The Johns Hopkins University Press, 1997.

Armstrong, H. *Blood on the Coal: The Origins and Future of New Zealand's Accident Compensation Scheme*. Wellington: Trade Union History Project, 2008.

Babcock, R. "Blood on the Factory Floor: The Workers' Compensation Movement in Canada and the United States." In *Social Fabric or Patchwork Quilt: The development of social policy in Canada*, edited by R. Blake and J. Keshan, 45–58. Peterborough: Broadview Press, 2006.

Bohme, S., J. Zorabedian, and D. Egilman. "Maximizing Profit and Endangering Health: Corporate Strategies to Avoid Litigation and Regulation," *International Journal of Occupational and Environmental Health* 11(6) (2005): 338–348.

Breslin, C., P. Smith, M. Koehoorn, and H. Lee, "Is the Workplace Becoming Safer?," *Perspectives on Labour and Income* 18(3) (2006): 36–42.

Brophy, J., M. Keith, and J. Schieman. "Canada's Asbestos Legacy at Home and Abroad," *International Journal of Occupational and Environmental Health* 13 (2007): 235–242.

Cutler, T., and P. James. "Does Safety Pay? A Critical Account of the Health and Safety Executive Document: 'The Cost of Accidents'," *Work, Employment and Society* 10(4) (1996): 755–765.

Davis, D. *The Secret History of the War on Cancer*. New York: Basic Books, 2007.

Dembe, A. *Occupation and Disease: How Social Factors Affect the Conception of Work-Related Disorders*. New Haven: Yale University Press, 1996.

Drache, D., and H. Glasbeek. *The Changing Workplace: Reshaping Canada's Industrial Relations System*. Toronto: Lorimer, 1992.

Eakin, J. "The Discourse of Abuse in Return to Work: A Hidden Epidemic of Suffering." In *Occupational Health and Safety: International Influences and the New Epidemics*, eds. C. Peterson and C. Mayhew, 159–174. Amityville, New York: Baywood Publishing, 2005.

Epstein, S. *The Politics of Cancer Revisited*. USA: East Ridge Press, 1998.

Fidler, R. "The Occupational Health and Safety Act and the Internal Responsibility System," *Osgood Hall Law Journal* 24(2) (1985): 315–352.

Firth, M., J. Brophy, and M. Keith, *Workplace Roulette: Gambling with Cancer*. Toronto: Between the Lines, 1997.

Glasbeek, H., and Tucker, E. "Death by consensus at Westray." In *The Westray Chronicles: A Case Study in Corporate Crime*, edited by C. McCormick, 71–96. Halifax: Fernwood, 1999.

Gray, G. "A Socio-legal Ethnography of the Right to Refuse Dangerous Work," *Studies in Law, Politics and Society* 24 (2002): 133–169.

———. "The Regulation of Corporate Violations: Punishment, Compliance, and the Blurring of Responsibility," *British Journal of Criminology* 46(5) (2006): 875–892.

———. "The Responsibilization Strategy of Health and Safety: Neoliberalism and the Reconfiguration of Individual Responsibility for Risk," *British Journal of Criminology* 49(3) (2009): 326–342.

Haddow, R., and T. Klassen. *Partisanship, Globalization and Canadian Labour Market Policy*. Toronto: University of Toronto Press, 2006.

Hall, A., A. Forrest, A. Sears, and N. Carlan. "Making a Difference: Knowledge Activism and Worker Representation in Joint OHS Committees," *Relations Industrielles/Industrial Relations* 64(3) (2006): 408–436.

Hyman, R. *The Political Economy of Industrial Relations: Theory and Practice in a Cold Climate*. MacMillan: Wiltshire, 1989.

Ison, T. "The Significance of Experience Rating," *Osgoode Hall Law Journal* 24(4) 1986): 723–742.

———. "Recognition of Occupational Disease in Workers' Compensation." Paper presented at the CCOHS Conference on the Recognition and Prevention of Occupational Disease, Toronto, Canada, March 3–4, 2005.

Kaminski, M. "Unintended Consequences: Organizational Practices and their Impact on Workplace Safety and Productivity," *Journal of Occupational Health Psychology* 6(2) (2001): 127–138.

Kome, P. *Wounded Workers: The Politics of Musculoskeletal Injuries*. Toronto: University of Toronto Press, 1998.

Lewchuck, W., M. Clarke, and A. de Wolff. "Working without Commitments: Precarious Employment and Health," *Work, Employment and Society* 22(3) (2008): 387–406.

Lippel, K. "Therapeutic and Anti-therapeutic Consequences of Workers' Compensation," *International Journal of Law and Psychiatry* 22(5–6) (1999a): 521–546.

————. "Workers Describe the Effect of the Workers' Compensation Process on their Health: A Quebec Study," *International Journal of Law and Psychiatry* 30 (2007): 427–443.

————. "Workers' Compensation and Controversial Illnesses." In *Contesting Illness: Process and Practices*, edited by P. Moss and K. Teghtsoonian, 47–68. Toronto: University of Toronto Press, 2008.

MacEachen, E., S. Ferrier, A. Kosny, and L. Chambers. "A Deliberation on 'Hurt versus Harm' in Early-Return-to-Work Policy," *Policy and Practice in Health and Safety* 5(2) (2007): 41–62.

McCluskey, M. "The Illusion of Efficiency in Workers' Compensation Reform," *Rutgers Law Journal* 50(3) (1998): 657–856.

Mehri, D. "The Darker Side of Lean: An Insider's Perspective on the Realities of the Toyota Production System," *Academy of Management Perspectives* May (2006): 21–42.

Messing, K. *One-Eyed Science: Occupational Health and Women Workers.* Philadelphia: Temple University Press, 1998.

Mogensen, V., ed. *Worker Safety Under Siege: Labor, Capital and the Politics of Workplace Safety in a Deregulated World.* Armonk: M.E. Sharpe, 2006.

Nelkin, D., ed. *The Language of Risk: Conflicting Perspectives on Occupational Health.* Beverly Hills: Sage, 1985.

Quinlan, M., and C. Mayhew. "Precarious Employment and Workers' Compensation," *International Journal of Law and Psychiatry* 22(5–6) (1999): 491–520.

————. C. Mayhew and P. Bohle, "The Global Expansion of Precarious Employment, Work Disorganisation, and Consequences for Occupational Health: A Review of Recent Research," *International Journal of Health Services* 31(2) (2001a): 335–414.

————. C. Mayhew and P. Bohle. "The Global Expansion of Precarious Employment, Work Disorganisation and Occupational Health: Placing the Debate in a Comparative Historical Context," *International Journal of Health Services* 31(3) (2001): 507–536.

Roach, S., and S. Rappaport. "But They Are Not Thresholds: A Critical Analysis of the Documentation of Threshold Limit Values," *American Journal of Industrial Medicine* 17 (1990): 728–753.

Roberts-Yates, C. "The Concerns and Issues of Injured Workers in Relation to Claims/Injury Management and Rehabilitation: The Need for New Operational Frameworks," *Disability and Rehabilitation* 25(16) (2003): 898–907.

Robinson, J. *Toil and Toxins: Workplace Struggles and Political Strategies for Occupational Health.* Berkeley: University of California Press, 1991.

Rosner, D., and G. Markowitz, eds. *Dying for a Living: Workers' Safety and Health in Twentieth-Century America.* Bloomington: Indiana University Press, 1989.

Sass, R. "The Limits of Workplace Health and Safety Reforms in Liberal Economics," *New Solutions* 3(1) (1992): 31–40.

Sharpe, A., and J. Hardt. *Five Deaths a Day: Workplace Fatalities in Canada, 1992–2005.* Ottawa: Centre for the Study of Living Standards, 2006.

Smith, D. *Consulted to Death: How Canada's Workplace Health and Safety System Fails Workers.* Winnipeg: Arbeiter Ring, 2000.

Storey, R. "From the Environment to the Workplace... and Back Again? Occupational Health and Safety Activism in Ontario, 1970s–2000+", *Canadian Review of Sociology and Anthropology* 41(4) (2004): 419–447.

———. "Their Only Power was Moral: The Injured Workers' Movement in Toronto," *Histoire sociale-social history* 41(81) (2008): 99–131.

Storey, R., and W. Lewchuk. "From Dust to DUST to Dust: Asbestos and the Struggle for Worker Health and Safety at Bendix Automotive," *Labour/Le Travail* (45) (2000): 103–140.

Thomason, T., T. Schmidle, and J. Burton. *Workers' Compensation: Benefits, Costs and Safety under Alternative Insurance Arrangements.* Kalamazoo: Updike Institute, 2001.

Tompa, E., S. Trevithick, and C. McLeod. "Systematic Review of the Prevention Incentives of Insurance and Regulatory Mechanisms for Occupational Health and Safety," *Scandinavian Journal of Work, Environment and Health* 33(2) (2007): 85–95.

Tucker, E. "The determination of occupational health and safety standards in Ontario, 1860–1982," *McGill Law Journal* 29 (1983/84): 260–311.

———. "Making the Workplace 'Safe' in Capitalism," *Labour/Le Travail* 21 (1988): 45–85.

———. *Administering Danger in the Workplace: The Law and Politics of Occupational Health and Safety Regulation in Ontario, 1850–1914.* Toronto: University of Toronto Press, 1990.

———. "And the Defeat Goes on: An Assessment of Third-Wave Health and Safety Regulation," in *Corporate Crime: Contemporary Debates*, edited by F. Pearce, 245–267. Toronto: University of Toronto Press, 1995.

———, ed. *Working Disasters: The Politics of Response and Recognition.* Amityville: Baywood Publishing, 2006.

Vosko, L., ed. *Precarious Employment: Understanding Labour Market Insecurity in Canada*. Montreal: McGill-Queen's University Press, 2006.

Walters, V. "Occupational health and safety legislation in Ontario: An analysis of its origins and content," *Canadian Review of Sociology and Anthropology* 20(4) (1983): 413–434.

————."The Politics of Occupational Health and Safety: Interviews with Workers' Health and Safety Representatives and Company Doctors," *Canadian Review of Sociology and Anthropology* 22(1) (1985): 57–79.

Walters, V., and M. Denton. "Workers' Knowledge of their Legal Rights and Resistance to Hazardous Work," *Relations Industrielles/Industrial Relations* 45(3) (1990): 531–547.

Walters, V., W. Lewchuk, J. Richardson, L. Moran, T. Haines, and D. Verma. "Judgments of Legitimacy Regarding Occupational Health and Safety: Regulating capitalism." In *Corporate Crime: Contemporary Debates*, ed. F. Pearce, 284–303. Toronto: University of Toronto Press, 1995.

Witt, J. *The Accidental Republic: Crippled Workingmen, Destitute Widows and the Remaking of American Law*. Cambridge: Harvard University Press, 2004.

Yates, M. *Naming the System: Inequality and Work in the Global Economy*. New York: Monthly Review Press, 2003.

Ziem, G., and B. Castleman. "Threshold Limit Values: Historical Perspectives and Current Practice." In *Illness and the Environment*, eds. S. Kroll-Smith, P. Brown, and V. Gunter, 120–134. New York: New York University Press, 2000.

INDEX

C

D

E

G

power in employment relationships, 14–15, 17, 42, 51–52, 62–63, 66–67, 93, 97, 149, 171–172, 177–178

precarious employment, 101–102, 103, 167–171

production process, 3, 18, 84, 90, 91, 100–101, 174–175

profitability and safety, 19, 24, 34, 66, 76–78, 174, 185

psychological injuries, 119–121, 181

R

repetitive strain injuries (RSI), 49–50, 100, 117

return-to-work programs, 129–133, 141, 181, 182

right
to manage, 91, 175
to refuse, 41, 45, 65–67, 178

role of the state, 17, 24, 38, 41–42, 64, 87, 91, 97, 124, 180, 185

S

social construction
of accidents, 32–33, 179, 186
of hazards, 51–52, 53, 71, 73, 85
of injuries, 51–52, 57–59, 83, 114–118, 120–121, 123–124, 138, 179,

social reproduction, 3, 37–38, 90, 124, 175, 181

social sanction of workplace injury, 94–95

T

threshold limit values, 43, 68–71, 91, 92, 183

U

unions, 36, 41, 98, 149–150, 185

W

worker response to injury, managing, 62, 103–104, 110, 124, 127–129, 133, 142–143, 148–157, 166–167, 170–171, 175, 180–181

Dr. Bob Barnetson is an assistant professor of labour relations at Athabasca University. He has worked for the Alberta Labour Relations Board, the Alberta Workers' Compensation Board, and the Alberta government.

Marquis Book Printing Inc.

Québec, Canada
2010